THE FALL OF FRANCE, 1940

TURNING POINTS
General Editor: Keith Robbins
Vice-Chancellor, University of Wales Lampeter

THE FALL OF FRANCE, 1940

This ambitious new programme of books under the direction of Professor Keith Robbins (already General Editor of Longman's very successful series of Profiles in Power*), examines moments and processes in history which have conventionally been seen as "turning points" in the emergence of the modern world. By looking at the causes and long-term consequences of these key events, the books illuminate the nature of both change and continuity in historical development.*

THE FALL OF FRANCE, 1940

ANDREW SHENNAN

Wellesley College

An imprint of **Pearson Education**

Harlow, England · London · New York · Reading, Massachusetts · San Francisco
Toronto · Don Mills, Ontario · Sydney · Tokyo · Singapore · Hong Kong · Seoul
Taipei · Cape Town · Madrid · Mexico City · Amsterdam · Munich · Paris · Milan

Pearson Education Limited
Edinburgh Gate
Harlow
Essex CM20 2JE
England

and Associated Companies throughout the world

Visit us on the World Wide Web at:
http://www.pearsoneduc.com

First published 2000

ISBN 0 582 29081 3 PPR
ISBN 0 582 29082 1 CSD

British Library Cataloguing in Publication Data
A catalogue record for this book is available from the British Library

Library of Congress Cataloging-in-Publication Data
Shennan, Andrew.
 The fall of France, 1940 / Andrew Shennan.
  p. cm. — (Turning points)
 Includes bibliographical references.
 ISBN 0–582–29082–1 — ISBN 0–582–29081–3 (pbk.)
  1. World War, 1939–1945—Campaigns—Western Front. 2. World War,
1939–1945—Campaigns—France. I. Turning points (Longman (Firm))

D756.S48 2000
940.54'214—dc21   00–042118

10 9 8 7 6 5 4 3 2 1
04 03 02 01 00

Typeset by 35 in 11/13pt Baskerville MT
Produced by Pearson Education Asia Pte Ltd.
Printed in Singapore

CONTENTS

SERIES EDITOR'S PREFACE

The success of the German offensive to the West which began on May 10, 1940 was one of the most dramatic events in the history of twentieth-century Europe, followed as it was by the armistice and the collapse of the French Third Republic. For contemporaries, it was impossible to escape the sensation of living through a decisive and perilous moment. Here indeed was a palpable turning point. In a few short weeks, assumptions about warfare and about Franco-British relations, to name only two, were shattered and could not easily recover. In Britain, finest hours beckoned. In France there was turmoil and trauma. Yet, in the end, though few could confidently predict that this would be the case, it was not the comprehensive turning point in the conflict which some supposed it to be at the time. Even so, above all in France itself, an inquest began into a strange defeat which still continues.

Turning points turn through time and gain fresh meaning in their afterlife. It is with that twisting path, whereby the present comes to interpret and accommodate a past upheaval, that Andrew Shennan is concerned in a study which illuminates not only the "Fall of France" itself but its significance still for France in the twenty-first century.

AUTHOR'S PREFACE

How did it feel to belong to a defeated nation? The word "trauma" is often invoked to describe the French experience in 1940 – with some justification, but also with the potential to mislead. These six weeks left over a hundred thousand citizens dead, millions more separated from their homes or families. They shocked a population and a government that had been anticipating an entirely different outcome. But neither the casualty toll (tragic as it was) nor the extent of physical or psychological damage nor the shock of the unexpected could be compared to that of the First War – four years of uninterrupted carnage that destroyed millions of bodies and minds, exploded all assumptions and conventions, and haunted the nation for decades to come. That had been a trauma of a different order.

Much of the shock and pain this time derived from the consequences of the war's abrupt ending rather than from the fighting itself. For individuals, these consequences ran the gamut from inconvenience and deprivation to deportation, imprisonment, exile, or death. For the nation, defeat entailed four years of foreign occupation, a change of regime, a drastic loss in collective status and power, deep rifts at every level of the national community. The trauma of 1940, in other words, was wrapped up in the traumatic experiences of the four years that followed.

The other part of it, of course, was the simple humiliation. Defeat forced individuals to reassess their country's place in the world and, by extension, their own significance and worth. One of the most frequently cited remarks about 1940 (by the late President, François Mitterrand) exemplifies this: "my feeling of belonging to a great people (great in the idea that it constructed of the world and of itself, and of itself in the world, according to a system of values that rested neither on number nor brute strength nor money) had taken some knocks. I lived through 1940: no need to say more."[1] Mitterrand expressed the sense, shared by many in his generation, that the defeat had cut to the core of national identity and self-esteem, that the nation was never quite the same after 1940. His final clause is also significant, however. The humiliation is a memory so vivid and so firmly impressed on the national consciousness that it scarcely needs to be expressed. Quite literally, it goes without saying.

Historians of France's "dark years" have always endorsed such a view. Take, for example, a recent study by the historian Robert Frank, one of the many to quote Mitterrand and also one of the most astute analysts of France's mid-century crisis.[2] In an essay about decline anxieties between the 1920s and 1960s, Frank argues that 1940 produced a "Copernican revolution" in French attitudes: it propelled state and society to embrace economic modernisation; it drove a generation of intellectuals to compensate for their impotence in 1940 by compulsive *engagement* after 1944; it woke the nation up to the harsh realities of its decline and confronted it with the imperative of renewal. What is striking about these familiar arguments, in addition to their intuitive common sense, is their generality. Even a well-informed historian like Frank can find relatively little historical evidence to demonstrate this presumed connection between postwar mentalities and the experience of 1940.

The problem is a structural one. An unspeakable memory tended to be a memory not much spoken about, except in occasional autobiographical asides like Mitterrand's. Collective remembering of the collapse proved very difficult. This was not the kind of inevitable, one-sided defeat that could be celebrated for its gallantry (since German and Allied forces had been fairly well matched in terms of numbers and equipment), nor could it be remembered as a sacrifice that advanced the cause of eventual victory. If anything, in fact, it proved harder to commemorate the defeat than to commemorate the crimes of the Occupation that ensued; the latter, at least, had identifiable victims and perpetrators, whereas in some sense everyone was both victimised by and implicated in the defeat. This diffusion of victimhood/complicity may help to explain why the fascination with the contested history of the Occupation (the now famous "Vichy syndrome") has not been replicated around the issue of 1940.[3] Whatever the reason (and this is an issue to which we will return later in the book), it is an undeniable fact that the causes of France's defeat and the culpability of individuals and organisations have not received the kind of intense historical and journalistic scrutiny directed at the Occupation experience. Nor have they become major issues in postwar politics. The Vichy regime that governed France under the Occupation tried to found its legitimacy on the "lessons of 1940". The experiment was, to say the least, not a success, and the two postwar republics have been loath to repeat it.

To write about such a deep, abiding but incommunicable hurt is no easy task. The purpose of this volume is not to challenge Mitterrand's claim so much as to explore what to him went without saying. This requires us to pose some rather prosaic questions about the significance of this trauma. In which respects precisely was France's public life transformed by the events of that May and June? What role did the defeat play in the succeeding years of Occupation? To what extent did it resurface as an issue after the war? And looking back from a distance of sixty years, how does 1940 now fit within the larger framework of twentieth-century French, and European, experience?

My interpretation of 1940 as a turning point proceeds along two axes. The first deals with the conscious politicisation of defeat and the various attempts by political elites to control and manipulate its meaning. Each of the rival wartime authorities, as well as their postwar successors, understood the defeat's transformative impact in ways that suited their political interests and reflected their ideologies and priorities. In general, I will argue that these attempts to politicise 1940 failed and that the defeat quickly lost salience in public debate. This outcome, which was truly remarkable in light of the scale of the disaster, can only be understood by a close reading of the political history of the decade after defeat.

On the other hand, it was to be expected that sooner or later – it just happened to be sooner in this case – the turning point would escape the control of those trying to manipulate its meaning for political ends. As the experience of defeat receded into the past and as the intervening years contextualised it in new ways, the issue of 1940's impact acquired new layers of complexity. To give some sense of this evolving historical significance, Part Two offers three views of it. A first takes defeat as "ground zero" and examines its immediate aftermath, adopting the short-term perspective of those who lived through the débâcle and exploring how they adapted to it. The second widens the angle, so as to see the defeat in what might be termed the medium term, that is within the context of a generation of crisis. It compares the trajectories that defeat interrupted with those that resumed after Liberation. And finally, taking the longest possible view, the third looks at the legacies of defeat in postwar decades and places them – and it – within the context of an entire century's history.

However traumatic and sadly memorable May and June 1940 were, it is well to remember that they were, after all, just two months: two months in the course of a six-year-long global conflagration (eight-year-long if one considers the pre-existing war in China); two months at the end of a harrowing decade and of a quarter-century of political, economic, and cultural turmoil. If we are not to turn the concept of a turning point into a straw man, we need to begin with realistic expectations as to how far the impact of this brief historic moment can be isolated from that of its tumultuous context. This book attempts to deepen our understanding of 1940's significance, by examining some of the intricate continuities that stretched across that transition and by observing how the event was, in a certain sense, absorbed into history. But to argue, for example, that the defeat was soon eclipsed as a political issue is not to deny that it was a turning point (if 1940 would not qualify as such, what could?); it is simply to describe the kind of turning-point it was or, rather, became.

Notes and references

1   *L'Abeille et l'architecte* (Paris: Flammarion, 1978), p. 281. (A literal translation would be ". . . had suffered some cuts".) All Mitterrand's statements about the war must now be read in light of the recent revelations about his own wartime record (see Chapter Seven below). One should note that his emphasis here on the intellectual and moral bases of French power was a traditional one, stretching back to the Revolution of 1789, and that the tradition had a particular resonance for the generation that grew up in the wake of the Great War and amid the depression of the 1930s – a period when, in varying degrees, the military, demographic and economic bases of national power were insecure. For some pertinent comments on the education that reinforced such conceptions of France's greatness, see C. Sellin, "L'image de la puissance française à travers les manuels scolaires", *Relations internationales*, 33 (1983), pp. 103–11.

2   *La Hantise du déclin. Le rang de la France en Europe, 1920–1960: finances, défense et identité nationale* (Paris: Belin, 1994).

3   S. Hoffmann, "The trauma of 1940", in J. Blatt (ed.), *The French Defeat of 1940, Reassessments* (Providence, Rhode Island: Berghahn, 1998), pp. 354–70. The term "Vichy Syndrome" was coined by the historian Henry Rousso.

AUTHOR'S ACKNOWLEDGEMENTS

I am grateful to Andrew MacLennan and Keith Robbins for giving me the impetus to write this book. At Wellesley College I have received invaluable assistance from several quarters: the President and Trustees granted me two semester-long sabbaticals; the staff of Clapp Library tracked down many arcane materials on my behalf; my colleagues in the History Department gave me constructive advice and moral support, and my new colleagues in the Dean's Office covered for me when I was writing rather than "deaning"; and Jeanine Yost was an exemplary research assistant. Several scholars at Wellesley and elsewhere kindly put their expertise at my disposal, either by reading part or all of the manuscript or by discussing the work with me. I particularly thank Martin Alexander, William Hitchcock, Frances Malino, and the graduate students and faculty in Steven Kaplan's modern Europe seminar at Cornell.

The first fragments of this work were written during the mid-1980s, while I was researching a doctoral thesis on a related theme. The bulk of it was written during the second half of the 1990s. Throughout that span of time, I have been fortunate enough to enjoy the companionship and support of Elizabeth Doherty and to be inspired by her critical intelligence. Our children have borne the trial of living with 1940 patiently (usually) and sympathetically (always).

This book is dedicated to the memory of two scholars who had a profound influence on my teaching and writing. Peter Morris, a friend from Cambridge days, sparked my interest in de Gaulle, helped me transplant to America, and from afar continued to show a generous interest in my work. Jonathan Knudsen was for eleven years my senior colleague at Wellesley, a teacher and historian who lived the scholarly life with rare intensity and passion. I know that both Peter and Jon would have volunteered to read this manuscript, and that it would have been a better book for their criticism.

PUBLISHER'S ACKNOWLEDGEMENTS

We are grateful to the following for permission to reproduce copyright material:

Calder Publications Ltd for adapted extracts from *La Route des Flandres* (*The Flanders Road*) by Claude Simon and Presses Universitaires de France for an abridged extract from *Les Evénements survenus en France*.

May–June 1940: fragments and impressions

> ... that inextricable, monotonous and enigmatic wake of disasters, in other
> words not even trucks or burned wagons, or men, or children, or soldiers,
> or women, or dead horses, but simply detritus, something like a vast public
> discharge ... exuding not the traditional and heroic odour of carrion, of
> corpses in a state of decomposition, but only of ordure, simply stinking, the
> way a pile of old tin cans, potato peels and burnt rags can stink ...
>
> Claude Simon, *La Route des Flandres* (1960)[1]

Before we address the impact of the defeat, it is vital to convey something of
the experience itself. Various aspects of it – its disorienting speed, the manner in which much of the civilian population was drawn into unwelcome
participation in it, the initial assumptions about its causes and implications
– shaped the politicisation that ensued. The history of these weeks is enorm-
ously complex and more thoroughly investigated by military and political
historians than by social historians. What follows here is not an attempt to
write the social history of May and June, which would require us to draw
systematic distinctions among the different regional or class or gender
experiences of defeat, but rather to offer certain somewhat impression-
istic observations about the experience writ large, the main source for these
impressions being the memoirs and diaries of participants.

Military collapse

It was shortly before dawn on May 10, 1940, that the forces of Nazi Germany finally set in motion their daring plan for the invasion of the Low

Countries and France. At first, their attack appeared to concentrate where the French had expected – in northern Belgium and southern Holland. It triggered the forward movement of strong French forces, together with the British Expeditionary Force (BEF), northwards into Belgium. Unexpectedly, however, the Germans also launched a major thrust in the densely wooded and hilly Ardennes region at the northern edge of the Maginot Line (a region which because of its topography had been left relatively poorly protected by the French army). Since the turn of the year there had been some intelligence indications that the Germans were contemplating an attack in that quarter and some recommendations (including one from a parliamentary source) that the defences around Sedan should be reinforced.[2] These recommendations had not been followed up, and on May 13, a German panzer division established a bridgehead on French territory at Sedan. In the days that followed, seven panzer divisions, closely supported by the Luftwaffe, cut a swathe across northern France, racing for the coast in order to cut off the Allied armies which had advanced into Belgium. The Germans reached the Channel on May 20. Four days before, unclear where the panzers were heading, the Commander-in-Chief, General Gamelin, had informed the Prime Minister, Paul Reynaud, that he did not have the forces to defend Paris. A week after the German assault began, the government was forced to contemplate abandoning the capital, and officials in the Foreign Ministry were hastily burning their archives on the lawns of the Quai d'Orsay (a sight and smell which almost instantaneously came to symbolise the French State's disarray in 1940).

After this first massive shock, the situation appeared to stabilise over the next couple of weeks. Reynaud tried to bolster morale by appointing the nation's two most venerable soldiers to prominent positions: 73-year-old Maxime Weygand replaced Gamelin as Commander-in-Chief, while 84-year-old Marshal Pétain was appointed Vice-Premier. In the field French forces launched a number of offensive operations against the "panzer corridor"; two of the more notable of them – at Montcornet during May 17–20 and at Abbeville at the end of the month – were led by Colonel Charles de Gaulle, who in early June was promoted to the rank of brigadier general and entered the government as Under-Secretary of State for National Defence. But these counter-measures were unsuccessful, and the German advance continued, quickly trapping several hundred thousand Allied troops in the vicinity of the port of Dunkirk. Though a sudden cautiousness on Hitler's part gave the Allies an opportunity to evacuate many of these troops, evacuation did nothing to alter the momentum of the campaign. What Dunkirk did do, besides improving British chances of survival, was further to strain already tense relations between the Allies. The British had withdrawn their forces to the coast in order to evacuate them; the French believed at first that they were there to form a bridgehead. For several days, French troops were prevented from embarking on rescue craft, and it was only at the end that large numbers were taken off. The memory of the brave and costly rearguard action that the French had fought while the bulk of the British forces were being evacuated was to be politically explosive after the defeat. In the heat of the moment, however, the tensions were partly overshadowed by news of the Belgian army's surrender (May 28), a decision that Reynaud immediately denounced.

The final stage of the German invasion began in early June, when their forces moved southwards to confront the remaining French forces, massed along the line of the Somme and the Aisne. It quickly became clear that the French could not contain the German advance. On June 10, the Reynaud government decided to leave Paris and head south to Tours, while General Weygand abandoned his headquarters at Vincennes. That same day, Hitler's Italian allies declared war on France – a symbolic blow more than a military disaster, since the thirty Italian divisions that invaded in the south-east achieved little. Four days later, on June 14, German forces entered the undefended capital. By that time, an itinerant and badly divided French government was preparing to head still further south, from Tours to Bordeaux. Backed by a majority of his ministers, who still favoured continuing the war in some form, Reynaud explored a variety of options – withdrawing the government to French North Africa or to a fortified "redoubt" in Brittany, appealing to the US government to intervene, or accepting a last-minute British proposal for a Franco-British union. In the late evening of June 16, after weeks of clutching at a variety of straws, Reynaud resigned the premiership. President Lebrun appointed the Vice-Premier, Pétain, as Reynaud's successor. Pétain had been convinced for weeks, if not from the very start of the campaign, that the war was lost and that an armistice was essential. At noon the next day (June 17), he broadcast to the nation, declaring that "the fighting must stop" ("il faut cesser le combat") and announcing that he had contacted the enemy to begin armistice negotiations. Then began several days of anxious waiting. French troops were not sure whether to lay down their weapons, and in some areas local authorities informed the population that the reports of armistice negotiations were a hoax.[3] The German authorities seemed in no hurry to agree to an armistice, and while they delayed, German troops continued to advance southwards, threatening the temporary French capital in Bordeaux. Meanwhile, various French politicians and government officials continued to search for a means of continuing the battle from North Africa. These attempts were cut short on June 22, when it was announced that the French and German governments had signed an armistice agreement. Three days later the French signed a second armistice with Italy.

Even when observed from a distance, these events were so shocking as to be scarcely credible. In Washington in mid-May, President Roosevelt sat up nights pondering the prospect of France's collapse and the possibility that Britain might be next. It was odd, he remarked to a State Department official, what images lodged in one's mind at a moment such as this. Roosevelt's thoughts went back to a trip he had made to Ireland during the First War. "[H]e had motored along Bantry Bay, seeing beautiful Irish girls along the road, who opened their mouths to curse as he went by, because he had British officers with him. When they did open their mouths, all their teeth were black and decayed."[4] Was it the incongruous and even sinister juxtaposition of beauty concealing anger and decay that had stuck in his memory, or just the unsettling sensation of the unexpected? There was a distinctly nightmarish cast to this fragmentary recollection that made it appropriate to a moment when events were hurtling uncontrollably towards a disastrous outcome.

Within France, virtually everyone – except perhaps those who took positive satisfaction in the bad news – had difficulty comprehending it. Rapid and overwhelming as the German victory appears in retrospect, the full extent of it did not sink in at first. The most mundane explanation for this lingering of illusions was French officialdom's continuing reluctance to break the bad news to its own people. Twice-daily communiqués in late May and early June were filled with obscure euphemisms about German "infiltrations" and "pockets", while the general tone of the official news was resolutely optimistic.[5] Well into June, newspapers continued to propagate old "news" – that Hitler lacked raw materials, that his soldiers did not have enough to eat, or that they were running out of munitions. On June 14, a teacher in Saint-Malo expressed a common bewilderment: "The Germans keep advancing. How can this advance be explained, when our newspapers encourage us and fill us with hope?"[6]

This official optimism was harshly criticised in the wake of defeat, on the grounds that it only exacerbated the population's subsequent sense of betrayal and alienation. Some, no doubt, were deceived by the communiqués. But one suspects that in many cases there was as much self-deception as deception. To put it another way, the government's stubborn optimism tapped into popular assumptions about the likely course that the fighting would take. Early setbacks in the north were disturbing, but tended to be seen within the context of the First World War and, in that light, were less troubling. The First War had begun as disastrously as this one, but the German advance had been stopped at the Marne. The question in 1940 was when and where would the second Marne occur.

Diaries written during the battle attest to how long this kind of hopeful-ness persisted.[7] In early June troops evacuated from Dunkirk and trans-ported to Cherbourg, directly or via England, were still hoping to staunch the German advance north of Paris.[8] Numerous observers remarked on the calmness of Paris at this time (often contrasted with the unhealthy frenzy in Bordeaux a week or two later). On June 3, for example, the Minister of Munitions, Raoul Dautry, visited a Parisian armaments factory that had been heavily bombed earlier in the day, and within a matter of hours was able to show admiring American journalists that the assembly lines were operating again at full output.[9] Even the fall of the capital ten days later did not end hopes of a last-minute recovery. Refugees heading south from Paris set their sights on the Loire, where they imagined substantial French forces lying in wait for the Germans (this time shades of 1870, when the repub-lican minister Gambetta had escaped from a besieged capital to rally a French force in the Loire).[10] Nor were such illusions confined to the unin-formed: in Bordeaux a deputy found plenty of his well-connected Parisian friends still believing in the possibility of a miracle on the Loire.[11] And on June 14, a critical-minded observer, the sociologist and philosopher Georges Friedmann, continued to believe that, if Roosevelt responded favourably to Reynaud's appeal, "we can be saved".[12] Friedmann understood that the alternative – "Pax Hitlérica", as he called it – loomed, but it is striking that he was still able to talk about defeat in the conditional. He was not alone. On the same day, an officer noted in his diary that news of the fall of Paris had prompted him to realise that France might be entirely defeated. "[B]etween ourselves we begin to discuss what the fate of France will be *if* she is beaten."[13]

In a perverse way, the very rapidity of the German invasion, once relayed to the French population, legitimised all kinds of compensatory illusions. As the novelist Jean Dutourd later put it, "Reality was so strange that it became indistinguishable from fiction."[14] Reports of the enemy advanc-ing hundreds of kilometres in a matter of hours were utterly improbable, yet turned out to be true.[15] So why not credit no less credible news – for example, rumours of a Soviet attack on Germany, which was hardly incon-ceivable given the history of animosity between Hitler and Stalin, not to mention their capacity for sudden volte-faces? Such rumours flared up continually, particularly in mid-June. Entering a post office on June 12, for example, the writer Arthur Koestler was accosted by a woman shouting that "the Russians have declared war on Germany and Italy. *C'est le miracle.*"[16] Almost always the rumour was attributed to a plausible source (like a BBC broadcast), and the story would rapidly make the rounds of a town or village. Then would come the let-down, usually when the next official broadcast made no mention of the news.

Civilian exodus

It may be that military defeat is bound to have an unreal quality for civilians, unless or until they actually see enemy soldiers in their streets. In one important respect, however, the reality of this defeat made itself felt well before the Germans arrived. In advance of the invading army, some 8–10 million people left their homes and fled south or west. For the refugees, but also for those who witnessed the refugees entering their communities and whose resources were stretched to the limit by the new arrivals, the defeat was inevitably conflated with this vast *"exode"* (as it came to be called).

A collective migration of such magnitude was certainly not an inevitable accompaniment to invasion. It was to be expected that those who had lived through German occupation two decades earlier should want to flee and that the well-to-do would take the precaution of heading to their summer places a month or two earlier than usual. Indeed, the government had drawn up detailed evacuation plans for those living in front-line areas, while in Paris civil defence brochures issued by the Prefecture of Police had long advised residents to head to the country as soon as danger threatened.[17] However, the mass flight which developed by early June far outstripped official preparations. The invasion's unexpected direction (east–west instead of north–south) and its equally unexpected rapidity, together with the uncontrollable flood of rumours and the incompetence or cowardice of local authorities, thwarted efforts to restore order. What struck observers was the sheer incongruousness of the phenomenon. It was "a peculiar sadistic irony of Fate", observed Arthur Koestler, that the war had turned "the most *petit-bourgeois*, fussy, stay-at-home people in the world into a nation of tramps".[18] A French observer had the same thought: "A sedentary, settled, civilised people, forced to become nomads."[19]

Various claims have been advanced about the significance of this experience. One of the first (made by a pioneering historian of the *exode*, Jean Vidalenc) was that the flight constituted "pre-resistance" or "an early referendum against collaboration, against coexistence with the invader".[20] In leaving their homes and most of their possessions, the refugees were demonstrating their faith in the French army's capacity to stop the enemy advance sooner or later; it was not so much the fear of total defeat that impelled them as the fear of being caught in a war zone when the front stabilised. Other writers detected in the *exode* a moment of regained social solidarity (to quote a Parisian metalworker on the road in mid-June, "Misfortune draws people together and overturns social barriers. We help each other, share our provisions, offer one another wine, tobacco, cigarettes."[21]) or an improvised, not always unwelcome, break from the monotony of everyday life.[22] In truth, the social history of this experience largely remains to be written. But it is certainly possible to identify the main impressions that it made and hypothesise as to their effect on initial perceptions of defeat.

The first impression was the sheer chaos and aimlessness of the migration. Refugees were constantly redirected, forced to circle back on themselves or change their itinerary. Their diaries are filled with the frustrations of thinking that they had reached a safe resting place, only to be warned that the Germans were close and that they had to move once more. Adrey, the metalworker quoted above, complained: "If . . . we had a target, if we knew where we were going, that would give us courage and ten times more strength. But nothing is more discouraging than this aimless walking. . . ."[23] Soldiers felt much the same about their continual withdrawals: in the words of one officer, "We always have the impression of marching blindly . . . we are always one step slower than the enemy."[24] Another asked a group of refugees where they were heading and was told that they had no idea: they were simply following the cart ahead.[25] Many, of course, did have destinations in mind, chosen for their symbolic significance (the Loire, for example) or because they had friends or relatives there. But the vagaries of the German advance, the state of the roads, the shortage of petrol, the infrequency of trains all conspired to ensure that plans continually evolved, and refugees who were not aimless at the outset soon became so.

A second impression was of general disorder. In a particularly perceptive war diary, Georges Sadoul called the refugees "locusts".[26] As they passed through communities from which, in many cases, the inhabitants had already fled, soldiers and civilians broke the locks and helped themselves – not just to food and alcohol (which was almost expected), but to clothing, bedding, furniture and valuables of all kinds. If the pots and pans and mattresses that the refugees had brought with them had an undeniable pathos, so too did the houses and gardens through which they passed – ransacked rooms, half-open drawers, dirty clothes and empty food containers strewn on the ground by anonymous strangers.

Contributing to the anonymity of the experience was the fragmentation of families and particularly the separation of children from their parents, which quickly became one of the most traumatic dimensions to the crisis. Within a week or two of May 10, chalked signs began to appear on walls in northern areas, rudimentary messages of the kind observed by Sadoul: "Edmond, keep going, we are waiting for you in Rouen."[27] Later, when the armistice had been signed, local newspapers in the south and west were filled for weeks with personal announcements placed by parents looking for children and children looking for parents. In the summer 90,000 children had to be reunited with their families; at year's end many children were still without news of their parents, and vice versa.[28]

Even when family members stayed together, the physical discomforts of hunger and exhaustion often strained familial ties. On June 15, Sadoul encountered a large family – several women, three men and five children – sitting beside the road having a snack. When a lorry came by and some soldiers offered the women and children a ride, they quickly jumped aboard. As the lorry took off, one of the men ran behind it: "Where are you going?" The women shouted back: "We don't know, but you'll catch up with us fine. . . ." The three men were left standing by the roadside with a pile of bags, bicycles and carts. One flew into a fit of rage and tried to catch up with the lorry; another wept and kicked his bicycle.[29] Such stories of desertion are not infrequent in the refugees' accounts. And it was not always female desertion: Adrey, for example, mentions a man who was so happy to get a ride on a military lorry that he left his wife and walking stick behind.[30]

Feelings of isolation or even desertion added to the overwhelming sense of vulnerability that refugees experienced. The pervasive images of the *exode* – German Stukas setting their sights on motley caravans of cars, bikes, carts and prams, refugees fleeing from their vehicles and throwing themselves on the ground under hedges, Fifth Columnists directing the Germans to their targets – all conveyed the refugees' essential powerlessness. Symbolic of such powerlessness were the animals caught up in this human disaster.[31] Refugee accounts are littered with horses lying dead beside the road, with swollen stomachs, decomposing in the hot sun, sometimes grotesquely posed with their hooves in the air; unmilked cows roaming the fields, lowing in pain, their full udders trailing on the ground; dogs and cats and caged birds brought by their loving owners and then abandoned on the road; heads or skins of rabbits and pigs eaten by refugees and carelessly discarded. On June 12, a Swiss journalist happened upon a herd of abandoned cows in central Paris. The surrounding streets, largely deserted of cars or other vehicles, now echoed with the bellowing of these hungry animals.[32] Such sights were pathetic and disconsoling: as contrast to the invulnerable German machines – the Stuka or the Panzer – they epitomised the one-sidedness of the fight; as images of innocent, vulnerable victims, they reminded the refugees (consciously or unconsciously) of their own helplessness. Reminisced one survivor: "All escape was impossible, we were going to be massacred there, senselessly, en masse . . . No-one even panicked. More curious than anguished, we awaited our imminent fate. . . ."[33]

The animals were also images of abandonment, of irresponsibility, of obligations broken. This struck a chord with civilians who felt abandoned by their own authority figures. "So where were the anti-riot police going on their trains?" wondered Georges Sadoul, like many others on the road in May and June. "The firemen left with all their equipment, the police took their badges and truncheons with them, and yet nowhere on the roads to retreat was there anyone to put out fires or direct the traffic at cross-roads."[34] Every family's experience was different, but many certainly felt that they had been left to fend for themselves, at best given a few minutes to evacuate their homes, without any indication of where to go or how to get there, at worst waking up one morning to find that the authorities had already vanished.

If the sight of animals dead or in pain was disgusting as well as sad or incongruous, equally hard to stomach was the sight of retreating soldiers in among the civilians (a sight which became increasingly commonplace in June). Amid a multitude of "cruel images", one refugee gave priority to her recollection of six haggard, ragged soldiers with a single object in their possession – a frying pan.[35] Another remembered the first time that he saw infantrymen without their weapons, heads down, scuffling along. At first, he and his companions took them to be stragglers, left behind by their units. The next day, the stragglers were more numerous and disconcerting: "Limping, ragged, only recognisable as soldiers (or former soldiers) by their caps."[36]

While civilians thus witnessed the army decomposing before their eyes, soldiers, and particularly officers, found it shaming and infuriating to have to share the road with horse-drawn carts, prams and bicycles. Sighed one officer, retreating from Belgium on May 18: "If only we were among ourselves, among soldiers, to act and manoeuvre. . . ."[37] The long, straggling lines of civilians, most of them women and children, were an impediment to military operations and a threat to military security (since the refugees were believed to be providing cover for thousands of enemy agents). They were also (to use gendered language that seems appropriate in the circumstances) a humiliating audience to the army's impotence and to Frenchmen's failure to perform their most basic role – protecting their country, their women, children, and elderly.

Explanations and recriminations

Politically speaking, the *exode* created ideal conditions for what was to become the Vichy backlash: frustration with officialdom;[38] the self-absorption of exhausted refugees;[39] the lurid fears of social disorder that hordes of refugees and inexplicable reverses and blunders aroused, especially in the minds of conservatives; and above all, the intuition that the defeat *must have been* more than a military event. Paradoxically, in fact, it was often easier for people to explain the defeat than to grasp that it had happened. The reality of the débâcle was still being resisted in mid-June, by which time almost everyone seemed to have an explanation for it. One suspects that the captain encountered by Arthur Koestler in July did not have to think long and hard before blaming the defeat on "an international conspiracy of plutocrats and Socialists, inspired by Jews",[40] nor the right-wing publisher Bernard Grasset before expostulating: "This is where your shitty republic has led us."[41]

Much of the blame, naturally, was directed at the nation's erstwhile leaders, men like Gamelin and the former Prime Minister Daladier. Gamelin's sacking on May 19 was widely applauded, and the rumours that he had committed suicide were received with an approving murmur. Daladier, too, became very unpopular very quickly. He was criticised for what now seemed an inadequate rearmament effort, over which, either as Minister of War or as Prime Minister, he had presided virtually throughout. By others he was held responsible for having declared an unwinnable war in September 1939 or for failing to take advantage of the eight-month breathing space that Hitler had given France. In May, he seems to have been more unpopular than Reynaud, perhaps because it was felt to be unpatriotic to attack the head of the government in a national crisis, perhaps because of Reynaud's gift for sounding tougher and more resolute than he was, but perhaps also because Daladier had commanded such trust and confidence in the late 1930s, had seemed the closest approximation to a strong national leader, and now had disappointed. In June, Reynaud's star fell as fast as Daladier's. On the roads, rumours spread to the effect that the Prime Minister had absconded with the proceeds of the National Lottery.[42]

The temptation to pass the buck was insuperable in circumstances such as these. Reynaud himself gave the lead: on May 28 he denounced the "treason" of King Leopold of Belgium, after the Belgians agreed to end hostilities. Reynaud's close adviser, Dominique Leca, insisted that the Prime Minister's real purpose was to fire a warning shot across the bows of French generals and politicians who wanted to emulate Leopold.[43] In any case, his speech both expressed and amplified a sensation of abandonment, a feeling that France had been left in the lurch by its allies. At the end of May, this translated into anger at the two million or so Belgian refugees in France, "Boches du Nord" as they were scornfully labelled.[44] The tone of this generally short-lived hostility was exemplified in some remarks of the historian Lucien Febvre: "millions of Belgians are inundating France; one sees a lot of luxury cars . . . wasting our petrol, carrying around arrogant fellows who . . . make faces at the fine wine offered them in the shops. . . ."[45] A couple of weeks later, one of these well-off refugees, a journalist from Brussels, recorded a typical tirade: "It was your king who opposed the extension of the Maginot Line in your direction, all so that he could surrender at his own convenience!"[46]

After Dunkirk, however, such resentments were redirected at the British. There was a widespread view that Britain's military effort in France had been inadequate and half-hearted.[47] Within certain sections of political opinion, later well represented in Vichy, British treachery provided the most straightforward explanation for what had befallen France. In early July, Admiral Darlan, the head of the French Navy and future Vichy Prime Minister, told a group of naval officers that the British had been secretly preparing the BEF's withdrawal long before it became militarily necessary. According to Darlan, the British had sabotaged Weygand's plans to reunite the northern and southern armies in late May. More fundamentally, from the outset they had manipulated France into declaring war and then taking the brunt of the German assault.[48] Darlan's Anglophobia was echoed by many other officers. General Voruz, the head of the French Mission to the BEF, concluded in retrospect that France had supported the wrong side and should have fought with the Germans against the British.[49] And one of Darlan's naval subordinates had a similar thought: "From the Treaty of Versailles [of 1919], they [the English] were our worst enemies . . . They sabotaged our currency; they bought our newspapers and our deputies to foster dissension, so that France became an English satellite in economic as well as diplomatic terms."[50] (Francophobic British officials expressed similarly ungracious feelings in the reverse direction. Thus Lord Hankey, minister without portfolio, on June 17: "The more I reflect on the events of recent years the more I realise that the French have been our evil genius from the Paris Peace Conference until today, inclusive."[51])

Betrayed by their allies, many of the troops also felt betrayed by their government. The government's own monitoring of mail found such sentiments frequently expressed. In a letter to his wife, an officer in the 61st Infantry Division complained of lack of aerial support and fire power: "It's simply shameful . . . It's as if you asked a horseman to stop an on-coming locomotive with his lance. The true culprits are not the soldiers, but the powers that be and the members of parliament who failed to give them planes, tanks, and anti-tank weapons capable of standing up to the enemy." A soldier in the same unit echoed this conclusion: "Reynaud lied odiously to save his Popular Front government, guilty of neglecting the airforce . . . The main culprit is the State. The State failed in its duty to prepare for war. Pulverised and shot to ribbons, the soldier did what he could."[52] "Those emasculated pygmies", expostulated one officer about politicians and "politician-generals": "Literally I have never met a single one of my *poilus* who has not expressed his disgust for the parliamentary regime and has not insisted on the Deputies and their policy as being solely responsible for the disaster."[53] This animosity towards the politicians did not necessarily let the military leadership off the hook. Even violently anti-republican officers were to be found criticising the top brass. "Certainly, [our generals] are guilty", admitted one such officer on June 15. "They knew how decrepit France was and they did nothing to make up for it . . . They were obsessed by the war of 1914."[54]

How could this sudden revelation of inadequacy be reconciled with the confidence that the army and navy had inspired just weeks before? Conspiracy theories of one kind or another provided easy answers. The idea that Germany had benefited from a covert "Fifth Column" was everywhere. Rumours abounded of spies signalling by morse code to German aircraft, Wehrmacht officers disguised as nuns or priests or nurses, or German parachutists dropping into Parisian parks. In early June, for example, it was reported that French troops in Belgium had had to remove the advertisement panels for a certain brand of chicory which, when treated with "a special chemical reagent", revealed information of use to the enemy.[55]

Six months after the defeat, André Morize, who had worked in the Ministry of Information before fleeing the country, published a much-remarked article in the American newspaper, *The Sunday Star*, claiming that the Fifth Column had been "not a legend but a deadly reality". Morize described "entire regiments of Germans" living in Holland as disguised civilians and paying off French Communists to sabotage war factories. Lest one suspect that such fantasies were uniquely French, one should note that France's allies took them equally seriously. The British government had reacted to rumours of Fifth Column treachery in Holland by interning enemy aliens in Britain. And after reading Morize's article, a high-ranking official in US military intelligence warned Washington that the Axis had plenty of agents in America ready to sabotage American preparedness just as they had done in France: "On good authority I am told that the typewriter industry is filled with fifth columnists", Major-General Robert Richardson noted to the Chief of Staff of the War Department.[56] As Paul Fussell has pointed out in his cultural history of the British and American experience during the Second World War, rumours and innuendo of this kind were commonplace at every stage of the fighting.[57] But they were particularly irresistible at a time when both left and right were struggling to make sense of improbable and embarrassing events. The Fifth Column was a politically malleable concept. Conservatives could use it to deflect blame away from the military hierarchy and towards supposed communist subversion (Weygand, for example, claimed at one point in mid-June that the Communist party leader Thorez had seized control of the Élysée). Antifascists, on the other hand, could use it to highlight the treachery of fascist sympathisers within the army or the civilian population, thereby exculpating the Republic itself.

For those disinclined to conspiracy theories, an alternative explanation for the unexpected reverses lay in the wasted opportunities of the "phony war", the period between the declaration of war in September 1939 and the German invasion. Returning to Paris in early May after serving in Syria, the parliamentarian Pierre Mendès-France found that the country's morale had deteriorated markedly during these months. Both in the army and among civilians he encountered a frightening complacency: "Little by little, the leaders gave up all initiative . . . Everyone, civilians and military alike, sought only to arrange their personal life as well as possible, so as to get through this seemingly indefinite period without too much risk, loss or discomfort. . . ."[58] Eight months of boredom, drinking, paper-pushing, and well-intended "diversions" had softened the troops' determination. An army of "card players" and "football champions" was no match for a real army.[59]

The only other way of reconciling defeat with prewar confidence was to acknowledge that the nation had been fooling itself in 1939 and for many years before. Most of the "large" cultural or structural explanations of the defeat that were to be popularised in Vichy or by the Resistance were first aired in the very midst of defeat. Thus, for example, the heavy moralising tone that Vichy virtually institutionalised in July was already finding expression in May and June. André Gide's reaction to events is well known but not atypical: "O incurably frivolous people of France! You are going to pay dearly today for your lack of application, your nonchalance, your smug reclining among so many charming qualities!"[60] Or to quote the less well known but equally representative sentiments of Hyacinthe Chobaut, an archivist from the Vaucluse: "The main culprit is the average Frenchman himself – spineless, selfish, unprolific"; "There's the result of fifty years of weakness, neglect, selfishness, the Republic of Pals ('République des camarades')."[61] In June, as Weygand famously blamed the defeat on "the spirit of pleasure and ease", church leaders told their congregations that the country could only recover "insofar as all Frenchmen of all classes and parties strike their breast [in confession of sins]".[62] Cardinal Gerlier of Lyons, Archbishop Feltin of Bordeaux, Monseigneur Caillot of Grenoble and other Catholic leaders suggested not just that defeat was God's punishment on an immoral, secular nation; they implied that it was a blessing in disguise ("if France had been victorious it would have remained the prisoner of its errors", to quote Gerlier).[63] While refusing to say that the war itself had been unjust, the Catholic writer François Mauriac echoed the hierarchy's call for contrition: "It is insofar as we acknowledge the proximate and the distant causes of this collapse that we will have a chance to recover from it; insofar also as all Frenchmen of all classes and parties strike their breast." (June 18)[64] The sin that was confessed most frequently was "egoism": an entire generation was alleged to have reacted against the

13

sufferings of the trenches by turning to hedonism and to have abandoned Christian values and morals in favour of materialism and individualism. Within a month Mauriac began to recognise the dangers of excessive "*mea culpa*-ism*", but the idea that national regeneration required confession was well and truly launched.[65]

A different kind of charge against the interwar generation was that it had been lazy and averse to change. This was one of Marc Bloch's main themes in a famous memoir that the historian wrote in the summer of 1940. Bloch argued that a lethargic, leisurely, too comfortable society had succumbed to a more dynamic, modern society. "If only to preserve what can, and ought to, be of value in our great heritage, we must adapt ourselves to the claims of a new age. The donkey-cart may be a friendly and a charming means of transport, but if we refuse to replace it by the motor-car, where the motor-car is desirable, we shall find ourselves stripped of everything – including the donkey."[66] Koestler picked up the same metaphor from a German journalist: "France . . . [was] travelling happily in a little mule cart, amidst the feverish stream of locomotives and automobiles on the highway of European destiny."[67] "Total ignorance of the new conditions of modern life", summed up the economist Charles Rist, who, like Bloch, singled out the bourgeoisie for particular blame in this regard. "Everywhere a lack of curiosity about new things made abroad and lack of information about things French. The rule is 'continue as is'."[68] It is hard to read such damning evocations of a country of donkey-carts without thinking of the *exode* – a society revealed to itself in all its archaic clutter of carts, wheelbarrows, barnyard animals, and mattresses. And yet, to complicate matters, the *exode* also confonted society with the limitations of modernity: cars and lorries often had to be abandoned because of petrol shortages and mechanical breakdowns, while the donkey-carts plodded on. The lessons of this experience were not straightforward.

Next steps

Then, finally, there was the question of: what next? As the extent and full meaning of defeat began to sink in, the French were faced by the need to accommodate themselves to the steadily encroaching disaster. The accommodations were shaped by a range of factors: personal or professional circumstances; accidents of location; political or ideological commitments; and, last but not least, a varying sense of personal connection to this national "event". The defeat hit home inescapably for some people – for example, relatives of the 90,000 soldiers and 30,000 civilians who had lost their lives, or the 250,000 who had been wounded or the more than one million who had been captured by the enemy. Others felt a greater distance from it – physically if they were lucky enough to live in an area that saw no fighting or few refugees, or sometimes just psychologically[69] (one of the effects of the conspiracy theories and wild rumours that were flying around in May and June was to relieve individuals of any sense of personal responsibility for what had happened).

A very few literally could not bear to go on. In his diary entry of May 9, Sadoul records the view of a Jewish officer hours before the invasion: "If we are defeated, I will kill myself at once."[70] We do not know what became of this particular officer, but there are plenty of reports of suicide in the wake of the invasion. On June 14, for example, the Prefect of Police in Paris, Roger Langeron, noted sixteen suicides in the city, including that of a famous neuro-surgeon, Thierry de Martel, son of the fin-de-siècle novelist, Gyp. Langeron reported that the surgeon could not tolerate the idea of defeat or the presence of the Germans in Paris.[71] Others killed themselves out of remorse for their own failings – for example, the managing director of a mining company in the North, who panicked and fled to Paris when he heard about the German victories and later felt ashamed of his flight.[72] (Perhaps it was a comparable sense of shame that prompted Daladier to contemplate suicide in June.[73]) Certain others were overwhelmed by a feeling of hopelessness: Arthur Koestler remembered the despair which gripped anti-Nazi refugees like himself in June, especially after they learned that Article 19 of the armistice obliged the French government to turn over all German nationals demanded by the Nazi authorities. "We thought that this time the defeat was final; we had been beaten out of one European country after another; this was the *coup de grâce*, journey's end."[74]

For others – a large number, though still only a small fraction of the population – the journey was just beginning. Those with the resources to travel, as well as the good fortune to avoid capture by the Germans, had the option to escape. In the first instance, escape – for government officials and politicians as for the mass of refugees – meant heading south or west in order to keep out of the German army's grasp. In mid-June, however, as the Germans advanced across the Loire and deep into central and western France, escape had to mean leaving metropolitan France altogether.

As Gérard Miller has observed, exile was really a very different choice from *exode*; the latter had been in essence a flight *towards* France (that is, an unoccupied France) rather than away from it.[75] Even for those who had the resources and the opportunity to leave French soil, this was a difficult step to take. The British journalist Alexander Werth, who left Bordeaux on June 18 aboard the British vessel *SS Madura* recorded the hesitations of French passengers, many of whom were seized by last minute *crises de conscience* about leaving.[76] Those who did not turn back no doubt felt the same wrenching emotion that Mendès-France expressed, on leaving Paris: "A loved one whom one meets again after several years of separation is no longer the same person. She has lived on, she has suffered, she has aged, she has changed . . . One day I will return to a free Paris, but she will no longer be the Paris that I have known."[77]

The arguments against leaving were powerful. Some were practical – how will I earn a living? what will become of my family? who will take care of my belongings and professional interests?[78] Other reasons could be principled. In a prison-cell in Chartres, the Prefect of Eure-et-Loir, Jean Moulin, reflected on a civil servant's obligation to the population: "Run away? . . . Wouldn't that be to act like the others, like all those who have run away from responsibilities, hunger or danger!"[79] The fact that Moulin, who within a matter of months became the first prefect involved in organised resistance, should have advised the elected officials and public servants in his department to remain at their posts and carry out their functions as best they could underlines the danger of automatically equating escape with pre-resistance or staying put with pre-collaboration. Indeed, many of the pioneers of resistance inside France were sharply critical of General de Gaulle and his supporters for leaving France. General Cochet, for example, who is credited with having made the first public appeal for resistance in mainland France (in September 1940) argued that "An *émigré* inevitably ends up losing sight of his country's interest and espousing the interests and feelings of the country that welcomed him, so that one day he finds himself taking up arms against his own fatherland."[80]

Some like Georges Mandel, Reynaud's Minister of the Interior, tried to draw a distinction between escaping to French North Africa (which could be rationalised as not really leaving France at all) and journeying to a foreign country. Mandel headed a group of twenty-seven politicians who left Bordeaux in late June on board the liner *Massilia* in the hope of establishing the French government in Morocco or Algeria. Nonetheless, this intransigent critic of the armistice was as attached to French soil as his arch-opponent Pétain,[81] and refused British invitations to come to London. "The struggle must go on on French soil, not in England."[82] The pro-Pétain press ignored Mandel's distinction and vilified the *Massilia* passengers as cowardly and unpatriotic. There were also unmistakably anti-semitic overtones in the wave of hostility that engulfed the "runaways".[83] It was perhaps a back-handed acknowledgement to the force of these stereotypes that many Jews in the still unoccupied south decided against departure precisely because such a step could be characterised as abandoning the *patrie en danger*.[84]

Why, then, did certain people overcome these inhibitions? Needless to say, no single factor was decisive in every case, but a number of factors seem relevant. One was youth: the average age of those who enlisted in the Free French forces in England was mid-20s.[85] Younger people presumably had fewer commitments back home. For older people, the opportunity to coordinate departure plans with family members was often crucial. One of the first members of the future Free France to reach London in June 1940, Pierre Denis, noted that many of the French servicemen who had been, as it were, washed up unexpectedly on British shores (for example, wounded troops ferried over to England from Dunkirk and then left behind by their units) were also the most eager to return to France. Not having planned their departure and being without news of their family, they tended to think of their absence not as escape but as abandonment.[86]

The conscious choice to come to Britain was most likely to be made by those who were not only able to plan it in advance but had some sense of what they were going to find abroad. Again according to Denis, people who had spent extended periods of time working outside France were both more confident about the ultimate outcome of the war and more likely to stay in Britain.[87] It was hardly coincidental, perhaps, that the first French officer to rally to de Gaulle's side (Claude Hettier de Boislambert) had been a liaison to the British Expeditionary Force, whose contacts with the British had secured him passage on a British vessel. As one of Reynaud's aides frankly admitted, in recollecting his own decision to leave Bordeaux, "If I had not lived twelve months of my life – between the ages of 24 and 25 – in the good city of London . . . doubtless I would not have taken the decisive step so easily."[88] Of course, there were countless French officials with experience abroad who did not opt to leave in 1940. But among those who did leave, some prior experience abroad probably eased the decision. In this regard, it is worth recalling that de Gaulle himself had served outside France during his military career (not to mention a year of youthful "exile" that he had undergone in 1907, when his Jesuit schoolteachers had been forced out of France), and that in the weeks before his departure for London he had made close contacts with British officials, which gave him some hope of being taken seriously.

An equally important factor was the means to escape, which most people did not have. Denis, for example, admitted in his memoirs that he had given up the idea of crossing the Channel until he happened to run into friends who offered him a seat on a plane heading to London. It was not surprising that the largest single group of civilians to make it to England were fishermen and merchant sailors, mostly from Brittany,[89] or that many air force pilots escaped to bases in North Africa, while those who flew planes with short flight ranges were forced to remain in metropolitan France.[90] The same applied to politicians. The 65 or so members of parliament who had reached Bordeaux by June 17 had a greater chance of getting out of France, if they so chose, than the 800 or so who were not in Bordeaux.

For the mass of the population who did not have the means or the opportunity to consider escape, the strongest impulse was to bring their personal nightmares to an end, to reunite their families and return home. Listening to Pétain's message was painful for any patriot; and it is perhaps revealing that memoirists so often recalled hearing the Marshal's June 17 broadcast wafting through an open window, as though such indirection minimised their own complicity. (Of course, many *were* living out of doors, but it was also psychologically easier to think of the news as just "in the air".) Still, the general reaction to the announcement seems to have been that it was long overdue. "Peace, peace, peace, what are they waiting for?" was the constant refrain that Sadoul heard on June 16.[91] The following day Hyacinthe Chobaut observed that people in the Vaucluse were "delighted to see the war end".[92] Others remarked on an atmosphere of relief. The phrase of the moment was "We must be done with it" ("Il faut en finir") – an obvious, ironic echo of the slogan with which the French had entered the war nine months earlier. Among refugees (even among the very few who actually heard de Gaulle's famous broadcast from London on June 18), the call to continued resistance elicited little enthusiasm. Sadoul heard de Gaulle's speech with a group of fellow soldiers: "Go fight yourself, you bastard. You've got your arse in an armchair and you want other people to go on getting themselves killed."[93] Civilians he met felt the same way.

The ending of hostilities confronted the French with the unheroic "detritus" of defeat. Encountering German soldiers for the first time was a trauma in itself: some gawked, others shook hands or tried to ingratiate themselves, others again were shocked or depressed by the sight of the enemy. When a German gave him a can of meat, Léon Werth felt a palpable humiliation: "Such is war, it imposes a rough and ready simplification . . . It opposes the victor and the vanquished . . . Nothing in this instant can prevent the soldier from being all victory and me from being all defeat."[94] There were other tangible signs of defeat to be absorbed: groups of French prisoners being guarded by German captors, clocks turned forward to Berlin time, German troops laden with cigarettes or sitting with their feet up, drinking champagne.

A second trauma was the realisation that, even after the armistice, it would not be so easy – literally or figuratively – to go back home. Trains were infrequent and petrol remained hard to come by in many areas. When the armistice terms were made public, millions of refugees found that a demarcation line and cumbersome procedures for travel now separated them from their homes – if they still had homes (400,000 houses had been destroyed). Those who had fled from sixteen northern and eastern departments found that the possibility of return was excluded altogether. In the northern zone, occupied by the Germans, the population had to adapt to a nightly curfew, to the sight of German posters on their walls and swastikas on public buildings.[95] 1.8 million soldiers were on their way to German prisoner-of-war camps; almost a million women learned that their husbands had been killed or captured. For them, as Sarah Fishman has said, "the real nightmare began after the armistice".[96] For many others, too.

Notes and references

1 *The Flanders Road* (London: John Calder, 1985), p. 152.

2 E. du Réau, *Edouard Daladier, 1884–1970* (Paris: Fayard, 1993), pp. 424, 518.

3 P. Béarn, *De Dunkerque en Liverpool* (Paris: Gallimard, 1941), p. 132.

4 Diary entry, 16 May 1940, *The Adolf A. Berle Diary* (Hyde Park, New York: Franklin D. Roosevelt Library, 1978), Roll 2, Frame 636.

5 P. Mendès-France, *Liberté, liberté chérie* (New York: Didier, 1943), p. 24.

6 J. de Riedmatten, *Quatre ans d'occupation sur la côte malouine et . . . ailleurs* (Rennes: Imprimerie de "La Voix de l'Ouest", 1946), p. 21.

7 See, for example, the works by Albert-Sorel, Barlone, Friedmann, Tony-Révillon, and Werth, cited below.

8 J. Albert-Sorel, *Le Chemin de Croix, 1939–1940* (Paris: R. Julliard, 1943), pp. 103–4.

9 *Les Evénements survenus en France de 1933 à 1945. Témoignages*, 9 vols (Paris: PUF, 1951–52), vol. 7, pp. 1967–8.

10 L. Werth, *33 jours* (Paris: Viviane Hamy, 1992), pp. 37, 46–7.

11 Tony-Révillon, *Mes carnets* (Paris: O. Lieutier, 1945), p. 17.

12 G. Friedmann, *Journal de guerre, 1939–1940* (Paris: Gallimard, 1987), pp. 267–8.

13 D. Barlone, *A French Officer's Diary* (Cambridge: Cambridge University Press, 1943), p. 74. Emphasis mine.

14 J. Dutourd, *Au bon beurre* (Paris: Gallimard, 1952), p. 84.

15 Werth, *33 jours*, p. 13.

16 A. Koestler, *Scum of the Earth* (New York: Macmillan, 1941), p. 184.

17 A. Meynier, *Les Déplacements de la population vers la Bretagne en 1940–1941* (Rennes: Les Nourritures Terrestres, 1950), pp. 5–7.

18 Koestler, *Scum of the Earth*, p. 182.

19 C. Jamet, *Carnets de déroute* (Paris: Sorlot, 1942), p. 130.

20 J. Vidalenc, *L'Exode de mai–juin 1940* (Paris: Presses Universitaires de France (PUF), 1957), pp. 415–16; Meynier, *Les Déplacements*, p. 97.

21 G. Adrey, *Journal d'un replié* (Paris: René Debresse, 1941), p. 52. In the next breath, this author recognised the dark side of solidarity – the lawlessness of anonymous crowds (discussed below).

22 R. Cobb, *Promenades* (Oxford: Oxford University Press, 1980), p. 53.

23 Adrey, *Journal*, pp. 62–3.

24 T. de Vibraye, *Avec mon groupe de reconnaissance* (Roanne: Ordres de Chevalerie, 1943), p. 146.

25 Jamet, *Carnets*, p. 130.

26 G. Sadoul, *Journal de guerre* (Paris: Les Editeurs Français Réunis, 1977), p. 336.

27 Sadoul, *Journal*, p. 234.

28 Meynier, *Les Déplacements*, p. 68.

29 Sadoul, *Journal*, pp. 335–6.

30 Adrey, *Journal*, p. 35. Notwithstanding this counter-example, it is striking how often contemporary accounts of the *exode* depicted the experience in terms of "inappropriate or deviant female behavior", as Miranda Pollard has pointed out in her recent study of Vichy's gender politics: *Reign of Virtue* (Chicago: University of Chicago Press, 1998), p. 30.

31 On this theme see, for example, the works by Vibraye, Jamet, Adrey, Langeron, and Werth cited in this chapter.

32 This episode from the postwar memoir of Edmond Dubois is recounted in M. Rajsfus, *Les Français de la débâcle* (Paris: Le Cherche Midi, 1997), p. 45.

33 Albert-Sorel, *Chemin de Croix*, p. 85.

34 Sadoul, *Journal*, p. 351.

35 A. Humbert, *Notre guerre* (Paris: Editions Emile-Paul Frères, 1946), p. 15.

36 Werth, *33 jours*, pp. 30–32.

37 Vibraye, *Avec mon groupe*, p. 142.

38 H. R. Kedward, "Patriots and patriotism in Vichy France", *Royal Historical Society Transactions* (5th ser.), 32 (1982), pp. 175–92.

39 Friedmann, *Journal*, p. 307.

40 Koestler, *Scum of the Earth*, pp. 237–8.

41 Quoted in J. Grenier, *Sous l'Occupation* (Paris: Ed. Claire Paulhan, 1997), p. 137.

42 R. Baudouin, quoted in *Paris-Match*, 24 May 1990.

43 D. Leca, *La Rupture de 1940* (Paris: Fayard, 1978), p. 163.

44 J. Vanwelkenhuyzen and J. Dumont, *1940, le grand exode* (Brussels: RTBF, 1983), p. 213. Anti-Belgian feeling was not uniform across the country. In certain southern departments where German-speaking evacuees from Alsace and Lorraine had been resettled at the outbreak of war, the francophone Belgians benefited from the popular hostility towards the earlier refugees. See L. Boswell, "Franco-Alsatian conflict and the crisis of national sentiment during the phoney war", *Journal of Modern History*, 71: 3 (1999), pp. 574–5.

45 Friedmann, *Journal*, p. 244.

46 D. Denuit, *L'Été ambigu de 1940* (Brussels: Louis Musin, 1978), p. 190.

47 J.-L. Crémieux-Brilhac, *Les Français de l'an 40*, 2 vols (Paris: Gallimard, 1990), vol. 1, pp. 570, 583.

48 H. Coutau-Bégarie and C. Huan, *Lettres et notes de l'Amiral Darlan* (Paris: Economica, 1992), pp. 214–19.

49 Quoted in F. Delpla (ed.), *Les Papiers secrets du Général Doumenc* (Paris: O. Orban, 1992), p. 143.

50 Béarn, *De Dunkerque*, pp. 161–2.

51 Quoted in M. Dockrill, *British Establishment Perspectives on France, 1936–40* (London: Macmillan, 1999), p. 156.

52 A. Lefébure, *Les Conversations secrètes des Français sous l'Occupation* (Paris: Plon, 1993), pp. 53–5.

53 Barlone, *Diary*, pp. 90, 97.

54 Béarn, *De Dunkerque*, p. 113.

55 Barlone, *Diary*, p. 66.

56 Major-Gen. R. Richardson, "Memorandum for the Chief of Staff", 3 Feb. 1941, in *US Military Intelligence Reports: France, 1919–1941* (Frederick, Maryland: University Publications of America, 1985), Roll 12.

57 P. Fussell, *Wartime. Understanding and behavior in the Second World War* (New York: Oxford University Press, 1989), pp. 35–51.

58 Mendès-France, *Liberté*, p. 11.

59 Sadoul, *Journal*, p. 207.

60 A. Gide, *Pages de journal 1939–1942* (New York: Pantheon, 1944), p. 27.

61 Crémieux-Brilhac, *Les Français*, vol. 1, p. 612.

62   P. Laborie, *L'Opinion française sous Vichy* (Paris: Seuil, 1990), pp. 225–6.

63   W. D. Halls, *Politics, Society and Christianity in Vichy France* (Oxford: Berg, 1995), pp. 38–9. Halls argues that French Protestants were more wary of this need for repentance.

64   D. Cordier, *Jean Moulin, l'inconnu du Panthéon*, 3 vols (Paris: J.-C. Lattès, 1989–93), vol. 3, pp. 147–8.

65   Cordier, *Jean Moulin*, vol. 3, pp. 175–6.

66   M. Bloch, *Strange Defeat* (New York: Norton, 1968), p. 149.

67   Koestler, *Scum of the Earth*, p. 270.

68   C. Rist, *Une Saison gâtée* (Paris: Fayard, 1983), pp. 88, 123.

69   Friedmann, *Journal*, pp. 253–4.

70   Sadoul, *Journal*, p. 191.

71   R. Langeron, *Paris juin 40* (Paris: Flammarion, 1946), pp. 53–4. Cf. W. Silverman, "Life and death of a 'non-conformist': Thierry de Martel (1875–1940)", *Modern and Contemporary France*, 5: 1 (1997), pp. 5–19.

72   Crémieux-Brilhac, *Les Français*, vol. 1, p. 574.

73   Du Réau, *Daladier*, p. 419.

74   Koestler, *Scum of the Earth*, p. 205.

75   *Les Pousse-au-jouir du Maréchal Pétain* (Paris: Seuil, 1975), p. 30.

76   A. Werth, *The Last Days of Paris* (London: Hamish Hamilton, 1940), pp. 208–9.

77   Mendès-France, *Liberté*, p. 40. Surprisingly, the English translation of this book, published well after the war, omitted these poignant lines.

78   C. Rimbaud, *L'Affaire du Massilia* (Paris: Seuil, 1984), p. 74.

79   Cordier, *Jean Moulin*, vol. 2, pp. 345–6.

80   Cordier, *Jean Moulin*, vol. 3, p. 194.

81   G. Palewski, *Mémoires d'action, 1924–1974* (Paris: Plon, 1988), p. 130.

82   Quoted in Rimbaud, *L'Affaire*, p. 37.

83   Rimbaud, *L'Affaire*, p. 193.

84   R. Poznanski, *Etre juif en France pendant la seconde guerre mondiale* (Paris: Hachette, 1994), pp. 60–61.

85   J.-L. Crémieux-Brilhac, *La France Libre* (Paris: Gallimard, 1996), p. 97.

86   P. Denis, *Souvenirs de la France Libre* (Paris: Berger-Levrault, 1947), pp. 29–31.

87   Denis, *Souvenirs*, p. 31.

88 Leca, *La Rupture*, p. 91.

89 Crémieux-Brilhac, *France Libre*, pp. 85–6.

90 Mendès-France, *Liberté*, p. 87.

91 Sadoul, *Journal*, p. 355.

92 Crémieux-Brilhac, *Les Français*, vol. 1, p. 613.

93 Sadoul, *Journal*, p. 378.

94 Werth, *33 jours*, pp. 65–6.

95 D. Veillon, *Vivre et survivre en France, 1939–1947* (Paris: Payot, 1995), pp. 62–70.

96 S. Fishman, *We Will Wait. Wives of French prisoners of war, 1940–1945* (New Haven, Connecticut: Yale University Press, 1991), p. 27.

PART ONE

The Politics of Defeat

CHAPTER ONE

Expectations

Every present has its future that illuminates and disappears with it, that
becomes past-future . . .

Jean-Paul Sartre, *Les Carnets de la drôle de guerre* (12 November 1939)[1]

One of the truisms about the fall of France is that defeat came out of the
blue. This is true, but it is not the whole truth. Certainly, the speed and
decisiveness of the German breakthrough confounded expectations. The
military had been prepared for an updated version of trench warfare, in
which they would hold the Germans at bay from strong, fixed positions.
Noted one officer in June 1940: "We were so accustomed to the idea of a
continuous front-line, like that of the last war, that it seems difficult to conceive how to organize resistance without it."[2] Civilians had been prepared,
quite simply, for victory. At times, it even sounded as though victory had
already been achieved. In February 1940, for instance, the minister in charge
of propaganda, Jean Giraudoux, told the members of the American Club of
Paris: "Our soldiers have set the pace; it is for us to keep it up when the war
is over."[3] A month earlier a well-known and reputedly well-informed journalist, Geneviève Tabouis, alleged that "the Allies have already won the war,
even though we do not yet see directly how the German defeat will unfold
and when it will begin".[4] Perhaps Tabouis's source came from the Third
Bureau of the French High Command, whose officers were busily engaged
in drawing up plans for Germany's postwar partition on the assumption
that "the war is over and we have won".[5] Re-reading phony war newspapers
in July 1940, the author Paul Léautaud found them comic, but also wretched:
"Such assurance, such decisiveness, such certainty, in all the forecasts . . . Not
the slightest dubious tone or slightest reserve as to the possibility of a new
development. No. The game played and won in advance."[6]

On the other hand, the bluff optimism of the press and of officialdom told only part of the story. One only had to probe a little deeper to detect an underlying ambivalence about French prospects, an ambivalence stemming from memories of the ghastly bloodshed of two decades earlier and from the steady pessimism of the 1930s. Defeat may not have been expected, but it was far from unimaginable. The politics of defeat cannot be understood unless one takes into account both its unexpectedness and its predictability.[7]

The unexpectedness intensified the shock and disorientation that gripped the parliamentary elite as well as the general public in the wake of the débâcle. Certainly, other aspects of their experience – such as the mass exodus of refugees and the virtual disintegration of the French State – contributed to the disorientation. But the contrast between expectation and experience was critical. Nothing did more to separate French society from its political moorings or to foster exaggerated or blatantly partisan constructions of the defeat's meaning.

Conversely, the predictability of the disaster helps to explain why the political vacuum created by defeat was filled almost instantaneously. Beneath the superficial optimism of the phony war, many people had, in fact, long doubted the capacity of the Republic and the nation to prevail. The defeat was strange, but to many it seemed – once it had happened – entirely natural. This fact is central to an understanding of the rapid politicisation of defeat. One could say that almost all the personalities who came to the fore in mid-1940 – with Pétain in Bordeaux and Vichy, with de Gaulle in London, with the Germans in Paris – were people who had long had their doubts about the vitality of their society or the soundness of their national institutions. These were people for whom, in short, defeat made sense.

Assumptions of victory

Recent studies of French attitudes at the outbreak of war (including the most comprehensive one by Jean-Louis Crémieux-Brilhac) have shown that the initial mobilisation took place in an atmosphere of relative calm and good order. William Bullitt, the American Ambassador in Paris, found the "self-control and quiet courage" so extraordinary that it had, in his words, "a dream quality" about it.[8] A French government official reported to Paris in early September 1939 that "no-one or almost no-one in the population has doubts about victory, even if they are afraid of the price it will cost". Another reported frequent comments to the effect that "We must be done with these people. This makes three wars that they have declared on us."[9] If observers detected less dash *("allant")* or enthusiasm *("ardeur")* than had been evidenced in 1914, one could hardly expect otherwise. The memory of the unimaginable losses of the previous war loomed much too large to allow for illusions about what modern war would be like; it also encouraged approval of the army's cautious strategy – "more reasonably economical with human blood than in 1914", to quote Marc Bloch.[10] Many of the reservists called up in 1939 had, like Bloch, fought in the earlier war. And the young soldiers had grown up amid memorials to the carnage, if they had no personal memories of it. One private from the south, arriving at the Maginot Line after passing by a Great War cemetery on the train, was greeted by a pep talk from his commander, who instructed the new recruits that in the Great War their fathers had gone into the trenches singing. "Yes," came the reply, "but the few who came back came out crying."[11] Notwithstanding such cynicism, the predominant view was that there was no alternative to war. And if war was inevitable, it was natural to assume that victory, too, was inevitable: to assume otherwise was to believe that France was fated for destruction. Beneath the surface of this "Il faut en finir" mentality, however, lay a complex set of expectations and assumptions, which need to be explored a little further in order to understand the subsequent reactions to defeat.

Once war had been declared, it became almost impossible to state publicly that France might be headed for defeat. Officers who expressed doubts were, in effect, guilty of insubordination. When General Montagne told the Duke of Windsor (on a visit to the French lines in December 1939) that "if we go on like this, we are f . . . !", he was promptly relieved of his command.[12] It may have been a little easier for politicians to whisper this sort of thing. Two former conservative Prime Ministers, Pierre Laval and Pierre-Etienne Flandin, certainly did so. So did Paul Faure, a leading figure in the Socialist party, neo-Socialists Marcel Déat and Gaston Bergery, and the trade union leader René Belin.[13] Even some of those at the centre of power had grave doubts about France's prospects. For example, the most senior permanent official in the Foreign Ministry, Alexis Léger, admitted in front of the US ambassador in late August that it was at the least "extremely doubtful" that France and Britain could win the war.[14] In October, Paul de Villelume, who served as liaison between the Foreign Ministry and General Gamelin, warned Reynaud that "it is not at all out of the question that the outcome of the conflict may be unfavourable to us". Privately, he termed the war "a venture beyond our means".[15] Several ministers, including the Foreign Minister Georges Bonnet, had long counselled against heroic commitments that the country was not, in his view, capable of honouring.[16] (Bonnet was moved from the Foreign Ministry ten days after war was declared.) Anatole de Monzie, the Minister of Public Works, assured a friend that France was heading for the greatest disaster in its history: "The first artillery shot will mean defeat!"[17]

Such "defeatism" rested less upon an informed understanding of the military balance than upon a set of perceptions of France's relative decline, themselves reflecting ideological presuppositions such as pacifism or anti-communism. As we shall see, these ideologically driven perceptions of French weakness were quite widely diffused in the prewar decade, and yet what is striking about the period leading up to May 1940 is how relatively few people read decline to mean more or less inevitable defeat in the war.

Simone de Beauvoir recalled how the general assumption at the outset was that the democracies would win the war: "Germany was short of food, steel, petrol, indeed of everything. The German populace had no wish to get themselves wiped out; they couldn't stand a war; the Reich would collapse."[18] In October 1939, an influential American supporter of the Anglo-French strategy, Henry Stimson, described it graphically (perhaps a little too graphically!) as follows: "It seems to me that their tactics should be and are to hold the line steadily and firmly both on land and at sea until the pressure squirts Hitler and his gang out of their posts in the way that you squeeze the pus out of an ulcer."[19] Throughout the autumn of 1939 there were press-inspired rumours of imminent collapse in Germany. Though this proved to be an illusion (and a damaging one insofar as it encouraged a belief that France could win the war without really fighting), it was not a mere product of journalists' wishful thinking. Many in official circles, not least the two Allied Prime Ministers Daladier and Chamberlain, shared the public's illusions.[20]

Just how large German vulnerabilities loomed in Paris is demonstrated in the diaries of Paul de Villelume. In late August, he reported the view of the French ambassador in Germany that Hitler was wavering because of "the hesitation and . . . anxiety which prevail among certain classes of the population". On August 27 he noted disorders in Cologne, and on August 30 rumours of demoralisation in the German army and growing indiscipline in the navy. On September 4 he noted that in Düsseldorf the declaration of war had been received with "astonishment".[21] (Around the same time, the Quai d'Orsay received reports via the British Foreign Office that Hitler was in a state of nervous collapse, that the German public's morale was as low as in late 1917 and 1918, that the harvest had been poor and coal production had fallen to a record low.[22]) Again in November (though now with more scepticism) Villelume was hearing of "internal crisis" in Germany, of the low morale of German troops, and of at least one small-scale mutiny.[23]

Such hopes for a German collapse had largely faded by the end of the year, but they were survived by the related hope that the Allies could defeat Germany through an economic blockade combined, if necessary, with peripheral operations in the Baltic and in southeast Europe. The priority attached to the strategy of choking off Germany's supplies of raw materials (particularly iron ore and petrol) reflected the Allies' realisation that they were in no position to launch a military offensive in the West in 1940. However, the blockade strategy, which had informed French war planning throughout the previous decade, was not in itself a form of defeatism. Though pessimistic about the prospects of an immediate offensive, the Allied leadership was confident in its ability to repel a German offensive. Even military leaders who were adamantly opposed to an offensive strategy (such as General Georges, the Commander-in-Chief on the northeastern front) believed that France could successfully resist a German invasion.[24]

French confidence had, in fact, grown significantly in the year immediately preceding the outbreak of war. Reassuring signs of German vulnerability were magnified by indications that France had experienced a *"redressement"* in its position since the Munich conference of September 1938. Before flying off to Munich, Daladier had been warned by the Air Force Chief of Staff, General Vuillemin, that if war broke out "there will be no French air force left at the end of two weeks".[25] By all accounts, Daladier was acutely conscious of French weakness throughout the Czech crisis, and this anxiety stimulated a dependence on Britain which both limited France's room for manoeuvre and disconcerted the British. Within a few months of Munich, however, there was a marked change in Daladier's outlook. The improvement is captured in the diary of a sympathetic British diplomat, Oliver Harvey. Visiting Paris in November, Harvey was disturbed by what he heard: "Daladier, who is said to be drinking heavily and certainly looks it, has much deteriorated. . . . France is in a bad way, I'm afraid, and the people are in a thoroughly non-cooperative mood." A couple of months later, however, Harvey found that the French had "weathered their storm". Suddenly there was "greater self-confidence than a few months ago, less defeatism, less self-criticism, better economic outlook".[26]

The economic recovery seemed particularly emblematic. Following an abortive general strike at the end of November 1938, Daladier's government presided over a vigorous spurt of industrial expansion (fuelled by rearmament). Encouraged by the final disintegration of the Popular Front and the restoration of management authority in industrial relations, business confidence soared. Capitalists' approval of Daladier's government was manifested in a steady increase in the Bank of France's gold holding. Capital that had fled the country in 1936 now returned. The precious metals in French vaults seemed to offer a critical reserve that France could draw upon in the long war of economic attrition that so many expected. The political parties of the centre and right, which supported Daladier, began to boast in 1939 that the nation's slide had been halted. "We are in the seventh month of the recovery", wrote one such author in June 1939.[27] Bolstered by this new-found confidence, the right returned to its traditional role as "the preeminent [advocate] of Germanophobic nationalism",[28] while foreigners marvelled at the "French miracle".[29]

Historians are not in agreement as to how widely this perception of recovery spread or how far it sank in. Perhaps its main significance was simply that it encouraged a view of France's glass as half-full rather than half-empty. The nation's ultimate protection was the strength of the army and the deterrent force of the recently constructed fortification system in eastern France (the Maginot Line). In the past, when observers had had their doubts about these assets, as some British officials had in 1937 and 1938, they had tended to worry not just about shortcomings of French equipment or strategy, but about the larger crisis of confidence in the nation as a whole.[30] Conversely – no more or less rationally – a perceived improvement in economic conditions and a restoration of a certain kind of social order under Daladier fostered an increasing confidence in the army and in the Maginot Line.

The other pillar on which public confidence rested in 1939 was the Empire. Beset by anxieties about the looming demographic and economic advantage enjoyed by Germany, the French expected their colonies to provide countervailing resources – hundreds of thousands or even millions of soldiers as well as strategic and economic assets throughout the world.[31] The pervasiveness of this compensating myth was well captured in the recollections of a prominent critic of colonialism, Robert Davezies: "Before the war when I was a youngster, whenever people spoke of Germany and said that it was powerful and had such a high population, and that Metropolitan France would be unable to stand up to Hitler and his armies, they would quickly add that fortunately there was the whole Empire to back us up: 110 million people, if I remember rightly. . . . That was reassuring. And the rag-and-bone merchants, shoe repairers, crockery sellers and country priests who . . . said these things in the small towns and villages in the south-west so as to boost their morale were not colonialists. They genuinely meant what they said."[32] Anthony Adamthwaite has noted how diplomatic setbacks inside Europe prompted a hardening of public and official opinion against appeasement outside Europe. Polls in the three months after Munich showed that the percentage of the French public opposing such appeasement jumped from forty to seventy.[33] Cultural historians have noted various traces of this psychological reliance on the Empire. In French cinema in the late 1930s, for example, the Empire played a starring role, and one that revolved increasingly around the tangible assistance that the Empire could provide to France.[34] It was a view that rested on memories of colonial contributions during the First War rather than on precise estimates of the military contribution that the Empire could provide in the future. Not all the men running the French war effort set as much store by these assets as the propagandists of Empire did;[35] like the pile of gold in the Bank of France and the millions of tons of poured concrete in the Maginot Line fortifications, the millions of hypothetical imperial soldiers were essentially symbols of national strength. Still, we should not underestimate the role that such symbols played in shaping both popular and elite expectations for the coming conflict.

This growing confidence reached a peak in the summer and autumn of 1939. In a series of highly publicised speeches, senior military figures, including the former Commander-in-Chief, General Weygand, proclaimed the army stronger than ever. When a war over Poland became probable, the military leaders informed the government that French forces were ready. At a critical meeting on August 23, the Air Force Minister, Guy La Chambre, told Daladier that aerial weakness was no longer an impediment to decisive action (as Daladier had been told it was before Munich).[36]

A high-ranking officer assigned in October 1939 to the General Staff Headquarters of the Ninth Army (the same army which was overwhelmed by the German Ardennes offensive seven months later) found "absolute confidence" there. In postwar testimony, General Véron enumerated the bases for this confidence as follows. First, the war was unavoidable and France's cause was a just one. Second, the fact that Germany had not attacked in the west demonstrated that the enemy acknowledged France's superiority. Third, all the critical vulnerabilities of the French position could be explained away or remedied. Of course, there was concern about the "hollow classes", the years when France's cohort of available conscripts was reduced by the bloodshed two decades before; but imperial troops were there to fill the shortfall. Of course, there were doubts about the combat effectiveness of the reservists; but Véron had heard the same doubts in the First War, and in his experience they had proved groundless. Of course, there were fears of a German armament advantage; but Véron saw steady improvement in the French position and felt that the phony war was working in France's favour. And like those around him he trusted in the competence and diligence of the army's commanders as well as in the aerial strength of France's British allies.[37]

By this point, the British largely subscribed to that optimistic assessment of French military strength (if not necessarily to its deterrent effect on Hitler). British military intelligence concluded that France was strong enough to fend off any German attack. Political leaders in Britain, including the Prime Minister, the Secretary of State for War Hore-Belisha, and the First Lord of the Admiralty Winston Churchill, all lauded the superiority of the French army and the effectiveness of the Maginot Line.[38] Not all the officers serving in the British Expeditionary Force that was despatched to France after the declaration of war were so impressed.[39] And yet the tendency at the higher levels was to suppress such doubts and trust unreservedly in the French army. To quote a recent historian of the BEF, "No-one who mattered in the Franco-British leadership believed that they were running a real danger of an early, quick and complete defeat."[40]

Undoubtedly, the assurance of the early months eroded as the phony war progressed. At the front, the morale of the troops dipped during the winter months. The universal rank-and-file complaints – resentment against officers, homesickness, boredom, lack of sex, sore feet, wet clothes – were exacerbated by the lack of real fighting. If there was to be no fighting, what was the point of being there?[41] There was also an undercurrent of subversive admiration for the German military and scepticism about the reports of impending collapse in Germany.[42] Some who remembered the First War noted that the press was recycling the same yarns (*"bobards"*) that had made the rounds in 1914–18.[43]

At higher levels, there were worries about poor coordination between French and British forces, about animosities among senior French commanders (for example, between Generals Gamelin and Georges), and about the shortage of armoured divisions. Some at least were disconcerted by the lethal effectiveness of German tactics – in Poland in September and again in Norway the following April.[44] And members of the government could not fail to be disturbed by the deep and widening rift between Reynaud and Gamelin. At a cabinet meeting on the morning of May 9, 1940, Reynaud excoriated Gamelin's handling of the recent Norwegian campaign and demanded the Commander-in-Chief's replacement. When Gamelin's main supporter, the ex-Prime Minister Daladier, objected, Reynaud announced that he would resign – a decision that was only revoked as a result of the news of Germany's attack a few hours later.

Despite this behind-the-scenes turmoil, the basic expectations of 1939 – that France had the strength not to be defeated and would somehow find a way, together with her allies, to win the war – survived until the defeat. French commanders convinced themselves that the German tactics which had proved so devastating in the open spaces of the East would not work as well in the tighter, more heavily fortified confines of northwest Europe, and that French troops were made of sterner stuff than the Poles.[45] To most observers, France's position seemed stronger than it had been in September.[46] Given the premise that Germany could only win a quick war, the protracted inactivity on the Western front reassured more than it disconcerted. It was giving the French and British economies, particularly their aircraft industries, desperately needed time to make up for their late start in mobilising for war. The Allies did not envisage parity with the German mobilisation until 1941, so every month that war did not break out in the West was perceived as a small step towards victory. The German strategy of delay could also be interpreted as hesitation, which in turn encouraged a belief (credited, it seems, even by some ministers and senior officers) that Germany would never attempt an invasion in the West.[47]

Intimations of defeat

Of course, the fact that defeat was not often predicted did not mean that it was never contemplated. On the contrary, it was conceivable in the sense that something which had happened before was bound to be conceivable. "1870 all over again!" the editor of the extreme right-wing paper *Gringoire* had trumpeted in September 1939.[48] Even for those who were not defeatists, 1870 and the early disasters in 1914 were memories to be reckoned with. In the instant of defeat, these memories were unleashed in a manner that suggested that they had been at the back of many minds all along. As soon as he received the order to retreat (on May 13 or 14), the philosopher Raymond Aron thought of images of 1870 that he had picked up from reading Zola. "The shadow of 1870 spreads over the country", wrote the conservative senator Jacques Bardoux a few days later.[49] For conservatives, this date evoked not only national defeat at the hands of the Prussians but the revolutionary Commune that had established itself in Paris early in the following year and had taught the right that there was a fate even worse than defeat. The experiences of 1870–71 bequeathed to conservatives a moralistic language for explaining military failure (as the punishment meted out to a sinful nation) that made it instantly explicable when it happened again. For the Republic's defenders, the tragic memory was equally rich in associations, mostly of patriotic defiance. When the government minister Raoul Dautry, a proponent of continued resistance, left Paris in June, he carried two books with him – an edition of Péguy and the letters of a Communard-to-be who had tried to rally the French army in Metz in 1870.[50]

Defeat was more than just conceivable, however. It was also predictable for the very good reason that it had been so often predicted (implicitly or explicitly) during the preceding decade. By 1939 the perception that France had become the new "sick man of Europe" had taken deep root and had propagated a set of frightening stereotypes of national decay. In the recovery of 1939 some of these anxieties had been dissolved, especially for the possessing classes who had been traumatised by the assertiveness of the working class during the Popular Front era and by the growth of communism and were correspondingly reassured by the reassertion of management's authority and the exclusion of the marxist parties from government. If the decline anxieties were now expressed in more muted form, that did not mean that they had been overcome.

Since talk of decline in wartime could be equated with defeatism or even with treason, we should not be surprised that the politicians and intellectuals who produced it expressed themselves in coded language after September 1939. The critics of prewar society and institutions adapted their rhetoric to wartime conditions. Of course (they now said) France would win the war against Germany. But military victory would not be enough. In January 1940 a group of Socialists established a review entitled *Europe Libre* with the following aim: "We had no doubts about eventual victory and wanted to work for it with all our might. However, we rejected the slogan 'War and nothing but war' because we believed that it was necessary, even during the war, to lay out and to tackle the problems of the peace."[51] In *Le Figaro* at the turn of the year, Jean Schlumberger warned that "once through with the fight, the hardest part of the work would still be ahead of us . . . after the victory which would save us from the other side, we would need a second to save us from ourselves".[52] Characteristic of many intellectuals' response to the phony war were the feelings expressed by Emmanuel Mounier, founder of one of the leading critical journals of the 1930s, *Esprit*: "As fast as we extricate ourselves from the chaos of hostilities . . . we will have to return progressively to our normal work, to think about and prepare the postwar world."[53] In such evocations of a postwar future, the assumption of victory – whether sincere or not – was a little too peremptory to be totally convincing. The idea that France had to overcome itself implied an underlying lack of confidence in the nation's capacities, in spite of the rhetoric by which the idea was rendered politically and psychologically acceptable. The truth was that for years such critics had been saying that France was in a state of decomposition or decline. These pessimistic diagnoses had left their mark on the collective self-image of the nation (and particularly of the nation's political and intellectual elites), and could be suppressed but not forgotten at the outbreak of war.

In what sense was France perceived to be in decline? To begin with, in the most elemental sense. For decades, the French had been warned that they were losing their vitality. After being bled white by four years of trench warfare, the French population had shown itself incapable of regeneration: the sagging of France's population (especially marked in the mid–late 1930s) was not only a symbol but a physical expression of decline. While so-called pro-natalist propagandists claimed that this was the great overlooked issue in French politics, the reality was that politicians and government officials were increasingly aware of it. It was characteristic of late Third Republic politics that in the wake of the Munich crisis the Commander-in-Chief should have told his Prime Minister that France needed to re-establish its domestic equilibrium, increase its military capability, and *first and foremost* build up its birth rate.[54] To the army, even more serious than the global figures was the paucity of 20–30-year-olds; France's supply of young men was less than half that available in Germany.

In general, the image of a lethargic, shrinking population of 42 million confronting a growing, energetic German population of 80 million was ever-present in the late thirties. It encouraged a caricatured contrast (which spilled into many areas besides demography) between youthful, purposeful societies like fascist Germany and senescent, self-doubting societies like France.[55] It also tapped into a long-standing association between population and national power (an association formed in the heyday of French power in the seventeenth, eighteenth and early nineteenth centuries). In the 1930s this association had profoundly defeatist implications: in 1810 France had had 15% of Europe's population, in 1939 8.8%, by the end of the century it would be another Belgium.

The omnipresence of this image of tiredness and contraction helps to explain the strong fears aroused by large-scale immigration into France (on the surface, a logical solution to France's demographic problems and one frequently advocated by demographic experts).[56] One physical image begot another: foreigners represented an alien, almost obscene, vitality in the midst of an enfeebled host society. From the early 1930s onwards, critics (primarily but by no means exclusively on the political right) warned that France was in danger of being overrun.[57] "Our land has become a land of invasion", wrote Jean Giraudoux in 1939 shortly before becoming a minister in Daladier's government.[58] Like a growing number of politicians and self-styled experts, Giraudoux professed to be particularly disturbed by the "invasion" of Jewish immigrants from Eastern Europe. As the international crisis deepened, such immigrants were increasingly suspect, feared either as potential Fifth Columnists planted by the Nazis or as warmongers bent on inveigling their reluctant hosts into war with Hitler.[59]

The spectre of this alien element was far from the only image of national decay preoccupying contemporaries. Throughout the preceding decade critics of the republican regime had lambasted the corruption of parliament and the inefficiency of political institutions which placed coalition governments at the mercy of parliamentary manoeuvring. The instability of French governments (of which there were no fewer than sixteen between 1932 and 1940) was perceived to limit the nation's capacity to respond to the challenges of economic crisis and international tension. Parliament was viewed as a closed world of byzantine intrigue – to the left, a bastion of bourgeois influence, to the right a conduit for dangerous marxist influences and pernicious ideologies of laicism and egalitarianism.

Another area of decay lay in the economy. Modernisers lamented an economy of inefficient producers, low investment and low productivity. Their figures were almost as stark and depressing as the demographic figures. In 1934, for example, a study conducted for the Ministry of War found that the average age of French machine tools was 20 years, compared with 7 in Germany and 3 in the US.[60] In 1937 French production levels were still 25% below those of 1929, whereas most of France's neighbours had regained or surpassed 1929 levels.[61] The persistence of depression de-legitimised the republican system, whose policies seemed incapable of ending it, and stimulated interest in a variety of alternative approaches to managing the economy.[62] Criticism of liberal capitalism led to a vogue for "planning" and corporatism. It also raised doubts about France's industrial vocation. On the eve of the war, Raoul Dautry (who was to be the key figure in France's industrial mobilisation effort in 1939–40) offered a sombre assessment of the nation's industrial performance. Decrying "our slow and serious industrial decline", he warned an audience of industrialists that France had steadily lost the leading position in the world economy that it had once occupied. If France was to win "the industrial war" which it had been quietly losing for years, it would have to raise the technological level of its industries, expand its modern machine tool sector, train more engineers and technicians. This, in turn, would require nothing less than the forma- tion of a new culture, in which technical expertise would have to be valued as highly as administrative expertise.[63]

Adding to the sense of deterioration was the increasing polarisation of French society. The emergence of a dangerous anti-parliamentary right by 1934 had brought together a broad anti-fascist coalition in the Popular Front, but the end result of this reflex of republican defence was a deepen- ing of the chasm between left and right. Social and political conservatives were horrified by the very idea of a Socialist-led government and resentful of the gains that the working class achieved under it. Overlooking the anaemic performance of the economy under right-centre governments be- fore 1936, conservatives blamed the continuing depression on the Popular Front, claiming that it had capitulated to the unions and the working class in general and, in pursuit of its social agenda, had ruined the nation's finances. Once evicted from power (by the spring of 1938) the parties of the left were, in their turn, outraged by the vindictive, reactionary policies of the centre-right coalition over which Daladier presided. Thus, even though they could not agree on who was responsible for the divisions, all parties acknowledged that they existed and that they were undermining France's international situation.[64] A graphic symbol of this seeming inability to set aside partisanship in the interests of the nation was provided by the pre- parations for the 1937 World's Fair in Paris. After the Popular Front came to power, construction of the pavilions was hampered by strikes and the new forty-hour work week. Intended as an event which would showcase French national cohesion as well as French products, the Fair became a highly politicised affair, claimed by the left as the "triumph of the working class, the Popular Front, and liberty" and denounced by the right as the "Popular Front's expo". When it opened in May 1937, most of the pavilions were still unfinished – an embarrassment that labour blamed on business footdragging and business blamed on working-class radicalism.[65]

Such episodes encouraged intellectuals and critics of the status quo to describe France as living under a cloud of national malaise. "During the years of decadence," reminisced Raymond Aron, "we felt France's ills personally . . . What struck all of us – appropriately – was the contrast between the paralysis of democratic regimes and the spectacular recovery of Hitler's Germany, as well as the rates of growth published by the Soviet Union."[66] The pessimism of these years was well captured in some remarks by one of the more influential advocates of reform, Auguste Detoeuf: "Let's not fool ourselves: France is not up to the idea that we want to present of France. Her glorious obstinacy in 1914–18 . . . deceived the world and all of us. We all believed that we were still a great people . . . Without children, without daring ideas in politics or in economics . . . what are we, in terms of power, by comparison with stupid peoples who persist in proliferating in too cramped an area, who are drunk with parades and rumours of war, who tighten their belts to be strong?"[67]

It is hard not to read this pessimism as an intimation of defeat, even if there was a tendency to suppress it during the phony war. On the other hand, it is also important to see it in its proper proportion, so as to understand how it could coexist with a certain level of confidence about French prospects in the war. Such decline anxieties had been a part of French political culture for decades; much of the language used in the 1930s had been applied to France's situation in the 1870s and 1890s, for example. The distinctive feature of this "declinist" trope was the fact that it combined apprehensions about decline of national power (as measured, for example, in the birth rate or in military capability *vis-à-vis* Germany) with a broader cultural critique of modern industrial society.[68] In the 1930s, as in earlier cycles, the decline fears raised by critics of the regime were wrapped up in their diagnosis of socio-cultural decadence. In reality, however, the two were not logically or necessarily linked: it was possible to believe that French democracy or French capitalism was morally rotten but that France could still win the war. In fact, many of the works that were most closely identified with the decline neurosis (for example, Robert Aron and Arnaud Dandieu's *Décadence de la nation française* (1931)) popularised disturbing stereotypes about French culture, but offered few concrete reasons to be apprehensive about the outcome of the war. The publication of Drieu la Rochelle's novel *Gilles* in the midst of the phony war gave fresh life to this intellectual debate about France's – and Europe's – decomposition since 1917. Sartre noted (somewhat disapprovingly) that the interwar generation was busy writing its own obituary.[69] But was it France's obituary? That was not clear until May 1940.

"The most ghastly of confirmations"

Naturally, the people who had felt most alienated from the republican establishment were also the ones most likely to feel personally vindicated by the events of May–June. Pierre Laval is an obvious example. He had been a central figure in republican government until the mid-1930s, but the election of the Popular Front had forced him into the political wilderness. Laval believed that if he had been allowed to pursue his policy of collaboration with Mussolini in the mid-1930s, the entire war and therefore the defeat would never have happened. Similarly, for admirers of the National Socialist new order or haters of the Republic (and the two categories were not necessarily synonymous), what happened in 1940 was "but the most ghastly of confirmations".[70] To quote one of the young Catholics who enlisted at Vichy's "leadership school" at Uriage in the hope of creating a new, spiritually revitalised nation: "I was completely fed up with the kind of parliamentary democracy we had had, with that circus of governments that broke a longevity record if they lasted two weeks! It made one sick. And rather than being astonished at the defeat, I was, on the contrary, prepared for it."[71] The Catholic hierarchy's immoderate enthusiasm for Marshal Pétain and his National Revolution reflected the depth of the Church's alienation from the pre-defeat Establishment.[72]

This sense of preparation for defeat explains a great deal about what was to follow. The defeat created an opening by destroying the regime which had led France into war. But it did not define the post-defeat regime. The form that the new State took and the policies it pursued reflected the long-standing ideological prejudices and politics of those who filled the vacuum. This was a case (in Déat's evocative phrase) of the Republic's long-standing enemies finding the old furrow and digging it deeper.[73]

In a sense, something similar might be said of the small minority who had the opposite reaction to defeat, refusing to reconcile themselves to it. Many future resisters had adopted some kind of critical or oppositional stance before 1940.[74] Either they had felt alienated from the status quo (for example because of their social catholicism or their communism) or they had dissented from policies which the majority of interwar society had supported. A significant number, for example, had been among the minority opposing the policy of appeasement. In a series of interviews with early resisters, the historian H. R. Kedward found "*anti-munichois*" across the political spectrum.[75] When it came to explaining their resistance in retrospect, resisters did so in various ways. Some emphasised religious principles (in the words of one Resistance leader, Pierre-Henri Teitgen, "I was not a resister in the first place because I was French, but because I was a Christian.").[76] Others cited long-standing anti-fascist commitments, going back to the Popular Front or to the Spanish Civil War or even before (the Free French spokesman Maurice Schumann said that his resistance began in 1935, when fascist Italy invaded Ethiopia)[77]. More traditional conservatives in the Resistance often attributed their reaction to family tradition, to military pride or to Germanophobia. In some cases, these resisters explained their actions in terms of an internal force (which one might call their "conscience" or "character"). Other resisters suggested that this revolt had been triggered by an external stimulus – de Gaulle's broadcasts, a chance encounter with like-minded friends, a piece of Vichy legislation, a photograph of Pétain and Hitler shaking hands. But for almost all resisters, the defeat was a shock that did not come entirely out of the blue. They had been just prepared enough for it to be able to respond not by total metamorphosis but by becoming more like themselves (even though doing so often entailed leaving home or family, turning one's back on a career or a political party).[78]

The fact that so many of those who were to be politically active under the Occupation could claim, often legitimately, to have expected or predicted the defeat in advance should give us pause. Does it not imply a certain a priori quality to their reading of the defeat, a lack of openness to its real and evolving significance? Too much of a shock not to provoke a revolution of sorts, 1940 was perhaps too little of a shock to be a new beginning.

Notes and references

1 *The War Diaries of Jean-Paul Sartre, November 1939/March 1940* (New York: Pantheon, 1984), p. 4.

2 D. Barlone, *A French Officer's Diary* (Cambridge: Cambridge University Press, 1943), p. 77.

3 J. Giraudoux, *The France of Tomorrow* (Paris: Centre d'Informations Documentaires, 1940), p. 6.

4 Quoted in J.-L. Crémieux-Brilhac, *Les Français de l'an 40*, 2 vols (Paris: Gallimard, 1990), vol. 1, p. 341.

5 P. de Villelume, *Journal d'une défaite* (Paris: Fayard, 1976), p. 103.

6 P. Léautaud, *Journal littéraire, février 1940–juin 1941* (Paris: Mercure de France, 1962), p. 117.

7 A recent work which stresses this theme of ambivalence in interwar France is: R. Young, *France and the Origins of the Second World War* (New York: St Martin's Press, 1996). It is extremely difficult to gauge reliably the expectations of those at the centre of power. So much of the evidence is retrospective and self-evidently tinged by the need to justify action (or inaction) in 1939–40 and to rehabilitate reputations. Retrospectively, so-called "bellicistes" (men like the Prime Minister, Reynaud) had an interest in stressing their lucidity about the shortcomings of the French position so as not to appear rash optimists; while so-called "defeatists", including many who ended up in Vichy, needed to present themselves as loyal pessimists in order to escape suspicion of having sabotaged national security in advance of the defeat.

8 O. H. Bullitt (ed.), *For the President: Personal and Secret* (Boston, Massachusetts: Houghton Mifflin, 1972), p. 369.

9 Crémieux-Brilhac, *Les Français*, vol. 1, p. 59.

10 Letter to Etienne Bloch, reprinted in *Cahiers de l'Institut du Temps Présent*, no. 19 (1991), p. 44. This quotation is taken from a letter dated September 1939.

11 G. Folcher, *Les Carnets de guerre de Gustave Folcher, paysan languedocien (1939–1945)* (Paris: F. Maspero, 1981), p. 43.

12 F. Pottecher, *Le Procès de la défaite. Riom, février–avril 1942* (Paris: Fayard, 1989), p. 198.

13 Crémieux-Brilhac, *Les Français*, vol. 1, pp. 114–15; *La France et les Français en 1938–1939* (Paris: Presses de la FNSP, 1978), pp. 218–19.

14 Quoted in Crémieux-Brilhac, *Les Français*, vol. 1, p. 115.

15 Villelume, *Journal*, pp. 50, 58.

16 R. Girault and R. Frank (eds), *La Puissance en Europe, 1938–1940* (Paris: Publications de la Sorbonne, 1984), pp. 36–7.

17 J. Le Roy Ladurie, *Mémoires 1902–1945* (Paris: Flammarion/Plon, 1997), p. 159.

18 S. de Beauvoir, *The Prime of Life* (Harmondsworth: Penguin, 1965), p. 377.

19 *Henry L. Stimson Diaries*, Microfilm edition, Roll 6 (New Haven, Connecticut: Yale University Library, 1973), vol. XXIX, pp. 28–9.

20 F. Bédarida, *La Stratégie secrète de la drôle de guerre. Le conseil suprême interallié* (Paris: Presses de la FNSP, 1979), pp. 92–3.

21 Villelume, *Journal*, pp. 9, 15–16, 22.

22 Testimony of Georges Bonnet to postwar commission of enquiry: *Les Evénements survenus en France de 1933 à 1945. Témoignages*, 9 vols (Paris: PUF, 1951–52), vol. 9, p. 2683.

23 Villelume, *Journal*, pp. 95, 99, 108.

24 Villelume, *Journal*, p. 13.

25 Quoted in E. du Réau, *Edouard Daladier, 1884–1970* (Paris: Fayard, 1993), p. 275.

26 J. Harvey (ed.), *The Diplomatic Diaries of Oliver Harvey, 1937–1940* (London: Collins, 1970), pp. 223, 250. For a recent analysis of British attitudes towards France in 1939, see M. Dockrill, *British Establishment Perspectives on France, 1936–40* (London: Macmillan, 1999), pp. 132–58.

27 G. Duhamel, *Positions françaises* (Paris: Mercure de France, 1940), p. 64.

28 W. Irvine, "Domestic politics and the fall of France in 1940", in J. Blatt (ed.), *The French Defeat of 1940. Reassessments* (Providence, Rhode Island: Berghahn, 1998), pp. 89–90.

29 Du Réau, *Daladier*, p. 313.

30 M. Alexander, *The Republic in Danger: General Maurice Gamelin and the Politics of French Defence, 1933–1940* (Cambridge: Cambridge University Press, 1992), pp. 271–2.

31 C.-R. Ageron, "La perception de la puissance française en 1938–1939: le mythe impérial", in Girault and Frank (eds), *La Puissance en Europe*, pp. 227–44.

32 Quoted in M. Evans, *The Memory of Resistance: French Opposition to the Algerian War (1954–1962)* (Oxford: Berg, 1997), p. 101.

33 A. Adamthwaite, *Grandeur and Misery. France's bid for power in Europe 1914–1940* (London: Arnold, 1995), p. 148.

34 M. Benteli *et al.*, "Le cinéma français: thèmes et public", in *La France et les Français*, pp. 33, 39. Along similar lines, Christine Sellin has noted how school textbooks stressed the Empire's essential contribution to French power: "L'image de la puissance française à travers les manuels scolaires", *Relations internationales*, 33 (1983), pp. 103–11.

35 Ageron, "La perception", p. 240.

36 Du Réau, *Daladier*, p. 359.

37 *Les Evénements . . . Témoignages*, vol. 5, pp. 1269–71. Admittedly, not all postwar witnesses recollected the situation in that light. Raoul Dautry, who as Minister of Munitions was singularly well placed to assess French preparedness, testified that by the spring of 1940 "Too many reasons led me to believe that we would not 'hold' as we had at the Marne.", *Les Evénements . . . Témoignages*, vol. 7, p. 1959.

38 Alexander, *Republic in Danger*, p. 277; F. Seager, "Les buts de guerre alliés devant l'opinion (1939–1940)", *Revue d'histoire moderne et contemporaine*, 32 (1985), p. 633.

39 For some highly critical remarks on French preparedness, see the quotations in Dockrill, pp. 147–9.

40 M. Alexander, "'Fighting to the last Frenchman'? Reflections on the BEF deployment to France and the strains in the Franco-British alliance, 1939–40", *Historical Reflections*, 22: 1 (1996), pp. 252, 254.

41 G. Sadoul, *Journal de guerre* (Paris: Les Editeurs Français Réunis, 1977).

42 Crémieux-Brilhac, *Les Français*, vol. 2, p. 367; Sadoul, *Journal*, p. 91.

43 See, for example, J. Galtier-Boissière, *Mémoires d'un parisien*, 3 vols (Paris: La Table Ronde, 1960–63), vol. 3, p. 25; L. Guilloux, *Carnets, 1921–1944* (Paris: Gallimard, 1978), p. 259.

44 Germany's daring invasion of Norway had begun on 9 April 1940 and enjoyed rapid success, largely because it confounded Allied strategic and tactical assumptions, just as the invasion a month later was to do.

45 For example, views of General Georges, quoted in *Les Evénements . . . Témoignages*, vol. 2, p. 362; and of General Véron in vol. 5, p. 1308.

46 J. Daridan, *Le Chemin de la défaite (1938–1940)* (Paris: Plon, 1980), pp. 203–4.

47 F. Delpla (ed.), *Les Papiers secrets du Général Doumenc* (Paris: O. Orban, 1992), pp. 206–7 (but see also Delpla's critical remarks on pp. 151–2).

48 Crémieux-Brilhac, *Les Français*, vol. 1, p. 114.

49 R. Aron, *Memoirs: Fifty Years of Political Reflection* (New York: Holmes and Meier, 1990), p. 112; J. Bardoux, *Journal d'un témoin de la Troisième* (Paris: Fayard, 1957), p. 332.

50 *Les Evénements . . . Témoignages*, vol. 7, p. 2029. Allusions to the patriotic resistance in 1870 were not infrequent in the resistance that developed after June 1940. For example, one of the major resistance movements in the south, Franc-Tireur ("The Sniper"), was named after pro-republican volunteers in the Franco-Prussian war: J.-P. Levy, *Mémoires d'un franc-tireur. Itinéraire d'un résistant (1940–1944)* (Brussels: Editions Complexe, 1998), p. 51.

51 A. Rossi [pseudonym of A. Tasca], *Physiologie du parti communiste français* (Paris: Editions Self, 1948), pp. xiii–xv.

52 J. Schlumberger, *Oeuvres*, 7 vols (Paris: Gallimard, 1958–61), vol. 6, p. 108.

53 *Esprit*, 85 (1939), pp. 8–9.

54 Memorandum quoted by Gamelin in *Servir*, 3 vols (Paris: Plon, 1946–47), vol. 1, p. 128.

55 J.-B. Duroselle, *La Décadence, 1932–1939* (Paris: Imprimerie Nationale, 1979), pp. 198–200.

56 A massive influx of immigrants in the decade after the First World War had brought the immigrant population to almost 7% of the total population by 1929. This percentage dropped as a result of the Depression, but the repatriations of foreign workers were partly offset by the arrival of political refugees from Germany, Eastern Europe and, above all, republican Spain.

57 R. Schor, *L'Opinion française et les étrangers en France, 1919–1939* (Paris: Publications de la Sorbonne, 1985), p. 663.

58 J. Giraudoux, *Pleins pouvoirs* (Paris: Gallimard, 1939), p. 59.

59 V. Caron, *Uneasy Asylum. France and the Jewish refugee crisis, 1933–1942* (Stanford, California: Stanford University Press, 1999), pp. 355–6.

60 Crémieux-Brilhac, *Les Français*, vol. 2, p. 32.

61 M. Margairaz, *L'Etat, les finances et l'économie. Histoire d'une conversion 1932–1952*, 2 vols (Paris: Comité pour l'Histoire Economique et Financière de la France, 1991), vol. 1, p. 421.

62 R. Kuisel, *Capitalism and the State in Modern France* (New York: Cambridge University Press, 1981), pp. 93–127.

63 Text of Dautry's speech is in *Les Evénements . . . Témoignages*, vol. 7, pp. 2009–13.

64 S. Berstein, in Girault and Frank, *Puissance en Europe*, p. 289.

65 S. Peer, *France on Display. Peasants, provincials, and folklore in the 1937 Paris World's Fair* (Albany, New York: SUNY Press, 1998), pp. 33–42. For a retrospective reflection on this unhappy episode, see the memoirs of the President of the Republic, Albert Lebrun: *Témoignage* (Paris: Plon, 1945), pp. 38–9.

66 Aron, *Memoirs*, pp. 106–7.

67 A. Detoeuf, 'Blasphèmes', *Nouveaux cahiers*, 22 (1938), pp. 1–2.

68 K. Swart, *The Sense of Decadence in Nineteenth-Century France* (The Hague: Martinus Nijhoff, 1964), p. 254.

69 J.-P. Sartre, *Les Carnets de la drôle de guerre* (Paris: Gallimard, 1983), pp. 214–17.

70 M. Déat, *Mémoires politiques* (Paris: Denoël, 1989), p. 512.

71 J. Hellman, *The Knight-Monks of Vichy France* (Montreal: McGill-Queen's University Press, 1993), p. 9.

72 W. Halls, *Politics, Society and Christianity in Vichy France* (Oxford: Berg, 1995), pp. 45–64.

73 Déat, *Mémoires*, p. 536.

74 H. R. Kedward, *Resistance in Vichy France* (Oxford: Oxford University Press, 1978), pp. 250–83; O. Wieviorka, *Nous entrerons dans la carrière* (Paris: Seuil, 1994), *passim*.

75 Kedward, *Resistance*, pp. 251, 272, 278, 282.

76 Wieviorka, *Nous entrerons*, p. 73.

77 Wieviorka, *Nous entrerons*, p. 143.

78 Kedward, *Resistance*, pp. 22–3. Laurent Douzou has made essentially this point about Emmanuel d'Astier de la Vigerie, founder of one of the major Resistance movements in the southern zone. Something of a dilettante before the war, d'Astier came into his own in 1940, as though the defeat had revealed his true potentialities as a leader. See Douzou, *La Désobéissance. Histoire du mouvement Libération-Sud* (Paris: Odile Jacob, 1995), p. 35.

CHAPTER TWO

Post-defeat politics:
impotence and improvisation

> We find ourselves to-day in this appalling situation – that the fate of
> France no longer depends upon the French.
>
> Marc Bloch, *L'étrange défaite* (1940)[1]

The disarray of the Third Republic by the time of the armistice would be
hard to overstate. It is enough simply to enumerate the options that the
Reynaud government was forced to consider in the first weeks of June:
a desperate last stand in Brittany; a bifurcation of the regime, with some
officials crossing to North Africa to form a government-in-exile while others
stayed behind to face the Germans; a union with Britain, in which the two
governments and parliaments would be consolidated into one and the two
peoples would adopt a common citizenship for the duration of the war. At
this point, Hitler's long-term plans were unclear, as was the future course of
the war, though the probability of a total German victory seemed strong.
While there was a natural tendency still to think in terms of prior experiences of invasion and defeat (1870 in particular), the mounting evidence of
the Nazi regime's ruthlessness and limitless ambition justified more extreme
apprehensions about what defeat might mean. The ultimate fear was that it
would lead literally to the end of France – *finis Franciae*.

The spectre of that "frightening void" (to use an expression of de Gaulle's)
was a critical element in the politics of the Occupation. One of the Vichy
regime's fundamental preoccupations – and certainly its main claim on the
loyalty of the French people – was its determination to perpetuate a sover-
eign French state. This determination was equally characteristic of General
de Gaulle's dissident movement in Britain. Though Gaullists disavowed any
political programme of their own (at least in the early years of the Occupation), they were adamant that they represented France and that France

remained, through their movement, a presence and a force in the world. Thus, at the root of both Vichy and Free France lay a double act of self-assertion, a claiming not just of legitimate authority for themselves but of continuing autonomy and sovereignty for the state they purported to embody. The rhetoric and ideologies of these new and competing authorities were anything but improvised, as we have noted. But their claims to authority had, of necessity, to be improvised.

The assertiveness of these claims should not blind us to the reality of extreme dependence noted by Bloch. Defeat forced the nation into an essentially reactive state, as Léon Werth pointed out in October 1940: "The stagnant armistice turns the Frenchman into a strange figure. He is dependent on Germany, on England, on Japan, on the United States and Russia. Some planes shot down, others victorious, a house in flames in London, a house in flames in Berlin, such things determine his fate . . . Events come to him, but he does not go to them."[2] In important respects, Werth's observation remained valid throughout the Occupation. In the tension between such fundamental dependence and the various attempts to overcome or transcend it lay the essence of post-defeat politics.

The realities of dependence

On June 25, the day that the armistice formally went into effect, a Belgian journalist who had been swept along in the *exode* found himself in the southern town of Castelnaudary, witness to a poignant ceremony. To mark this official day of national mourning, a group of local veterans from the First War had gathered at the war memorial – re-enacting on the occasion of this new armistice a ritual associated with the other armistice day. School-children laid wreaths at the base of the monument, the cathedral bell tolled, flags were lowered. Before the hushed crowd, the mayor proclaimed: "Let us swear to restore France." To which the veterans of the First War replied "We swear it!", while younger "veterans" of the more recent fighting stood silently by.[3]

Moments such as this tell us a good deal about the atmosphere in France in the aftermath of the armistice. The differentiation between older and younger participants hints at the intergenerational divisions produced by defeat. Predictably enough, the journalist overheard some of the older men grumbling that their sons had not held up well against the enemy. This was a common complaint. Veterans of the First War not infrequently remembered their comrades as uncomplaining and stoical in contrast to the supposedly pampered troops of 1939–40.[4] We may be certain that the resentment was reciprocated: plenty of the young soldiers taken prisoner in 1940 complained that they had been let down by fossilised officers trying to fight the previous war over again.[5] The instinctive recourse to symbols from the First War also helps to explain what was so consoling about the leadership of a man who had symbolised victory in that war. Much of the magic of the word "armistice" came from an assumed analogy with 1918: that is, the assumption (made not only by the public but also by the government) that it would be followed in short order by a peace settlement. Above all, in the oath to remake France – an oath made, not coincidentally, in a place unoccupied by Germans – we hear a rhetoric which flourished in the early stages of occupation. This rhetoric suggested that in spite of the defeat, and yet because the defeat had been so exemplary, national reconstruction could begin immediately.

Much in France's situation after the signing of the armistice makes this claim appear delusional. Objectively speaking, France had become a helpless spectator in the war. By the terms of the armistice agreement, Pétain had given up 60% of the country to German occupation in return for the privilege of an unoccupied zone in the south. The northern departments of Nord and Pas-de-Calais were detached from the rest of the country and administered by the German military authorities in Belgium. Alsace and Lorraine, which were not mentioned in the armistice, were incorporated as a matter of course into the Reich, while a large area of northeast France was converted into a so-called *zone interdite* (prohibited zone), which was reserved for future German colonisation. The occupied zone as a whole extended down the entire Atlantic coastline and included not only Paris and most of the major industrial centres but also the richest agricultural regions (75% of the country's wheat, sugar and butter, for example, was produced in the occupied zone).[6] A demarcation line, which initially took on the character of a virtual frontier, separated occupied France from the unoccupied zone.

In addition to losing effective control over most of the national territory, the French government was compelled to disarm itself. The army was reduced to 100,000 men (the same number imposed on Germany's army in 1919). Its activities, as well as its armaments and munitions, were closely monitored by an Armistice Commission that the Germans established at Wiesbaden, the Rhineland town where a French-run commission had operated after the First World War. This commission also supervised the payment of a massive indemnity (20 million marks or 400 million francs per day), supposedly levied on France to cover the costs of occupation, but in reality far exceeding such costs.

Almost more important (certainly for understanding Vichy's history) than the immediately quantifiable costs of defeat were the "swords of Damocles" that the armistice suspended over the French government.[7] At any moment Hitler could tear up the agreement and occupy the southern zone (as eventually he did in November 1942). Germany continued to hold almost two million French prisoners of war as well as an ever growing mountain of French currency. The zone system and demarcation lines gave German authorities the capacity to control the movement of people and goods and thereby to modulate the impact of occupation on the French population. In the North, Germany's control over the economic and human resources of the richest and most populous regions of the country was essentially unrestricted. Exercising "all the rights of the occupying power" (in the words of the armistice), the German military authorities in Paris could intervene at will in virtually any aspect of civilian life or civil administration.

The subsequent history of Vichy–German dealings amply demonstrates the lopsidedness of their relationship. Once it became clear that Vichy's expectations of rapid British submission would not be realised, the defeated state had no choice but to cooperate with its occupiers if it wished to survive. This fact was publicly acknowledged in October 1940, when Pétain had his first face-to-face meeting with Hitler at Montoire and pronounced the fateful word "collaboration" (his Prime Minister, Laval, had already used it in July). In early 1941 a new Prime Minister, Admiral Darlan, tried to institutionalise collaboration by bartering French assistance to the German war effort in exchange for a 50% reduction in occupation costs, relaxation of the demarcation line, return of some prisoners of war, and improvement in the food supply. This bartering arrangement never bore fruit, even though Darlan persisted with the effort throughout his fourteen months at the head of the government. As one of his ministers, Jacques Benoist-Méchin, later acknowledged, the imbalance in power relations made any *quid pro quo* impracticable. The Germans were always the ones who set the terms; they demanded the French concessions immediately and then could release the prisoners or relax the demarcation line (or not) as they saw fit.[8]

The failure of Darlan's collaboration, like the equal failure of more overtly pro-fascist collaborationism, underscored the reality of French dependence. It was not French footdragging that doomed the collaborationists' dream of Vichy partnership in a Nazi-dominated Europe, but rather Hitler's disdain. The Führer never felt that he needed an alliance with France. His only interest was in exploiting French resources at the lowest cost and with the least risk to himself. During Darlan's premiership, he secured French concessions without significant counterpart. With Darlan's departure and the return of Laval to power in April 1942, that pattern continued. It was telling that when the head of France's largest collaborationist party, Jacques Doriot of the *Parti Populaire Français*, tried to force his way into Laval's government, it was Hitler who blocked the move. Like other collaborators before and after him, Doriot found that no amount of identification with National Socialist ideals or zealous participation in its anti-Bolshevik or anti-Jewish crusades could induce Hitler or other German authorities to treat him as an equal.[9]

Vichy claims

To go back to June 1940, however, the lure of the armistice from the French perspective had been that it was just "generous" enough to hold this reality of powerlessness at bay and to keep alive hopes of limited sovereignty and autonomy.[10] In addition to the substantial area of unoccupied territory that Hitler had left under sole French control and to the small armistice army, the Pétain government commanded a powerful fleet. Hitler had intended to demobilise and disarm Vichy's naval forces as drastically as he disarmed the army and air force, but in early July 1940 a British attack on the French squadron stationed at Oran in Algeria (an attack intended to preempt its falling into Axis control) encouraged the German authorities to rethink. Recognising the intense Anglophobia of the French navy and its determination to defend the French Empire from British (or British-sponsored) incursion, the Germans allowed it to remain close to its considerable pre-armistice strength. (Even after the British attack at Oran, Vichy's navy was larger than Italy's.) For the next couple of years the navy provided Vichy with a critical lifeline to its Empire.[11]

That the overwhelming majority of France's protectorates, mandates and colonies (including those in North Africa, West Africa, the Caribbean, the Middle East and Indochina) should have rallied to the Pétain government was not inevitable.[12] Viewed from a colonial perspective, the defeat at first looked rather less definitive than it appeared inside France. Distance insulated the colonies from some of the disorienting and disheartening effects of the collapse and made resistance seem at least a conceivable option. In mid–late June there were serious rumblings of defiance from senior officers and officials throughout the Empire (including from General Noguès, the Resident-General in Morocco and military commander in French North Africa, from General Mittelhauser, commander of the army in Syria, and from General Catroux, Governor-General in Indochina). But by the end of the month the government in France had reined in most such defiance. Of the imperial "proconsuls", only Catroux decided to continue the fight, and he was not able to bring Indochina with him. The armistice terms (in particular, the leniency of the colonial clauses) reassured imperial officials as to Pétain's capacity to preserve the Empire from German or Italian encroachment. A strong sense of hierarchy, combined with scepticism about the likelihood of British assistance, did the rest. The Empire fell into line, thereby giving Vichy crucial credibility with third-party governments and with its own population, and also (at least in the minds of some Vichy officials, such as Laval) giving the regime something really substantial to bargain over with Germany.

These tangible assets bolstered Vichy's claim to sovereignty, as did the intangible choice that Pétain represented in June 1940 – the choice to stay put. The idea of transporting the government and the armed forces, or at least a portion of both, out of France appealed to some politicians and military leaders, but it was viewed by most of the population as unrealistic.[13] Pétain himself was viscerally opposed to it. He believed that the responsibility of a government was to stay with its people. This *"politique de présence"* was institutionalised in the armistice – not just in the creation of the unoccupied zone, but also in the terminology of occupation as opposed to annexation (implying that the territory remained French) and in the stipulation that French administrators in the occupied zone would remain in place. In other words, the armistice preserved the fiction of French sovereignty, a fiction which gained external validation from the decision of foreign governments, including those of the USA, Canada and the Soviet Union, to send diplomatic representatives to Vichy. While Vichy governments recognised that this sovereignty was precarious, they could never bring themselves to view it as illusory. Indeed they focused much of their energy on the effort to safeguard it and to limit, or at least monitor, German incursions on it.

The creation of a "free" zone made possible a second kind of claim – that the government now had the space (physical as well as legal) in which to establish a whole new political and social order. For the foreseeable future the government could do nothing to free the country from German military control. But it could claim the autonomy to remake France, as the veterans in Castelnaudary had urged. And it immediately set about realising this claim via its so-called National Revolution. The logic of National Revolution was that recovery could be achieved through a kind of silent, internal regeneration that could compensate, at least in the short term, for the relative lack of military and political means. Typical of this notion of a silent regeneration was the official attention lavished on the French family. The regime's focus on this institution was not just an outgrowth of pre-existing ideological commitments (though long-time advocates of a pro-family policy certainly abounded in Vichy). It also reflected the fact that the armistice had redefined the political role of the family, suddenly making it a space uniquely impervious to the occupiers' surveillance and control and thus a potential locus of national renewal.[14] To quote a Vichy propagandist: "Behind the door of each French home, France continues to live, even in the Occupied Zone, even in the prohibited zone. It is still necessary that in each house lives a French family worthy of the name." This gives a sense both of the constraints within which the National Revolution was being attempted and of its expansive ambitions.

The constitutional revolution of July 10

The prerequisite for such social regeneration was the establishment of a new constitutional order to replace the Republic which had brought France into the war and was now blamed for having lost it. Supervising the transition was Pierre Laval, who became Deputy Prime Minister in late June 1940. Conditions were ideal for Laval's settling of accounts with the Popular Front legislature. Public respect for the Republic had sunk to a new low. The Pétain government was composed of men hostile to the regime that they now served. Vilified in the press and, in many cases, genuinely shamed or contrite, republican politicians themselves favoured granting full powers to the Marshal.[15] Not surprisingly in a country which had seen so many regimes come and go, even good republicans acknowledged that disasters on this scale were bound to be followed by a change of regime.[16] Most of the politicians who might conceivably have obstructed Laval's plans in early July were in prison (in the case of Communist deputies), in North Africa (in the case of those who had sailed on the *Massilia*), incapacitated (like Reynaud, who had been seriously injured in a car accident on June 28) or too scared to show their faces in Vichy.

It was, therefore, more a question of how, rather than whether, a constitutional revolution would occur. Some members of the new government, like the monarchist-inclined Weygand, would have preferred a unilateral dissolution of the Republic. Others, like Baudouin and Bouthillier, favoured quietly suspending parliamentary sessions.[17] But Laval persuaded Pétain that the best procedure would be to convene the members of the National Assembly and have them dissolve the Third Republic and transfer constituent authority to Pétain. It took just two days to implement this procedure. On July 9, parliamentarians voted 624 to 4 to revise the constitution. On July 10, they voted 569 to 80 to grant Pétain the authority to draw up a new constitution. The day after that, the government promulgated the first of a dozen "constitutional acts", which vested almost total executive and legislative power in the Marshal. Theoretically, these constitutional acts represented an interim regime which would operate until Pétain had produced a new constitution; in fact, since the new constitution never materialised, this was to be the regime under which the French lived for the remainder of the Occupation.

The legend that this revolution was entirely the doing of Laval and a handful of co-conspirators has long since been exposed. In the end, July 10 was far less a coup than an act of collective abdication. Certainly, Laval's expertise as a parliamentarian facilitated this abdication. He employed carrot and stick with equal adroitness, compromising on the language of the government's bill, while exploiting rumours of an impending military inter-vention (allegedly being contemplated by General Weygand) and managing the parliamentary procedure so as to prevent dissenters from airing their opinions. Nonetheless, the historian Robert Paxton was surely right when he concluded that "Laval did not really have to work very hard."[18] Among parliamentarians, as among the public at large, the prevailing emotions in the summer of 1940 were those of embarrassment, humiliation and self-disgust. All the illusions of the past two decades had been exposed; all the unkept resolutions and the lost opportunities flooded back to mind. In these circumstances, there was broad sympathy for the goals of National Revolu-tion outlined in the preamble to the July 10 bill: restoring the principle of authority in government, correcting the "intellectual and moral perversion" of French youth, respecting the elemental social institutions of family, pro-fession, commune and region, reestablishing the agricultural basis of the French economy, healing class antagonisms.

Though this "morning after" mood contributed to the initial acceptance of Vichy, in retrospect we can see that it was not the solid foundation that the regime hoped and claimed it to be. The public's disgust with the de-funct republican institutions and with the former leadership did not mean that it had permanently rejected republicanism *per se*. At the end of June, an army major noted that his men blamed the disaster squarely on the parlia-mentary system, yet remained "so profoundly attached to the Republic, so accustomed to make use of their deputy, that when they return home, they will write him for a grant of money to rebuild their houses or in order to get a job on the railways".[19] This was a rather jaundiced observation, but a perceptive one. In the months that followed, as the punitive and sectarian dimensions of the National Revolution were revealed, the public's enthusi-asm for it waned – not that there was much active resistance to Vichy's policies for many months, but there was a widespread loss of interest even by the first half of 1941.[20]

Within the regime, the waning of popular enthusiasm was perceived as a problem, but not as a reason to change course. Vichy was filled with people for whom the "achievement" of July 10 offered a first taste of what quickly became an addictive temptation – compensating for lack of freedom in relation to the occupied zone or to the outside world by exercising their autonomy "at home".[21] This temptation particularly afflicted two kinds of people. One was the motley collection of activists, intellectuals and politicians who were drawn to Vichy out of ambition or by intellectual affinity with the ideals of the National Revolution (which will be discussed further in Chapter Three). The elimination of parliamentary institutions and political parties created the perfect conditions for such people to implement their schemes. The other group were civil servants, to whom fell the vast and complex job of administering scarcity and managing the relationship with the occupiers on a day-to-day basis. In carrying out this task, they, too, were no longer constrained by parliaments or political parties. Defeat provided them with a perfect reason to discard laws or practices that they regarded as irrational or antiquated. The lure of the *tabula rasa* has been well described by François Bloch-Lainé, a senior official (with a long and distinguished career ahead of him) who went to work in the Ministry of Industrial Production in August 1940. Bloch-Lainé was assigned the important task of compiling a nationwide statistical inventory of French industry. Like many senior officials, he had long deplored the lack of such statistics in France, but he quickly began to have misgivings about his assignment. "I started . . . preparing the questionnaire, brought it to Bichelonne [the minister] and told him that what was bothering me was that I could not see how we were going to achieve all this without the Germans knowing. Bichelonne fired back: 'What do you mean? We are doing this work for the occupation authorities and for ourselves.'"[22] At that point, Bloch-Lainé opted for a transfer. But many others could not resist the temptation to implement projects that they had been nursing through the protracted death throes of the Third Republic.

Clearly, Vichy's claim to autonomy was far from entirely unfounded. In the first two years after defeat, the regime was given plenty of latitude by the Germans to introduce domestic reforms. The occupiers' complacency reflected their ruthless sense of priorities: the purpose of the armistice was to maintain order and exploit French resources, not to proselytise. When Germany won the war, France's future would be determined from Berlin, and the irrelevance of Vichy's reformism would be manifest. Until that time, allowing Vichy to distract itself with domestic policy made good sense, especially as many of Vichy's policies ran so parallel to German plans. As Paxton long ago demonstrated, Germany made no effort to foist the National Revolution on France.[23] It was a French initiative, and the suggestion that it had been implemented under German duress was largely an alibi.

Still, it cannot be denied that this initiative took place on German sufferance. Even when the occupation authorities did not impose their preferences directly, they could and did exert indirect pressure. Some of the best testimony to this pressure comes from committed collaborators in Vichy who were frustrated by the German authorities' divide-and-conquer tactics, for example their habit of favouring collaborationist factions in Paris, who made a sport out of attacking Vichy.[24] Similarly, by refusing Vichy's requests – for example, its request to release prisoners of war categorised as essential to its programme (such as students of the elite "*grandes écoles*") – the German authorities could thwart the National Revolution.[25] On a more fundamental level, however much legislative and administrative latitude the French government possessed, it always had to contend with the political reality that its actions were *perceived* within the context of occupation. In a factual sense, for example, Vichy's anti-Jewish measures were neither extorted by German pressure nor modelled on German practice, but the fact that the first group of such measures (the *statut des juifs* of October 1940) was announced in the same month that Pétain and Hitler exchanged handshakes after their meeting at Montoire created a perception of collusion. It would be naïve not to recognise that in time such perceptions could perform a useful political and psychological function for supporters and servants of the regime (inasmuch as they could be used to corroborate the alibi about German pressure). The immediate effect, nevertheless, was to undermine the credibility of the regime's programme. Within a few months of the armistice, there was widespread public cynicism about Vichy's claim (reiterated by Admiral Darlan after meeting with Hitler in May 1941) that a defeated nation could control its own fate. In seeking to justify this claim, Vichy locked itself into a vicious cycle. In order to demonstrate its autonomy, the regime became hyperactive in the elaboration and implementation of policy. But the substance of this policy tended to confirm the public's growing impression that Vichy was a puppet of Germany.

A similar vicious cycle was triggered by Vichy's claim to sovereignty. This was typified by the regime's attempts to maintain control over French industry. Within a month or two of the armistice, the officials whom Pétain placed in charge of industrial production formed the view that German authorities were intent on integrating the entire occupied zone into the German economy. In August 1940, one of these officials, René Belin, warned Pétain that "the occupied zone is already becoming an annexed country, exploited by the victors, instead of a region subjected to military occupation, as provided for in the armistice agreement".[26] To forestall this takeover, the government hastily established a new *French* industrial control system which would apply to the entire French economy, north and south. The price of implementing this new system was considerable: in exchange for permitting the French committees to function in the occupied zone, the Germans compelled Vichy to open up access to the industrial resources of the "free" zone; and much of the industrial control system itself was modelled on German practices.[27]

The willingness to pay virtually any price in order to maintain sovereignty over the entire country proved to be a recurrent theme in Vichy's history. In time, it guided the regime to some of its most notorious decisions. In 1941, the government agreed to select and execute Communist prisoners in retaliation for anti-German sabotage so as to preempt German retaliation. It also created a special department devoted to Jewish policy (*Commissariat Général Aux Questions Juives* or CGQJ), so that a French authority would be able to supervise anti-Jewish measures in both zones.[28] Most of Vichy's domestic initiatives had home-grown political or ideological roots – neither the *dirigisme* of the Ministry of Industrial Production nor the antisemitism of the CGQJ was fundamentally imitative – but such inclinations were strongly reinforced by a bureaucratic imperative to retain as much control as possible over the country.

Gaullist counter-claims

If one looks across the Channel at the dissident movement constituted by Charles de Gaulle during the same weeks in June and July 1940 that Laval and Pétain were pushing through their revolution, one sees a comparable process of self-assertion.

De Gaulle's message (first broadcast to France in the famous *appel* of June 18) was neither original nor wholly improvised. He told his listeners that the human and material resources of the French and British empires, backed by the productive capacity of the USA, would ultimately prevail in the war. That was essentially to recapitulate the Daladier/Reynaud strategy of the phony war – i.e. superior resources would eventually wear down Germany.[29] This was also the conviction of other members of the Reynaud government who wanted to carry on fighting, for example Georges Mandel[30] and Raoul Dautry: Dautry had distributed a memorandum to that effect just the week before.[31] The more novel aspect of de Gaulle's initiative was his closing appeal to French servicemen, engineers and skilled workers to join him in London. This was the first stage in the creation of what became Free France.

At the outset, the status of this movement was unclear. De Gaulle could have conceived of it simply as a French contribution to the Allied war effort, as some of the French refugees in Britain (Jean Monnet, for example) urged him to do. But he adamantly refused. Instead, de Gaulle, too, laid claim to sovereignty. "We are France", he insisted privately in June 1940, in spite of the tiny size of his dissident movement (fewer than 10,000 in the first summer, 35,000 by the end of 1940).[32] At the end of October 1940, in a manifesto issued from his African base in Brazzaville, he made this claim official. "[T]here is no longer a truly French government . . . the body that has its seat at Vichy and claims to bear that name is unconstitutional . . . It is, therefore, necessary for a new authority to assume the responsibility of directing the French war effort. Events impose this sacred duty upon me . . . I will exercise my powers in the name of France and solely in her defence."[33] This expressed a characteristically Gaullist conception of France as something more than a geographic entity, as a great nation that could never, by definition, reconcile itself to defeat.

The disproportion between the ambition of the claim and the powerlessness of those making it was even more extreme than in Vichy's case. The Brazzaville declaration was made just weeks after Gaullist forces had been rebuffed from the West African port of Dakar by colonial forces loyal to Vichy. At the time Dakar was viewed as a humiliating and, in the eyes of many Allied observers, potentially fatal setback. In 1940 de Gaulle confronted the same collapse in France's international power and stature that Vichy confronted. But even more than Pétain (who at least retained an administrative apparatus, a navy, and an Empire, and whose regime had won widespread diplomatic recognition), de Gaulle lacked the military and political resources to restore the nation's pre-defeat status, or even to influence when it would be restored. Unlike the Marshal, he also lacked both the aura of constitutional legitimacy that the vote of July 10 had conferred on Pétain and the latter's intense popularity with the French population.

As an exile movement, Free France was heavily dependent on the goodwill of its hosts. In the summer and autumn of 1940 this support, in particular the personal backing that de Gaulle received from Churchill, was sufficient to launch the movement. Thereafter, however, relations between Free France and the British government, as between de Gaulle and Churchill, steadily deteriorated. After January 1941 a series of crises in Anglo–Free French relations led British officials to contemplate replacing de Gaulle or breaking with his movement. With the Americans (who maintained diplomatic ties with Vichy), relations were strained from the outset, and became much more so after the United States entered the war in December 1941. Of course, the suspicion or hostility of friendly powers was a less oppressive constraint than the proximity and frequent interventions of foreign occupiers. But it nonetheless imposed real limits on the exercise of Free French "sovereignty". These limits were manifested at particular moments, for example when Free France was virtually excluded from military operations to liberate French territory (in Madagascar and North Africa in 1942, as in Normandy in 1944). More broadly, the Allies' mistrust of de Gaulle and the fundamental weakness of his position (belied though it was by his remarkable capacity to stand up to his patrons privately or even in public) meant that the main military and political decisions in the war against Hitler were made without French participation.

The other danger of exile, often cited by resisters who opted to stay behind in France, was that the Free French would lose touch with French realities and public opinion. The Empire offered one kind of symbolic connection to France – hence de Gaulle's continual efforts to rally even the most far-flung territories to his movement. But after promising early developments (notably the August 1940 rallying of territories in Equatorial Africa), most of the Empire remained loyal to Pétain. De Gaulle had to wait until the middle of 1943 before he was in a position to base his movement on French-controlled soil (in liberated Algeria). Meanwhile, his main connection to the population inside France came via the BBC. Free French radio broadcasts played a critical role in converting him, over the course of four years, from a little-known soldier/junior minister into the national symbol of resistance that he had become by the time of his return.[34] The BBC not only allowed Free France to communicate with, and thereby to influence, the French population; to a limited extent, it also allowed the movement to orchestrate public displays of allegiance, for example by instructing listeners to adopt the V (for victory) symbol or to gather in public at certain symbolic moments. On the other hand, these legitimating demonstrations were hardly comparable to those that Vichy could organise on a daily basis in the streets of French cities, in French schools and public places. And the communication was largely one-way. It was not until 1942 that de Gaulle was able to receive reliable information about political developments inside France.

If one takes a longer view of the Occupation, however, it becomes clear that what was initially a disadvantage for the London exiles ultimately worked to their great advantage. At the outset, Vichy's physical presence on French soil gave it the opportunity to orchestrate a legitimate-seeming transfer of authority from the Republic, to legislate and begin to implement an expressly political agenda. Over the longer term, however, this presence implicated Vichy so closely with the enemy that it destroyed the credibility of the regime's claims to independence. Free France's history was precisely the opposite. At the outset, its physical distance from metropolitan France seemed to be a critical handicap. It was extremely difficult for Gaullists in 1940 and 1941 to convince third-party governments that they represented the "true" France, when Pétain's popularity was patent, the legitimacy of his regime hard to deny, and his control over at least part of French territory an established fact. But the effect of this initial powerlessness was to compel de Gaulle and his movement to follow the trend of public opinion rather than attempt to lead it. In 1940 and 1941, when the old regime was still largely discredited, de Gaulle adopted a determinedly apolitical stance. In 1942 and 1943, as public opinion evolved inside France and inside the Resistance in particular, he gave his movement a more pro-republican and socially progressive cast. This permitted an ideological and (in the person of Jean Moulin, de Gaulle's chief delegate to the Resistance) institutional fusion between internal and external resistances – a fusion that did more than anything else to consolidate de Gaulle's status as symbol of national resistance. The organisational form of his movement evolved accordingly. In 1940 the organisation was skeletal and improvised, a collection of volunteers headed by a small Committee of Imperial Defence (in which military people figured prominently). By 1944, it had become a provisional government, with a sizeable bureaucracy organised into ministries (or "commissariats"), mostly civilian ministers, and a Consultative Assembly symbolising a commitment to representative government.

Distance had preserved Gaullists from the temptation which ruined Vichy – the temptation to rush to judgement. The people who gathered in London in July 1940 were almost as heterogeneous a crowd as those who went to Vichy: they included non-conformist socialists, technocrats, authoritarian conservatives, military officers, journalists and businessmen. Many of them had anti-republican, anti-Popular Front and anti-Jewish prejudices similar to those to be found in Vichy.[35] Nor were they immune to the moralising of defeat that was so pronounced inside France. To quote from a popular Penguin book published in 1941 by a left-wing French journalist, Louis Lévy: "The ordinary men and women of France were not wholly compounded of virtue. . . . The café, the motor-cycle and indifferent films played too large a part in their lives; they did not read as much as they used to . . .".[36] If the émigrés had had the power to act on their prejudices in 1940 or 1941, the choices might have compromised them almost as fatally as the National Revolution compromised Vichy.

It can be argued (indeed will be argued in later chapters of this book) that the experiences of resistance and collaboration restored – at least to those who participated in them – something that had been lost in June 1940: a sense of agency and control over events. This was the need that drew people towards the National Revolution in 1940, and that de Gaulle's movement and the Resistance in later years satisfied. By any standards, it was a remarkable achievement on the Resistance's part and on de Gaulle's part to find a way (using Werth's terms again) of "going to the event" rather than having "the event come to them". But we should also recognise that there was more to real autonomy and sovereignty than the sensation of control. The defeat had forced France – both Frances – into an unprecedented dependence on other nations. Difficult as it was to restore the sensation of control, it was even more difficult to restore its reality.

Notes and references

1 *Strange Defeat* (New York: Norton, 1968), p. 174.

2 L. Werth, *Déposition. Journal 1940–1944* (Paris: B. Grasset, 1946), p. 21.

3 D. Denuit, *L'Eté ambigu de 1940* (Brussels: Louis Musin, 1978), p. 202.

4 See, for example, the testimony of Marcel Héraud to the postwar commission of enquiry: *Les Evénements survenus en France de 1933 à 1945. Témoignages*, 9 vols (Paris: PUF, 1951–52), vol. 6, p. 1498.

5 For example, A. Lefébure, *Les Conversations secrètes des Français sous l'Occupation* (Paris: Plon, 1993), p. 313.

6 D. Veillon, *Vivre et survivre en France 1939–1947* (Paris: Payot, 1995), p. 102.

7 J.-B. Duroselle, *L'Abîme, 1939–1945* (Paris: Imprimerie Nationale, 1982), pp. 212–13.

8 J. Benoist-Méchin, *De la défaite au désastre*, 2 vols (Paris: Albin Michel, 1984–85), vol. 1, pp. 237–9.

9 B. Gordon, *Collaborationism in France during the Second World War* (Ithaca, New York: Cornell University Press, 1980), pp. 148–9. As Gordon notes, it was only after the collapse of the German position in the West (in the autumn of 1944) that a desperate Hitler turned again to Doriot.

10 This "generosity", of course, reflected Hitler's own interest in a rapid conclusion to the campaign and, in particular, in an arrangement that might prevent the French navy and Empire from falling under British influence or control. Gerhard Weinberg has noted that the Germans "saw the possible danger to themselves of continued French resistance very much more clearly than many of those now coming to power in France". Weinberg, *A World at Arms. A global history of World War II* (Cambridge: Cambridge University Press, 1994), p. 140.

11 M. Thomas, "After Mers-el-Kébir: the armed neutrality of the Vichy French Navy, 1940–43", *English Historical Review*, no. 447 (1997), pp. 643–70.

12 The major exception was in French Equatorial Africa, where three territories (Chad, Cameroon and Congo) rallied to de Gaulle in August 1940.

13 R. Rémond, "L'opinion française des années 1930 aux années 1940. Poids de l'événement, permanence des mentalités", in J.-P. Azéma and F. Bédarida (eds), *Le Régime de Vichy et les Français* (Paris: Fayard, 1992), pp. 484–5.

14 M. Pollard, *Reign of Virtue* (Chicago: University of Chicago Press, 1998), pp. 35–6, 52. The Vichy source is quoted on p. 35.

15 See, for example, testimony of M. Boivin-Champeaux, in *Les Evénements . . . Témoignages*, vol. 7, pp. 2198–9.

16 See Léon Blum's testimony at Pétain's postwar trial: *Procès du Maréchal Pétain* (Paris: Imprimerie des Journaux Officiels, 1945), p. 78.

17 E. Berl, *La Fin de la Troisième République* (Paris: Gallimard, 1968), p. 208; H. Michel, *Vichy année 40* (Paris: R. Laffont, 1966), pp. 59–60.

18 R. Paxton, *Vichy France: Old Guard and New Order* (New York: Columbia University Press, 1972), p. 31.

19 D. Barlone, *A French Officer's Diary* (Cambridge: Cambridge University Press, 1943), p. 97.

20 J. Sweets, *Choices in Vichy France* (New York: Oxford University Press, 1986), pp. 146–69; R. Rémond, "Introduction", in *Le Régime de Vichy et les Français*, p. 16. Rémond's generalisation about the findings of recent research into French public opinion – findings which suggest that broad-based support for Vichy disappeared in 1941 rather than 1942 – is amplified in several of the other contributions to this volume.

21 H. R. Kedward, *Resistance in Vichy France* (Oxford: Oxford University Press, 1978), p. 83. One of the defining characteristics of the Vichy regime was its legislative hyperactivity. Whatever else doomed the National Revolution, it was not a failure to convert ideology into law. In family policy, for example, the government issued 99 laws and decrees in just fourteen months (Oct. 1940–Dec. 1941). See F. Muel-Dreyfus, *Vichy et l'éternel féminin* (Paris: Seuil, 1996), p. 196.

22 *Le Régime de Vichy et les Français*, p. 367.

23 Paxton, *Vichy France*, pp. 142–3.

24 Benoist-Méchin, *De la défaite*, vol. 1, pp. 134–5.

25 W. Halls, *The Youth of Vichy France* (Oxford: Oxford University Press, 1981), pp. 54–5.

26 M. Margairaz, *L'Etat, les finances et l'économie. Histoire d'une conversion 1932–1952*, 2 vols (Paris: Comité pour l'Histoire Economique et Financière de la France, 1991), vol. 1, p. 505.

27 Margairaz, *L'Etat, les finances*, vol. 1, pp. 523–33.

28 P. Burrin, *La France à l'heure allemande 1940–1944* (Paris: Seuil, 1995), pp. 136–49.

29 Robert Frank has noted the paradox that de Gaulle, who had been the most forceful critic of Daladier's military strategy, should now have adopted the global, long view of the war's course: *La Hantise du déclin. Le rang de la France en Europe, 1920–1960: finances, défense et identité nationale* (Paris: Belin, 1994), p. 92.

30 Tony-Révillon, *Mes carnets* (Paris: O. Lieutier, 1945), p. 23.

31 *Les Evénements . . . Témoignages*, vol. 7, pp. 1970–1.

32 R. Cassin, *Les Hommes partis de rien* (Paris: Plon, 1975), p. 77.

33 C. de Gaulle, *Mémoires de guerre*, 3 vols (Paris: Plon, 1954–59), vol. 1, pp. 303–5.

34 A. Shennan, *De Gaulle* (London: Longman, 1993), pp. 16–38.

35 J.-L. Crémieux-Brilhac, *La France Libre* (Paris: Gallimard, 1996), pp. 195–7.

36 L. Lévy, *The Truth about France* (Harmondsworth: Penguin, 1941), p. 190.

CHAPTER THREE

Vichy, resistance and the lessons of defeat

It was in the tragedy of defeat that our thoughts came to fruition, that the last veils were torn away and we saw clearly.

Renaissances (November 1943)

Along with the aspiration to transcend defeat by perpetuating a French state went the rather different, one might almost say contradictory, impulse to acknowledge defeat and base France's future squarely upon it. The fiction here (paralleling the fictions of sovereignty and autonomy) was that defeat had brought about a collective awakening, exposing the nation's fundamental problems and clarifying the right way to tackle them. The reality was that the "lessons of defeat" were anything but self-evident; they were weapons in the hands of contending political forces. Each of the main elements in Occupation-era politics had distinct opinions about what had gone wrong in 1940 and deployed these views to advance their political interests and claims.

The National Revolution

Nobody was more adamant about the need to learn from the events of 1940 than Pétain and his government. In 1942, the Marshal remarked that he reminded himself every day that he belonged to a defeated people.[1] His ministers often echoed him. Thus, for example, Admiral Darlan in September 1940: "We must not forget that we have been defeated and that every defeat has its price."[2] Such talk no doubt reflected the conservative values of the people who gravitated to Vichy; a rhetoric of sin and contrition came quite naturally to them. But there was also a political basis for it. In the instant of defeat – as it were, in that flash of lightning – the nation had been forced to confront a new reality. Everything that Pétain had said in June 1940 had seemed uncontested. Recapturing that moment of imagined consensus became Vichy's perennial aspiration. To quote the memoirs of Pétain's first Minister of Finance, Yves Bouthillier, "The very great difficulty of our task was to get . . . the French to continue in the state of mind that the harsh lesson of defeat had engendered."[3] The more opposition Vichy encountered, the more desperately it sought to remind the public of the lessons which had seemed so self-evident in June 1940.

Before we sketch out the Vichy view of these lessons, it is important to make two preliminary observations. The first is to acknowledge the gross simplification involved in describing Vichy politics in the singular. If two generations of scholarship on this subject have done anything, they have "pluralised" Vichy – demonstrating how many different ideological strands and factions were represented there. This was a place in which traditionalists and reactionaries of many varieties rubbed elbows with modernisers and futurists of equally varied provenance. Every aspect of the National Revolution was contested within the regime – if not in substance, then certainly in relative priority. There was no more complete agreement about the lessons of 1940 than about anything else. The second observation, already made, is that little, if anything, in Vichy's reaction to defeat was truly new. Taken individually, the ideologies and attitudes that found expression there were deeply rooted in the past, either in the political movements of the interwar era (anti-communism, pacifism, pro-natalism, *planisme*[4]) or in still older reactionary or radical traditions (such as anti-semitism, integral nationalism, regionalism, anti-republicanism). The originality, such as it was, lay in the perpetually shifting and unstable mixture in which these various ideologies combined. The continuity between pre-defeat politics and post-defeat politics was something of which the Vichy leadership was fully conscious, even proud. A minor but telling manifestation of this was the citation accompanying the highest decoration that the regime could bestow on its servants. To be eligible for the *francisque*, the recipient had to demonstrate an active attachment to the work and person of the Marshal, to possess a distinguished service record, and to have compiled *before the war* a political record "conforming to the principles of the National Revolution". There could be no clearer expression of Vichy's reluctance to see itself as a mere product of defeat, even as it claimed to identify and act on the lessons of defeat.

The essential lesson, of course, was the need to rebuild the crumbling and dilapidated "house of France" (to borrow one of Vichy's favourite metaphors for the National Revolution). The process of rebuilding involved a number of stages. The first was to place the nation back on a firm foundation. Vichy's motto of *Travail, Famille, Patrie* (Work, Family, Fatherland) gave a good indication of what it had in mind by that: in contrast to *Liberté, Egalité, Fraternité*, these three concepts were grounded in real, existing institutions. Realism, in fact, was the basic theme of the National Revolution. It established a set of fundamental antinomies. The individual was an artificial concept; communities such as family, workplace, profession, region were real. Industrial capitalism rested on fictions like the "free market" and produced paper wealth; agriculture and artisan crafts produced real goods. Urban living was sterile and parasitic; country life was fertile and life-giving. Mothers were fulfilled, real women; childless women were unfulfilled, unnatural beings.[5] The Republic was an abstraction, artificially dividing the country into parties, departments, classes; the *patrie* was grounded in history and experience, uniting all who belonged. This realist conceit, which was no doubt encouraged by retrospective feelings of embarrassment at the fool's paradise in which France had been living before defeat, found its way into most areas of Vichy legislation. It guided the regime's attempt to reconstruct the polity as a community of communities rather than a conglomeration of individuals – an effort which required the government to give new institutional form to "natural" communities of family, profession and region. It also justified a so-called "retour à la terre" ("return to the land"), which was intended to restore the economy's agricultural basis and limit industrialisation. It was variously invoked by technocrats proposing to rationalise economic organisation and apply technical expertise to public policy, or by cultural conservatives demanding that schools place more stress on real-life or physical education and that boys' education be more sharply differentiated from girls'.

One of the chief virtues of "real" institutions was that they were, in Vichy's eyes, inherently orderly and hierarchical. That meant, first of all, that they were internally ordered: to be natural a family must have a father at its head and a mother at its heart; a workplace must have a master; a region must have a capital; or in the words of Article 8 of Vichy's Principles of Community (its alternative to the Declaration of the Rights of Man), "Every community requires a leader." Real institutions were also naturally ordered among themselves. They formed a perfect pyramid: the family was at the base, then came the workplace, the commune, the region, the profession, the nation. This inherent orderliness was essential to Vichy's second aspiration, which was to end what it viewed as the anarchy of republican France and restore the principle of authority in every area of national life. To quote Pétain himself (July 12, 1940): "We will make an organised France where the discipline of the subordinates corresponds to the authority of the leaders ... In every order, we will strive to create elites and to confer command on them, without consideration to anything but their abilities and merit."[6] This principle required a reorganisation of the relationship between state and society. Under the Third Republic, according to Vichy, politics had seeped into every aspect of society, and society (in the form of powerful interests) had seeped into politics. The self-proclaimed goal of Pétain's regime was to be a strong state, but strong within a limited sphere. According to one of the regime's legal theoreticians, the constitution of 1940 was a reaction against the idea of "restrained government", intended to restore "the strength of the political authority" so that it could act against those pernicious special interests that were perpetually seeking to insinuate themselves into positions of influence.[7] On the other hand, in order to empower the better kind of special interest, that is the various natural communities that Vichy wanted to promote, the state also needed to devolve power. A recent study of this politics (which was more traditionalist Catholic than fascist) expresses the crucial distinction as follows: "The State's role was to inspire and coordinate, not regulate. . . ."[8] If honoured in practice, this required the state to work with and through elites generated from within natural communities. Having rejected the elective principle and being opposed, at least on a sentimental level, to equating authority with wealth or social status, the regime was bound to take the identification and formation of elites very seriously. Characteristic of its aspirations were the schools that it created in order to train new leaders (the so-called "*écoles des cadres*" or "leadership schools") and, in general, its heavy emphasis on youth and education.

The model of the ideal relationship between elite and subordinate was that of Pétain and the *patrie* – total authority but authority willingly submitted to. The hierarchical principle would create a functional structure, but something more was needed to create a truly cohesive edifice. That something (Vichy's third aspiration) was a closer identification of the individual with the various communities to which he or she belonged, above all with the national community. In 1942 a prominent communitarian described the nation's problem as nothing less than "the integration of the people into France".[9] Undoubtedly, one of the popular regrets that Vichy exploited in 1940 was the feeling that, in marked contrast to the generation of the Great War, contemporary generations had failed to subordinate their sectarian interests to the interest of the nation as a whole. A left-wing Pétainist (a rare but not very rare bird in 1940) viewed such internal divisions as the principal cause of the defeat and quoted the bitter words of an officer in the defeated army: "How could we win the war . . . with an army in which half did not want to fight for capitalism and the other half did not want to fight for democracy?"[10] Vichy's remedy, proposed (depending on the source) in more or less good faith, was to transcend the social barriers between classes and recover a mystique of unity. In its idealised natural communities there were no class conflicts, just as in its idealised national community all gladly obeyed the Marshal's voice.

The corollary of this aspiration to reconstruct a cohesive society was a fourth aspiration – to clean off unsightly excrescences that had attached themselves to the *patrie*. Vichy representations of the defeated nation stressed not just its decrepitude but its insalubrity. Often, this made the National Revolution sound like spring-cleaning.[11] France was an ugly sight – intoxicated (literally) by alcohol and (figuratively) by materialism and self-indulgence, gradually losing its vitality and creativity. The regime wasted no time in displaying its determination to clean up the mess, by cracking down on alcohol consumption, by reintroducing religious instruction into state schools, by awarding various economic and political privileges to the fathers of large families, above all by punishing very visibly those who were alleged to have corrupted the nation. Civil servants who were accused of putting their political or trade union affiliation before the national interest were purged. Primary school teachers who were alleged to have crammed young men's heads with "the spirit of pleasure-seeking" were dismissed from their posts. The masonic societies which had supposedly been pulling all the strings in the defunct Republic and had drawn the nation into an anti-fascist crusade were declared a "cancer" and an "abscess" and outlawed as a "necessary public health precaution".[12] Punitive activism was clothed in the benignly clinical rhetoric of staunching infection or amputating diseased limbs. To quote Adrien Marquet, Pétain's second Minister of the Interior, speaking in August 1940: "France is truly sick . . . We need to operate. . . ."[13]

Given the mounting xenophobia and anti-semitism of the late 1930s, not to mention the prejudices of key members of the new regime, it was hardly surprising that this insalubrity should have been associated primarily with foreign or Jewish influence. Still, it was striking how quickly and how far the xenophobia and anti-semitism escalated. In July 1940, the Minister of Justice began reviewing the cases of recently naturalised citizens, with a view to reversing as many as possible. In early August, Vichy radio broadcast the names of Jewish "runaways" who had left at the armistice and thereby proved that they were Jews first and Frenchmen second. The Marshal spoke publicly of the need to purge the administration of "too many recently naturalised citizens" and authorised the repeal of a 1939 law prohibiting newspapers from inciting racial hatred. A little over a month later, in early October, the government adopted its "*statut des juifs*" – sweeping legislation which barred Jews from a variety of professions, including the officer corps, the media and senior civil service positions, on the grounds that Jewish influence had contributed significantly to French defeat.

Already, the finger of suspicion was directed not just at the recently natural-ised Jews or at foreign Jews (whom Vichy interned in special camps), but at all Jews. Léon Blum became a symbol of Jewish sabotage of national defence, while Mandel became the symbol of Jews who had pushed France into an unwinnable war.[14] In Vichy rhetoric, Jewishness was equated culturally and even racially with foreignness. To quote the *statut*'s preamble: "Our disaster compels us to regroup those French forces whose character-istics have been fixed by a long heritage."[15] This regrouping of truly French forces was placed on a par with the measures against alcoholism: they were all part of an effort to purge French society of corrupting influences.

It would be anachronistic to assume that this purging mentality was unpopular or restricted to right-wing circles. In fact, the belief that Jews had exercised too much economic and political influence in prewar France was widely held and had been gaining ground ever since 1936.[16] Pétain's initial steps in this direction were not necessarily viewed as divisive or unwar-ranted. The main complaint with the *statut des juifs* was that it fostered the impression that Vichy was becoming a German puppet. But otherwise the rhetoric of rebuilding (including its punitive elements) struck a chord with many segments of French society, not just in the opening months of occupation but throughout the period 1940–44. The communitarianism, the stress on revitalising the family and reviving patriotism, the desire to harmonise industrial relations and check unbridled competition, to attack corruption, to establish clearer lines of authority, to moralise public life – these aspirations were as evident in 1944 as in 1940.

The main obstacle to rebuilding was not its unpopularity in principle so much as its sheer irrelevance under conditions of occupation. As soon as the spectre of imminent German victory ceased to loom so menacingly, the argument of the Gaullists – that when a house is on fire is hardly the right moment to repair its foundations – seemed irrefutable. It was not necessary to disagree with Pétain's rhetoric to believe that this was simply not the right time for it. Within a year, such feelings were, by all accounts, wide-spread even in the unoccupied zone.[17] They explain the unreality that surrounded so much of the National Revolution, the lack of any popular engagement in these grandiose reforms, when just a couple of years later similarly grandiose projects were to arouse great public interest.

The other problem was the inauthenticity of Vichy's rhetoric. The re-gime quickly revealed that its prime motivation was neither integrative, constructive idealism nor pragmatic realism, but rather sectarianism. It is a trait of authoritarian regimes to confess their true inclinations by way of denial. Thus when we find Pétain denying in October 1940 that the National Revolution was a form of "moral order" (i.e. a traditionalist, catholic reaction) or a revenge for the events of 1936, we may read this as a tacit acknowledgement that it was, in fact, both these things. The tone of the early Vichy period was strikingly expressed by one of the regime's many clerical supporters, the Bishop of Dax (speaking in February 1941): "The accursed year for us was not the year of our external defeat, but the year of our internal defeat, 1936."[18] Symmetry required Vichy to dissolve employers' associations at the same time as it dissolved trade unions, but dissolution had incomparably greater impact on the working class than on the *patrons*. The latter were given a significant role in the Organisation Committees set up in August 1940, whereas the former were excluded from representation on these critical institutions. And Vichy's comprehensive reordering of labour relations, promised in 1940 and finally unveiled in October 1941 (the "*Charte du Travail*"), was concerned far more with controlling workers than with giving them power. As for the meritocratic ideal, the only "representative" body that Vichy created on the national level suggested that its conception of the elite was extremely traditional: the membership of the 1941 National Council read, in Paxton's words, "like an honors list of 'la vieille France'".[19]

The Riom trial

The clearest evidence of Vichy's sectarian motives was the regime's persistent effort to criminalise the defeat by prosecuting specific individuals whom it regarded as responsible for the disaster. The search for guilty parties had begun as early as May 1940, when Reynaud had promised the public that the government would identify and punish those who had been responsible for the catastrophic collapse around Sedan. At that point, Weygand and Pétain had objected to Reynaud's implication that the military leaders rather than the politicians were responsible for the defeat.[20] Once in power, the Marshal launched what one hyperbolic apologist termed "the greatest trial in history",[21] in which six men (Blum, Daladier, Gamelin, the two prewar Air Ministers Pierre Cot and Guy La Chambre, and a former official in the Ministry of National Defence) were tried on charges of having undermined the nation's preparation for war between 1936 and 1940. The political purpose of these charges was frankly admitted by the government. In the instructions that it issued to the press in February 1942, the government advised journalists to explain that the purpose of the trial was "to allow the French people in their misfortune to pass enlightened judgement on the methods of government by which they had been victimised".[22] Certainly this fact was not lost on the civilian defendants, who found themselves outnumbering the sole general five to one. In his prison diary, Daladier wrote that "In the minds of the people who engineered this – Pétain, Laval, and their valets – the Republic and the Republic alone was to be put on trial."[23]

The strategy of putting the Republic on trial was fashioned, as we have noted, in the early days of Vichy rule, when the universal disaffection towards the former regime made it seem an uncontroversial project. In one of his first Constitutional Acts (July 30, 1940), Pétain created a *Cour Suprême de Justice*, responsible for judging former ministers or government officials "accused of having committed crimes in the discharge of their duties or of having betrayed the responsibilities of their office". In July and August 1940 the Vichy propaganda machine held out to the public the prospect of swift retribution for those responsible for the defeat, and clearly the government did not need its own magistrates to pinpoint the guilty parties. While the Supreme Court was setting itself up in the town of Riom, the government announced a new law (September 3, 1940) granting the Minister of the Interior power to intern individuals without charging them. In a château specially leased by Vichy for the purpose, the government interned a number of prominent republican politicians (including Reynaud, Daladier, Blum, and Mandel) as well as General Gamelin.

The roster of detainees made perfectly clear which direction the government wanted the Riom court's proceedings to take. Gamelin, the former Commander-in-Chief, and Daladier, the long-time Minister of National Defence, were to be the symbolic scapegoats for a defeated army; their incompetence would exonerate all the other members of the General Staff and military leaders past and present (including Pétain and Weygand[24]). Reynaud and Mandel were the so-called "bellicists", the most notorious and high-ranking critics of the defeatist option in June 1940; their irresponsibility would vindicate Pétain's armistice policy. And Blum and a handful of fellow socialists were the symbols of the hated Popular Front, whose divisive social legislation and nationalisations were to be blamed for undermining national unity (thus justifying the "revenge for 1936" as something more than class politics).

It has been suggested that Pétain, in his ignorance of judicial procedures, may have assumed that the Riom court would complete its business within a very short period, while the nation's anger with its former leaders was still white-hot (the kind of expeditious political trial that Pétain himself and Laval were to receive five years later).[25] That was probably the only way in which Vichy could have staged a successful trial of these defendants. In fact, however, the magistrates on the court, who were appointed for life, set about their task rather conscientiously, gathering testimony from more than six hundred witnesses. The more carefully they constructed their case, the more precarious (politically speaking) the whole enterprise became.

The guilt of the Republic was essentially a slogan – plausible in a general sense but difficult, if not impossible, to prove in a judicial context. In pressing on with a trial, Vichy ended up highlighting the internal contradictions that lay beneath the simple and superficially appealing slogan. These contradictions stemmed from the basic fact that, for political reasons of its own, the regime could only put part of the past on trial.

It certainly could not afford to put the army on trial, when so many of its senior officers had found their way to Vichy. Not only was just one general indicted, but even this indictment said absolutely nothing about the conduct of military operations: Gamelin was charged simply with failing to ensure adequate levels of armament and equipment. Furthermore, the former Commander-in-Chief declined to speak at the trial. Whatever his motives,[26] the effect of Gamelin's silence was to focus attention on the political defendants. The absurdity and hypocrisy of assigning responsibility for the defeat without even considering the army's strategic planning or the military decision-making during the campaign itself were blatant. "What a pathetic lot [the generals] are", noted a scornful Daladier in October 1940. "On my brief official visits to the front, each of them had expressed the utmost confidence. Now they claim they didn't have any weapons to fight with and that the battle was lost before the first shot was fired."[27]

Another significant complication was introduced by the government's determination to place most of the blame at the door of the Popular Front. Since Blum had not even been in office in September 1939, it was difficult to hold him directly accountable for the declaration of war (which Hitler and many French collaborators, including Laval, considered the real "crime"). The fall-back was to blame Blum and the Popular Front for France's unpreparedness in 1939. This charge, as developed in the court's indictment of Blum and Daladier, held that the legislation of 1936 (nationalising war industries and introducing paid holidays and a forty-hour work week) had combined with the strikes and factory occupations of 1936–38 to produce a critical shortfall in the supply of military-related equipment and armaments. Though politically attractive to supporters of the regime, the unpreparedness argument played into the defendants' hands. If this was to be the main charge, there were no good grounds – beyond pure partisanship – to restrict the scrutiny to the post-1936 years (after all, Hitler had come to power in January 1933). In retrospect, the chief prosecutor at Riom tried to justify the 1936 cut-off by arguing that Germany's remilitarisation of the Rhineland in that year constituted a fundamental turning point; after March 1936 war was likely and, therefore, preparedness for war became a more pressing issue.[28] The members of the postwar enquiry commission found this as unconvincing as the Riom defendants had. As Daladier the prisoner repeatedly pointed out, the Popular Front had been preceded by a series of right-centre governments (one including Pétain as Minister of War), which had done infinitely less than the Popular Front to rearm France against the threat of Hitler: "If Doumergue, Flandin, and Laval, who knew of and in fact denounced Germany's massive rearmament, had made a serious effort to rearm the nation, it wouldn't have fallen to me, beginning in 1936, to organize the war industry and produce all the equipment with which our armies went into battle." (September 14, 1940)[29] Before the court in 1942 Daladier was even more pointed: "Was it the Republic that cut armaments funding in 1934? Was it the Republic that prevented Marshal Pétain, Minister of War in 1934, from combatting the German rearmament programme with a French programme?"[30]

Vichy's strategy began to unravel well before the ill-fated trial began in Riom. The press (particularly the collaborationist press in Paris) quickly became frustrated with the stately pace of the Supreme Court's enquiry. It was further infuriated by the court's decision not to indict Reynaud and Mandel (on the grounds that Reynaud had brought Pétain into the government in 1940 and that Mandel's long association with Clemenceau made it implausible to question his patriotism).[31] In response to these setbacks, Pétain announced in August 1941 that he was creating a second court – this one styled the *Conseil de Justice Politique* – to judge those responsible for the defeat. The Council, composed not of magistrates but of judicial amateurs, mostly war veterans, conducted no independent enquiry of its own. Plagiarising the Supreme Court's indictment, it rendered its judgement in just two months. In October 1941 the Marshal announced the convictions not just of Daladier, Blum, Gamelin and two of the other Riom defendants, but also of Reynaud and Mandel.[32] Illogically, and against the advice of his Justice Minister, Pétain decided that this guilty finding should not preclude the Supreme Court trial.

So in February 1942 Vichy's "trial of the century" finally got under way. Within weeks, the incoherence of the indictments became manifest, largely as a result of the unexpectedly aggressive defence offered by Blum and Daladier. In mid-March Hitler, who had wanted a show trial in which the French would saddle themselves with war guilt, expressed his anger that the charges dealt only with France's unpreparedness, not with the decision to declare war. Recognising that the proceedings were rehabilitating the defendants rather than exposing them to ridicule, Vichy was happy to accommodate Hitler by suspending the trial *sine die*. As one of the fullest studies of the Riom trial has noted, this judicial fiasco typified the Vichy regime's entire history, beginning in righteous euphoria and consensus, ending in confusion and division.[33] It also reflected the inner logic of a government driven to legitimise itself on the basis of national defeat. In view of the manifest disadvantages of the strategy (the platform it offered former republicans, the anger it aroused in Berlin, the internal dissensions it created in Vichy), Riom becomes explicable only if one remembers that the defeat provided the regime with its foundation myth.

Well before the trial began, many of those who had been baying loudest for the defendants' blood had given up on Vichy. Most of the collaborationists (a term used to describe people who pursued collaboration out of ideological zeal rather than mere expediency) had gravitated back to Paris, where they congregated in a variety of pro-collaboration parties, organisations and coteries, with the active encouragement of the German ambassador Otto Abetz or other Nazi authorities. As much as Vichyites, these collaborationists defined their politics in terms of the lessons of defeat. As Philippe Burrin has recently noted, they were not so much anti-Pétainist as ultra-Pétainist.[34] They believed that National Revolution was the proper response to defeat, but accused the Marshal's ministers of subverting this revolution.

In the collaborationist camp, one finds the Vichy discourse on defeat rendered with the literalness and pungency of extremists. Thus, for example, a collaborationist post-mortem written by a journalist from the far-right paper *Gringoire* directed a torrent of racist abuse at Léon Blum and his "pro-Jewish" Popular Front: "That poor man's Nero, straying from literature into politics, is basically a destructive genius – as sometimes happens with those of his race – devious, affected, narcissistic, inclined to consider himself the centre of the universe, devoured by ambition or rather by a patholo-gical vanity, feeling a veritable aversion for all that is fundamentally and deeply French."[35] This "born destroyer" had dragged France into war to save his "race" and bolshevise the nation "which was only half his own". Or to quote another such rant, from a journalist on the collaborationist newspaper *La Gerbe*: "Blum prepared the Defeat: 1. By corrupting moral standards; 2. By sabotaging the workers' conscience; 3. By killing confid-ence; 4. By disarming France; 5. By promoting war; 6. By sacrificing the Franco-German alliance demanded by the Socialist party since 1871 to the interests of Jewish High Finance. In a word, by carrying out in France the programme of the war-mongering Communist party."[36] In its extreme, at times obscene, vituperation against Blum, as well as in its implication of a Jewish–Communist conspiracy to foment war, this retrospective rhetoric largely restated the far right's "prophecies" of 1936–39.

As one might expect of people who threw in their lot unambiguously with the Nazi victors, collaborationists expressed in even more black and white terms than Vichy the contrast between the defeated society and the victorious one. They viewed the defeat as a judgement of history on an anachronistic civilisation. Prewar France had been more than decrepit; it had been dying on its feet. In the words of the fascist intellectual Drieu la

Rochelle: "The French people asked for but one thing – to be left to grow old in peace, like the Dutch, amid their museums and deposit banks . . . This awful cancer that [France] produced in its breast, the inescapable cancer of decay and death. Oh, how France *wanted* to die."[37] Some collaborationists were more disdainful of the old bourgeois France than others, but virtually all viewed National Socialism as representing vitality, purpose, a sense of mission, in short the future. The defeat had given France an opportunity to participate actively in the building of the new Europe and in the crusade against Jews and bolshevism.

Resistance and Free French perspectives on 1939–40

Resisters shared Vichy's belief that the defeat had opened the nation's eyes. But their assumptions about what the nation now saw naturally diverged. The lessons that defeat held for the Resistance were inherently more complex than for Vichy or for collaborationists. Vichy, it is true, had to explain away the role that several of its luminaries (not least Pétain and Weygand) had played in the construction of the disastrous prewar defence strategy. Hence the regime's persistent efforts to shift blame on to others – the Riom defendants or, more generically, Jews, immigrants or Communists. It also had to negotiate between its own agenda (the discrediting of the Third Republic and a recasting of French society) and the German desire to transfer responsibility for the war, i.e. war guilt, on to France. But the regime's fundamental assumption about the defeat, as we have noted, was quite straightforward: defeat was a fact. Resisters, on the other hand, were contesting the defeat and/or what had flowed from it (the armistice, the vote of July 10, the policy of collaboration) at the same time as they shared the almost universal urge to assign responsibility for the débâcle. This put them in the difficult situation of contesting something while simultaneously confronting it, denying that defeat was final while acknowledging that it contained certain lessons. Vichy's quarrel was solely and monotonously with the regime that had led France to defeat. Resisters, however, had to balance their own anger with the prewar regime against their rejection of the post-armistice status quo.

In the early phase of Occupation, there was some apparent convergence between the Resistance and Vichy. In tactical terms, resisters had little to gain by attacking the goal of national rebuilding or the Marshal himself, while both were so popular.[38] Furthermore, in principle, a number of the early Resistance organisations were not unsympathetic to the goals of the National Revolution. Their objection in 1940 was only that, until the nation had been liberated, a National Revolution was premature.[39] There was a widespread belief among resisters that Pétain was secretly sympathetic to their aims, just as many imagined that Pétain and de Gaulle were secretly colluding (one imaginative rumour had it that de Gaulle was Pétain's nephew[40]).

Though de Gaulle himself knew better than anyone the military flaws that had been exposed in defeat and was not averse to pointing them out in order to embarrass the generals in Vichy,[41] he also appreciated that the French public blamed the former Republic as much as the army for the disaster. For more than a year after the armistice, he refused to identify his movement with republican politics except in the most general terms (i.e. by indicating that the French people should be free to decide their own institutions after Liberation).[42] But he also refused to echo the allegations being made at Riom. Asked by a journalist to comment in print on the events of June 1940, de Gaulle declined. Privately, he acknowledged to the journalist the degradation of political authority in the crisis and the malign influence of Fifth Columnists, but he staunchly defended Reynaud and insisted that "this is not the moment to open proceedings".[43] This was the line articulated in the same month (February 1941) by General de Larminat, a prominent Free French officer of distinctly anti-republican leanings: "We refuse to weaken ourselves in a crisis such as this by diverting our attention and our energy towards the investigation and tracking down of those responsible for the disaster. The political disorders which engendered this disaster are dead and buried, and it is too late to do anything about them, whereas France is alive and in need of rescue from a great peril."[44]

Some Free French leaders would have liked to hold to this apolitical position. In 1942, when de Gaulle publicly aligned his movement with the progressive ideology of Resistance movements inside France, notable Gaullists such as General Leclerc and Colonel Rémy expressed their regret.[45] But the politicisation, outside as well as inside metropolitan France, was inexorable. The widening of the anti-Axis alliance in 1941, first to encompass the Soviet Union and then the United States, reinjected ideological purpose into the war. The growing probability of Allied victory directed resisters' thoughts towards the postwar future. Above all, Vichy's determination to construe internal reconstruction in a partisan way and to combine it with a foreign policy of collaboration (political, economic and even military) forced resisters to realise that resisting the occupiers also meant resisting Vichy. By the end of 1941, the authoritarianism, social conservatism and repressiveness of Vichy's politics, all tinged with the stain of collaboration, were impelling resisters towards republicanism and socialism.

This Resistance politics embedded the defeat within a larger crisis of liberal capitalism and democratic institutions. The essence of this crisis was the failure of the bourgeoisie as a ruling class. "The defeat of June 1940", observed one resistance author, "marks above all the collapse of the bourgeois class which has provided the nation with its rulers, managers and leaders ever since 1789: the bourgeois class has failed in its mission as a ruling class."[46] The Resistance saw 1940 as a watershed separating two eras: the era of bourgeois domination (1789–1939) yielding to an era of social transformation, heralded by the Resistance and embodied in the working class, "the Third Estate of our time".[47]

How exactly was the bourgeoisie implicated in the defeat? The most direct connection lay in the manifest mistakes, inefficiencies and oversights that had characterised officialdom's preparation for and conduct of the war. Resisters pointed to the half-hearted economic mobilisation by big business and the incompetent strategic planning: "No boldness of vision, no disinterestedness . . . universal mediocrity", in the words of Léon Blum.[48] Like many others, Blum felt that the bourgeoisie had put its animosity towards the working class ahead of patriotism. A related accusation was advanced by Communists, who stressed the malevolent influence of the "trusts" – the economic potentates who had stifled the development of the French economy since 1870, and in recent times had whipped up anti-Communism and sabotaged the nation's economic mobilisation in order to discredit the working class and aid Hitler.[49] Perhaps the most comprehensive and (outside France at least) influential inventory of prewar elites' failures was that compiled by an émigré journalist André Géraud, writing under the pen-name Pertinax. In his two-volume work *The Gravediggers of France* (first published in English in 1942 and in French the following year under the title *Les Fossoyeurs*), Pertinax spared virtually no member of the political and military establishment, as he detailed the shortcomings (or betrayals) of one after another – Gamelin, Weygand, Pétain, Daladier, Reynaud, Blum, Bonnet, Flandin, Laval, and so on. If there was a fundamental cause for the mediocrity of French leadership, Géraud located it (as did Blum) in the obsessive fear of socialism which had gripped the bourgeoisie throughout the interwar decades but especially in the wake of the Popular Front's election victory in 1936.[50]

In the underground press, it was perhaps more common to see the bourgeoisie's failure depicted in terms of its pernicious values. This ethical focus was convenient, since in purely social terms, most of the non-Communist Resistance leaders themselves emanated from the university-educated bourgeoisie. (The same may be said of ideologues of the National Revolution such as the leaders of the Uriage school, whose bourgeois origins did not preclude a sharply anti-bourgeois rhetoric.[51]) Thus, for the underground newspaper *Combat*, while the Resistance represented "the spirit of generosity, greatness and audacity", the bourgeois elites had been motivated by "egoism", "narrow-mindedness" and "fear".[52] It became a Resistance cliché that the bourgeoisie had been risk-averse and backward-looking, while the working class (identified as the class most sympathetic to resistance) was forward-looking and idealistic. Not surprisingly, resisters often made the leap from this kind of argument to broader denunciations of prewar culture. Lamenting "France's perpetual temptation . . . to adopt bourgeois values",[53] they explained the defeat as the outcome of a hopelessly "bourgeoisified" culture. "To Restore France, Let's Stop Being a Petit Bourgeois People!" declared the group *Libérer et Fédérer*.[54] Or to quote a prominent intellectual resister, Professor André Hauriou: "Our defeat in 1940 was due in part to a lack of material means. Most importantly, it was the consequence of a spiritual subsidence which had afflicted both the Nation and its leaders. But it was also the consequence of the spirit's abdication in the face of material progress and its false certainties."[55]

There were certainly points of commonality between this Resistance tendency to "moralise" the defeat and de Gaulle's attitude towards it. For *Combat*, an essential cause of the disaster had been "the lack of sincerity in public, as in private, life".[56] De Gaulle shared this sense of a general moral decay. As he explained to the Catholic writer Jacques Maritain, the fact that he had been forced, in 1940–41, to counteract Vichy propaganda by stressing the purely military dimension of the defeat did not mean that he was blind to the "moral subsidence" which had been the fundamental cause of defeat. "The loss of the Rhine in '36, the abandonment of the Austrians in '37, and of the Czechs in '39, the incoherence of the policy and the mediocrity of the strategy, were effects before they became causes. The nation was tottering for many years."[57] For de Gaulle, this moral weakness was associated with the decay of the French State, the nation's natural moral compass. In an interesting letter to Pertinax in 1943, the General gently chided the journalist for being too severe on Daladier and Gamelin. "Not that I deny their failure! But my feeling is that that head of government and that military commander suffered the effects of a deplorable general system which overwhelmed them. The fact is that it had become almost impossible truly to govern and to command in France because of the State's chronic paralysis."[58]

It is important to add that neither the underground in France nor the Gaullists limited the bourgeoisie's culpability to the defeat alone. In fact, it was the elites' conduct *after* 1940 which seemed to provide the most damning evidence of their guilt as a class. The message conveyed to de Gaulle by virtually all the Resistance leaders who journeyed to meet him in London in 1941 and 1942 was that the bourgeoisie was either pro-Vichy or at best *"attentiste"* (adopting a strategy of wait and see). As a class, the bourgeoisie seemed intent on exploiting the nation's defeat in order to crush rival classes.[59] The judgement of a prominent Resistance intellectual, whose personal views were distinctly unsocialist, typified the Resistance's indictment: "The bourgeoisie's short-sighted egoism, cynically displayed since the armistice, if not since Munich . . . its resignation in the face of France's decline, its lack of faith and imagination, and lastly its incredible adherence to the cult of the Marshal, the slogans of the National Revolution, and, all too often, the lies of collaboration, have brought into sharp relief the problem of the elite."[60]

This concept of bourgeois France, encompassing both the pre-defeat republican establishment and the post-defeat regime in Vichy, allowed the Resistance to lump the Third Republic and Vichy together. Historically speaking, this was not unjustifiable – the easy transition of many *hauts fonctionnaires* and business leaders to Pétain's *État Français* was notorious. But it also performed a crucial tactical function, by enabling resisters to escape the logic that the enemy of their enemy was their friend. On the whole, resisters no more wanted their antipathy to Vichy to be mistaken for sympathy for the Third Republic than they wanted their antipathy to the Third Republic to be interpreted as pro-Vichy. Their preference was to keep their distance from both. That was very evident during the Riom trial, when Resistance publications attacked the Vichy government's corrupt judicial procedures and stressed Pétain's heavy responsibility in the defeat, but did not associate themselves too closely with the defendants.[61]

The Resistance's hostility towards the prewar regime came from several sources. The most basic, of course, were the bitter memories of 1940. Another was the Resistance's view of itself as a self-selected, moral elite; insofar as resisters defined themselves in opposition to their republican predecessors, it was inevitable that their view of the latter should remain caricatured and unsympathetic. As the Occupation wore on, however, an even more critical factor became the Resistance's concern for its political future. Whereas Vichy had constructed its interpretation of the defeat from a position of strength in the present (albeit a precarious present), both the Gaullists and the Resistance movements inside France had to think forward to their postwar roles as they were looking back to 1940.

In 1942 and 1943 de Gaulle was embroiled in power struggles within his movement, and at the same time was attempting to secure international recognition of his movement's legitimacy. To fend off the challenge of an American-backed rival, General Giraud, de Gaulle needed to win the support of Resistance leaders who were, for the most part, newcomers to national politics. This required a strong rhetoric about the failings of the prewar system and prewar elites (a rhetoric which, it must be said, came easily to de Gaulle). On the other hand, to win international recognition, he needed the endorsement of the broadest possible range of politicians and political parties, which, in practice, often meant familiar figures from the prewar regime. In other words, de Gaulle's political predicament required him to square the circle on the issue of 1940 – combining a reformist, even revolutionary, rhetoric about the impossibility of returning to the past with a pragmatic rehabilitation of well-known parties and political figures not too closely associated with Vichy.

For leaders of the Resistance movements inside France, the challenge was to secure a permanent role for themselves and their organisations in the postwar nation. By mid-1943, when de Gaulle and Moulin agreed to make room for representatives of several of the leading prewar parties in the newly formed Conseil National de la Résistance (CNR), the leaders of the major Resistance movements could have little doubt that they would find themselves in competition with Third Republic parties. This would have seemed an implausible scenario in 1940, when all the parties (the strong parties of the left as well as the loosely structured parties of the centre and right) had been torn apart by the shock of defeat. The parties' unexpectedly rapid rise from the ashes (beginning with the Communists' resurgence after June 1941, continuing with the emergence of a Socialist Resistance committee, and culminating in the representation of the Radical party and conservative parties within the CNR) confronted Resistance movements with a major threat. To make a case for their new organisations and for new leadership in postwar France, it became more essential than ever to stress the defunct Republic's responsibility for the disaster of 1940. This re-emphasis on the guilt of the Republic was reflected in Resistance rhetoric in 1943–44. It was evident, for example, in a series of responses that Resistance groups gave to a questionnaire sent out by de Gaulle's administration in late 1943. Asked about their political preferences for the postwar period, resisters were critical, often abusive, about the personnel and parties of the Third Republic. One group's summary expressed the consensus view: "there is no doubt that the overwhelming majority of the French people feel a total disaffection towards the parliamentarians of 1939 . . . All the parties failed."[62] Some groups were willing to admit the possibility that former republican leaders, who had been active in the Resistance or had voted against Pétain in July 1940, could be rehabilitated; others believed that no member of the parliament of 1939 should ever be allowed into public life again. Significantly, the main target of resisters' animus tended not to be those former leaders (Daladier, Reynaud, Blum, and so on) who were in French or

German prisons, but people who had been prominent in the later Third Republic *and* had reappeared in or around de Gaulle's provisional government in North Africa (socialists such as Vincent Auriol and André Le Troquer, or radicals such as Pierre Mendès-France and, in particular, the much-detested prewar Air Force Minister, Pierre Cot). By 1944 resisters were vilifying such people in as categorical and almost as nasty terms as Vichy had in 1940–42: "It is absolutely essential that the prewar political elite be completely and definitively eliminated. Through their incompetence, weakness and demagoguery, they were responsible for the moral and material condition in which France found herself on September 1st, 1939."

The frequent references to 1939 to denote "pre-defeat" France suggested a view of the defeat as largely conditioned by prewar structures and virtually inevitable from the outset. It thereby shifted the burden from the army's failure in 1940 to the Republic's failure in the 1930s. The rhetoric of Resistance leaders, notwithstanding their mostly bourgeois origins, was that they were "unknowns" who could distance themselves entirely from the old establishment.[63] Implicit or explicit in this rhetoric was a generational argument: a rising elite, too young to have attained power before 1939 or ill-suited to the old regime, had now emerged to think through the future. The situation of this youthful elite was different from that of more established republican leaders who had refused to capitulate to Vichy. Figures like Blum, Daladier or the prewar Education Minister Jean Zay (all of whom saw imprisonment) had been too closely implicated in the past to blame defeat so casually on the older generation or "*les gens en place*" (the people in power). But they shared with the emergent Resistance elite a conviction that France needed a new Republic "freed of the fetters, the rust, and the parliamentary demagoguery that eventually made the Third Republic unrecognisable".[64]

The situation of the Communist party (PCF) was different again. They had been victims of official repression before Vichy came on the scene, and had their own scores to settle with the Third Republic. Furthermore, the defeat had come at a time when the official line emanating from Moscow was calling for neutrality in the conflict between fascism and Anglo-American plutocracy. Together, these factors led the party hierarchy into an awkward timidity on the issue of resistance to the occupier. In the immediate aftermath of defeat, the party tentatively explored the possibility that an accommodation could be reached with the Occupation authorities which would lead to the legalisation of the party. By the late summer of 1940 these hopes had already been dashed, and the party withdrew to a position of what might be termed neutralist opposition – opposition to Vichy, opposition to the former Republic, opposition to the capitalist interests of the

City of London. If this isolation was not the outright collaboration that postwar anti-Communists alleged, and if the party line did not preclude individual members from adopting a more active anti-German resistance, still it was certainly an uncomfortable position. It was not until the German attack on the Soviet Union in June 1941 that French Communists were released from this position and could subordinate all other priorities to the immediate struggle against the occupiers and their collaborators and to building up a broad-based National Front against fascism. This strategy was a phenomenal success: it brought millions of new members and voters to the party, identified the PCF as the quintessential party of resistance, and gave it leverage in the post-Liberation era. Still, 1940 remained a difficult memory for the party. After 1944 it had to rewrite the history of 1939–41 in order to demonstrate that its patriotic resistance to occupation had begun at the moment of defeat.

The PCF's quietism in 1939–41 and its aggressive infiltration and manipulation of the Resistance after June 1941 left many non-Communist resisters intensely suspicious of the party's motives. For some such resisters (especially the more conservative), this anti-Communism ultimately trumped their resentment of the Third Republic. Thus Jacques Lecompte-Boinet, a leader in the *Ceux de la Résistance* movement, decided that he preferred "the republican order of the Third Republic to the adventure and the probable dictatorship of the Fourth Republic".[65] This view was not the norm in 1944, but it became progressively more common in the later years of the decade, as the Resistance alliance disintegrated and containment of Communism came to be the defining challenge of French politics.

The defeat of 1940, like that of 1870, spawned a huge literature diagnosing the causes of the nation's collapse and recommending remedies.[66] Books and articles in this vein appeared throughout the Occupation, and indeed throughout the entire decade of the 1940s. But in spite of all the talk, responsibility for the defeat had ceased to be a burning political issue well before the end of the Occupation. Vichy's partisan assault on the Third Republic, in particular its mismanaged show trial at Riom, had drained the issue of much of its credibility. Though many resisters eyed the reemergence of Third Republic celebrities and parties with unease or hostility, the main targets of their animus remained the policies of the German occupiers, of Vichy and of the collaborators. In a certain sense, as we will argue in Chapter Five, the occupied nation had adjusted to the fact of defeat – adjusted not in the sense of accepting it but of no longer being immobilised by it. As a result of the development of significant movements of resistance and collaboration, the political landscape had shifted. The issues that were in the forefront of public consciousness by 1944 were those of the preceding four years rather than of 1939–40.

Notes and references

1 Quoted in P. Burrin, *La France à l'heure allemande 1940–1944* (Paris: Seuil, 1995), p. 81. Pétain's remark was cited in the indictment against him at his postwar trial.

2 H. Coutau-Bégarie and C. Huan, *Lettres et notes de l'Amiral Darlan* (Paris: Economica, 1992), p. 231.

3 Y. Bouthillier, *Le Drame de Vichy*, 2 vols (Paris: Plon, 1950–51), vol. 2, p. 6.

4 Pro-natalists campaigned to increase France's flagging birthrate, and *planistes* advocated managing the economy through some kind of concerted programme or plan.

5 Many of these ideas about order/disorder, especially relating to the role of women, the dangers of urban life, and individualism, recycled the conservative soul-searching that had followed the Franco-Prussian war (1870) and the Paris Commune (1871). See F. Muel-Dreyfus, *Vichy et l'éternel féminin* (Paris: Seuil, 1996), pp. 18–19, 23–32, 66.

6 P. Pétain, *Actes et écrits* (Paris: Flammarion, 1974), p. 456.

7 R. Bonnard, *Les Actes constitutionnels de 1940* (Paris: R. Pichon, 1942), p. 59.

8 M. Pollard, *Reign of Virtue* (Chicago: University of Chicago Press, 1998), p. 109.

9 François Perroux, writing in a publication of the Institut d'Etudes Corporatives et Sociales (I.E.C.S.): *Vers la construction corporative française* (Paris: I.E.C.S.), p. 93.

10 *Vichy 1940–1944. Quaderni e documenti inediti di Angelo Tasca/Archives de guerre d'Angelo Tasca* (Milan: Feltrinelli, 1986), p. 237.

11 G. Miller, *Les Pousse-au-jouir du Maréchal Pétain* (Paris: Seuil, 1975), p. 104. Miller notes the conservative subtext in turning revolution into housework. At the same time, as I observe below, the homespun rhetoric masked a reality of persecution.

12 D. Rossignol, *Vichy et les Francs-Maçons* (Paris: J.-C. Lattès, 1981), pp. 94, 137.

13 Quoted in G. Pernot, *Journal de guerre (1940–1941)* (Paris: Les Belles-Lettres, 1971), p. 119.

14 R. Poznanski, *Etre juif en France pendant la seconde guerre mondiale* (Paris: Hachette, 1994), p. 129.

15 C. Singer, *Vichy, l'université et les juifs* (Paris: Les Belles Lettres, 1992), pp. 73–4.

16 V. Caron, *Uneasy Asylum. France and the Jewish refugee crisis, 1933–1942* (Stanford, California: Stanford University Press, 1999), pp. 268–301.

17 For a useful summary of the evolution of public opinion under occupation, see the article by J.-M. Flonneau, in J.-P. Azéma and F. Bédarida (eds), *Le Régime de Vichy et les Français* (Paris: Fayard, 1992), pp. 506–22.

18 Quoted in Burrin, *La France*, p. 223.

19 R. Paxton, *Vichy France: Old Guard and New Order* (New York: Columbia University Press, 1972), p. 192.

20 P. Baudouin, *Neuf mois au gouvernement (avril–décembre 1940)* (Paris: La Table Ronde, 1948), p. 90.

21 J. Picavet, *Le Procès des responsables de la défaite* (Amiens: Journal d'Amiens, 1941), p. 5.

22 F. Pottecher, *Le Procès de la défaite. Riom, février–avril 1942* (Paris: Fayard, 1989), p. 28.

23 E. Daladier, *Prison Journal, 1940–1945* (Boulder, Colorado: Westview Press, 1995), p. 128.

24 Weygand later claimed that he had disapproved of the trials and tried to dissuade the government from going forward with them: *Les Evénements survenus en France de 1933 à 1945. Témoignages*, 9 vols (Paris: PUF, 1951–52), vol. 6, p. 1569.

25 Pottecher, *Le Procès*, p. 17.

26 Nicole Jordan has unearthed a "fire-breathing" anti-Popular Front memorandum that Gamelin circulated at Riom, a document that suggests, at the very least, a capacity for opportunism on his part. *The Popular Front and Central Europe: The Dilemmas of French Impotence, 1918–1940* (Cambridge: Cambridge University Press, 1992), pp. 54, 105 n., 305 n.

27 Daladier, *Prison Journal*, pp. 28–9.

28 Testimony of M. Cassagnau, in *Les Evénements . . . Témoignages*, vol. 9, p. 2833.

29 Daladier, *Prison Journal*, p. 19.

30 Pottecher, *Le Procès*, p. 52.

31 H. Michel, *Le Procès de Riom* (Paris: Albin Michel, 1979), pp. 55–60.

32 Reynaud, like Daladier and Blum, survived the war, but Mandel was assassinated in 1944 by the pro-collaboration *Milice*.

33 Michel, *Le Procès*, p. 402.

34 Burrin, *La France*, p. 389.

35 R. Recouly, *Les Causes de notre effondrement* (Paris: Editions de France, 1941), p. 10.

36 H. Ghilini, *A la barre de Riom* (Paris: Jean-Renard, 1942), p. 127.

37 P. Drieu la Rochelle, *Journal 1939–1945* (Paris: Gallimard, 1992), pp. 210, 212.

38 P.-H. Teitgen, *Faites entrer le témoin suivant* (Rennes: Ouest-France, 1988), p. 31.

39 See, for example, the manifesto of the Mouvement de Libération Nationale, reprinted in D. Cordier, *Jean Moulin, l'inconnu du Panthéon*, 3 vols (Paris: J.-C. Lattès, 1989–93), vol. 3, pp. 1286–9.

40 J. Grenier, *Sous l'Occupation* (Paris: Claire Paulhan, 1997), p. 115.

41 For example, speech of 15 Aug. 1940, in de Gaulle, *Lettres, notes et carnets*, 12 vols (Paris: Plon, 1980–88), vol. 3, p. 83.

42 See his telegram of 8 July 1941, in *Lettres, notes et carnets*, vol. 3, pp. 384–5.

43 Letter of 1 Feb. 1941, in *Lettres, notes et carnets*, vol. 3, pp. 243–4.

44 "Position des Français Libres *vis-à-vis* des problèmes nationaux", in Archives Nationales (Paris) (hereafter AN), F60 1728.

45 J.-L. Crémieux-Brilhac, *La France Libre* (Paris: Gallimard, 1996), pp. 370–1.

46 "Projet de manifeste pour une union politique de la Résistance", Sept. 1943, in AN F1a 3755.

47 Jacquier-Bruère, *Refaire la France* (Paris: Plon, 1945), p. 63. Michel Debré, the future Gaullist eminence and Prime Minister under the Fifth Republic, was one of the co-authors of this work.

48 L. Blum, *A l'échelle humaine* (1945), translated as *For All Mankind* (Gloucester, Massachusetts: Peter Smith, 1969), pp. 80–4.

49 PCF, "Un acte d'accusation contre les traîtres" (spring 1944), in AN F1a 3751.

50 Pertinax, *The Gravediggers of France*, 2nd edn (Garden City, New York: Doubleday, 1944), p. 578.

51 Disgust with bourgeois mediocrity and materialism gave some early advocates of the National Revolution (François Mitterrand would be an apt example) a point of affinity with the Resistance. This ideological affinity – a shared taste for heroic engagement, a shared distaste for capitalist greed and bourgeois prudence – may help to explain the comfortable transition that people like Mitterrand made from one side to the other. On Mitterrand's hatred of his own class, see Stanley Hoffmann's comments in *French Politics and Society*, 13: 1 (1995), pp. 9–10.

52 *Combat*, 34 (Sept. 1942).

53 *Cahiers du témoignage chrétien*, 28–29 (July 1944), p. 14.

54 *Libérer et Fédérer*, 2 (1 Sept. 1942).

55 A. Hauriou, *Vers une doctrine de la Résistance, le socialisme humaniste* (Algiers: Fontaine, 1944), p. 14.

56 *Combat*, 34 (Sept. 1942).

57 Letter of 7 Jan. 1942, in *Lettres, notes et carnets*, vol. 4, pp. 174–5.

58 *Lettres, notes et carnets*, vol. 4, p. 595.

59 Crémieux-Brilhac, *France Libre*, pp. 373–4.

60 R. Courtin, *Rapport sur la politique économique d'après-guerre* (Algiers: Editions Combat, 1944), p. 8.

61 Michel, *Le Procès*, pp. 350–3.

62 All these responses are in AN F1a 3756.

63 *Défense de la France*, 18 (17 June 1942); *Combat*, 51 (15 Nov. 1943).

64 Daladier, *Prison Journal*, pp. 114, 121–2, 197; J. Zay, *Souvenirs et solitude* (Paris: R. Julliard, 1945), pp. 189–95.

65 Quoted in R. Vinen, *Bourgeois Politics in France, 1945–1951* (Cambridge: Cambridge University Press, 1995), p. 190.

66 This literature is discussed at length in my book *Rethinking France: Plans for Renewal, 1940–1946* (Oxford: Oxford University Press, 1989).

CHAPTER FOUR

1940 after Liberation

... and now it was summer – not the first but the second after it had all come to an end, that is, had closed over, formed a scar, or rather . . . readjusted, mended, and so perfectly that you could no longer detect the least crack, the way the surface of the water closes over a pebble, the landscape that had been reflected for a moment broken, fractured, splintered into an incoherent multitude of fragments . . . recomposing . . . still undulating a little like dangerous serpents, then motionless, and then nothing but the varnished perfidious surface serene and mysterious . . .

Claude Simon, *La Route des Flandres* (1960)[1]

The resurfacing of the defeat

Liberation closed the chapter in national history that had begun in 1940. In the process, it could not help but recall the experience of four years before. "Revenge for 1940", shouted the crowd in newly liberated Coutances at the end of July 1944.[2] As in any such inversion, part of the satisfaction lay in savouring the contrast between the two experiences. The liberators' propaganda juxtaposed images of sad and serious faces in 1940 with images of elated, victorious faces in 1944, or set images of arrogant Germans goose-stepping into Paris in 1940 alongside images of chaotic skedaddlers four years later.[3] Alain Brossat has likened the scenes of Liberation to a frightening film being run backwards: Germans being harried and hunted from west to east, as they had harried and hunted in 1940 from east to west.[4]

Though memories of defeat could heighten the elation of revenge, they also revived painful emotions. Civilians in Normandy and other combat areas were reduced, as in 1940, to the role of spectators and had to see again the columns of exhausted, demoralised soldiers in retreat, caravans of hapless civilians caught up in the battle, carcasses of dead animals in the fields, random deaths and casual plundering. Even though there was the vast satisfaction of knowing that this time it was the Germans who were in retreat, the sights and sounds were uncomfortably familiar. Encountering German troops in Neuilly on August 19, a schoolteacher recorded her impressions as follows: "I pass one of those stray cars driving in circles, panic-stricken. The driver stops alongside me. In the front of the car is a soldier in green. His stiff arms must have been holding the same machine-gun for days. His dazed head hangs forward . . . Where have I seen this before? . . . Ah yes! June 1940."[5] Other diarists record similarly uneasy feelings of recognition. Martine Rouchaud, for example, a young *bourgeoise* who had seen the *exode* in 1940, watched a group of bedraggled Germans heading towards Paris, one pushing a comrade in an old baby carriage, and found her thoughts slipping back four years. "All the faces fade . . . It is French women and children streaming along the road. Some are dying, others cry out in fear or moan from hunger. I see again the little pale-faced girl with solemn eyes among our refugees."[6] Similarly, the Free French journalist, Pierre Bourdan, who was with General Leclerc's armoured division near Argentan commented on how "that first day [back in France] . . . awoke many old echoes. . . . In that same plain on June 10th 1940 there had been a cavalry charge and I remembered how my brother had died, covered with wounds, after just such a charge. Its antiquated futility was brought into relief to-day by all this armoured might, when, four years after, the same enemy was on the defensive . . ."[7] Another journalist (Albert Desile from Saint-Lô) noted the same "stigmata" of defeat on German soldiers that he remembered from 1940 – bare, helmet-less heads, boots and trousers caked with dried mud, dirty bandages leaking blood.[8] No doubt, there was something self-consciously literary in some of these evocations of the reversal of fortune. But the echoes of the past were undeniable, so self-evident that they hardly needed to be stated: "June 25, 1944. At 8 p.m., sad traffic past the house, of unfortunates fleeing Biéville, where the shells rain down, animals all killed or wounded. Vehicles loaded with mattresses and everything that they're trying to save."[9]

In the months that followed, there were to be other moments when the experience of the defeat broke through to the surface again. In the spring of 1945, the repatriation of hundreds of thousands of prisoners of war brought French society face to face with the men who had disappeared from view in 1940. It was, on both sides, an uncomfortable reunion. Having been cut off from the rest of French society during the Occupation, the ex-POWs had missed the evolution that had occurred in their absence – the emergence of the Resistance as the main focus for patriotic sentiment, the discrediting of Pétain and the partial rehabilitation of republicanism, the eclipse of the memory of May–June 1940 by other memories, both more traumatic and more uplifting. In the camps, the POWs had had ample time to reflect on the causes of the defeat and to build up idealised expectations for postwar change. To judge by their newspapers, they found much of French society ungrateful for their sacrifices and depressingly unconcerned about learning the lessons of the defeat.[10] And indeed it was true that both the elite and the general public had moved on since 1940 and no longer viewed their situation as they had in the immediate aftermath of defeat.

The postwar purge: Riom redux?

Another kind of uncomfortable reunion with the past took place in courtrooms, where former members of the Vichy regime were forced to answer for their actions after June 1940, and in some cases before. In 1943, de Gaulle's authorities had prosecuted an ex-Vichy minister, Pierre Pucheu, on the grounds that he had plotted the illegal modification of a legal regime in 1940.[11] In the wake of Liberation they levelled similar charges against Pétain and other prominent Vichyites. Perhaps more than any other event, the trial of Marshal Pétain in July–August 1945 focused the public's attention back to the circumstances preceding the armistice. The former head of state was tried before a newly created *Haute Cour de Justice*, whose jurors were selected by the members of the Consultative Assembly. The indictment contained two counts: that Pétain had engaged in a premeditated plot to undermine the security of the French State; and that he had colluded with the enemy to advance the latter's interest as well as his own. In fact, the charges said more about Pétain's alleged prewar plotting than about his conduct under the Occupation. Collaboration was largely construed as the outgrowth of a pre-defeat conspiracy, the means whereby the conspirators maintained themselves in power.[12] In line with these priorities, the prosecution began the trial by focusing on the first charge. Prosecutors argued that both the armistice and the parliamentary vote of July 10 had been the product of an organised anti-republican conspiracy involving Pétain, Laval, and a motley collection of French right-wing extremists, and assisted by Franco, Mussolini and Hitler. A series of witnesses testified to Pétain's associations with members of a notorious pro-fascist terrorist group called the *Cagoule*. They also testified to the Marshal's suspicious prescience about the events of May 1940: in March 1940, for example, while still ambassador to Madrid, he was alleged to have told a government minister, Anatole de Monzie, that "in the second half of May, they will need me".[13] The former President of the Republic, Albert Lebrun, bolstered the premeditation theory by recalling that, when he asked Pétain to form a government on June 16, 1940, the latter pulled out a piece of paper with his list of ministers already written. Other witnesses, who had worked under him in the embassy in Madrid, testified that in the fall of 1939 he had been drafting lists of ministers (always including Laval) in the event that he would be called back to Paris to head the government. Some evidence (all of it hearsay) was presented to establish that Pétain and Laval had been in contact throughout the phony war.

The implication of all this testimony, much of it inconclusive or unsubstantiated, was that Pétain and Laval had been in active collusion with France's enemies, including Hitler himself. How else could Pétain have known that he would be needed back in Paris in May rather than April or June? The prosecution was clear that Pétain had seized the opportunity of defeat to carry out a premeditated coup, and that it was, therefore, in Pétain's interest not to put the defeat in doubt once it had happened (hence his refusal to allow the government to escape to North Africa). But less clear was Pétain's (or the Pétainist conspiracy's) role in the defeat itself. The prosecution's two star witnesses, Reynaud and Daladier, strongly implied that Pétain was heavily implicated in the defeat, without specifying the extent of his treason. Both pointed to Pétain's record as Minister of War in 1934 as evidence of a reckless neglect of French security. Daladier went further, by citing various sinister episodes before the 1940 campaign, in which an unspecified Fifth Column in the military hierarchy had sabotaged French preparedness. While he could not say that Pétain was aware of or approving of the actions of this Fifth Column, he did not disagree with the gloss put on his evidence by one of the jury members: "there was a Fifth Column whose intrigues had terrible consequences . . . Men belonging to the Marshal's entourage were among the elements in this Fifth Column."[14]

This attempt to blame Pétain for the defeat, either on the grounds (not wholly unjustified) that he had been responsible for the disastrous strategy employed by the army in 1939–40 or on the more far-fetched grounds that he or his supporters had actively facilitated Hitler's invasion, backfired. It threatened to turn the trial into precisely what critics had warned it might become: Riom in reverse. Even before the trial began, the spectre of Riom hung over the proceedings. In June and July, members of the Consultative Assembly tried (unsuccessfully) to persuade de Gaulle to move the trial from a somewhat cramped courtroom in the Palais de Justice to a venue more suitable for a political trial. They suggested the Palais Bourbon (the site of the prewar Chamber of Deputies) and complained that holding the trial in a normal courtroom, closed to the nation, would invite comparisons with Riom.[15] Once the proceedings got under way, the echoes of Riom became unavoidable: a mute Pétain replacing the mute Gamelin; Daladier repeating the same arguments for the prosecution that he had offered at Riom in his own defence; Pétain and Laval in the dock instead of orchestrating the prosecution. When it was revealed that the chief prosecutor himself had accepted an appointment to the Riom court in 1940, the irony of the proceedings was complete. The Resistance press fumed at the bungling. Raymond Aron warned that, just as Vichy's attempt to pin blame for the defeat on the Third Republic had ended up rehabilitating the Republic, so the equally implausible attempt to blame Pétain could only rehabilitate Vichy.[16] In the influential Resistance newspaper *Combat*, the editorialist predicted that "we will not disarm the Pétainist faithful by pitting against them the leaders of another regime which capitulated".[17] In the pro-Communist weekly *Les Lettres Françaises*, Claude Morgan called the trial an "ignoble farce",[18] while *Le Monde* opted for a tone of bemusement: "One cannot escape the impression that we have been witness to a sort of preamble to related trials – trials involving the armistice, the conspiracy against the Republic, the causes of the defeat – rather than a trial to determine the accused's responsibilities in the policy of collaboration."[19]

What this initial detour in the Pétain trial demonstrated was the risk involved in reopening the debate about 1940 and the minimal enthusiasm for doing so. Conspiracy theories about the defeat and the circumstances surrounding the vote of July 10 could only have the effect of exonerating a prewar regime which was still widely viewed as discredited. Furthermore, it was difficult to dwell on the events of mid-1940 without recalling the unpleasant truth (highlighted by the defence lawyers) that most of the people testifying against the Marshal in 1945 had put their faith in him in 1940. The Court apparently recognised these facts. For the remainder of the trial, the prosecution tried to focus on what most people regarded as the essence of the case, that is what Pétain had done with his power after July 11, 1940: "It is a question of establishing if Pétain served Germany, if his policies strengthened the odds of a Hitler victory, if he is responsible for deportations, tortures and shootings . . . if he was, in the end, whether he liked it or not, the enemy's servant."[20]

That the defeat had become a judicial distraction was made clear again in the autumn of 1945, when it was Laval's turn to appear before the High Court. As in Pétain's case, the indictment included the charge of having sought an armistice with a view to overthrowing the Republic and having conspired to prevent the government from leaving French soil. But while the prosecution plainly believed that Laval had attempted to sabotage the nation's war effort, the Court was adamant that the question of the defeat and Laval's responsibility for it was not relevant to the trial.[21] "The trial over responsibility [for the defeat] was the Riom trial, and we are not at Riom now."[22]

The Riom trial had permanently tainted the idea of prosecuting those who had led the nation to defeat. Even without that taint, the criminalising of responsibility would have been problematic. Unless the authorities could uncover evidence of deliberate sabotaging of the war effort or collusion with the enemy (of the kind that made prosecution of collaborators feasible), they were left with negligence or incompetence or simple bad luck. In the civilian cases, how could one abstract an individual's errors from the flaws of the political system? (This was de Gaulle's backhanded defence of the Third Republic's leadership.) And in a democracy could one punish politicians for making decisions that, at the time they were made, met with the approval of public opinion? Self-serving as Reynaud's postwar comments were, they were hard to rebut:

> After each of the catastrophes in our history, the French people has always looked for a scapegoat in order to escape its own collective responsibility . . . Don't you think that Pétain's slogan "Fire kills" ("Le feu tue") and the system of only fighting from behind concrete defences appealed to the French people? Don't you retain, as I do, the painful and humiliating memory of the enthusiastic reception of the Munich agreement? . . . True courage, for elected officials, consists in telling the sovereign people: "You are a sovereign like the others, you make mistakes like the others, and the only profit that you can draw from this great disaster is to face up to your failings and mistakes and change your ways."[23]

It was not much easier to criminalise military incompetence. The mere fact of defeat could scarcely qualify as a crime. Lack of imagination or failure to adapt to modern techniques of warfare were institutional as much as individual failings. And so unless one could demonstrate that officers had deliberately compromised national security or voluntarily acquiesced in defeat (which is certainly what their critics suspected, since so many high-ranking officers reappeared in positions of authority in Vichy[24]), one was left again in the grey area of incompetence, a professional failing but not easy to construe as a crime.

All this is to say that the project of criminalising defeat soon petered out after Liberation, while the task of prosecuting collaborators for post-armistice actions continued for several more years. Most of the "grave-diggers" still felt the need to defend their records; they could do so now not as defendants but as witnesses before a long-running parliamentary enquiry (discussed below) or, better yet, as memoirists. The late 1940s and early 1950s saw the publication of a series of lengthy, self-justificatory memoirs by many of the principal decision-makers in 1939–40 (including Gamelin,

Weygand and Reynaud).[25] In effect, these memoirs constituted the continuation by other means of the investigation that had begun at Riom in 1940.

The entire first volume of Gamelin's three-volume memoir, for example, purported to express what the author would have said at Riom if he had felt free to speak. Point by point, Gamelin refuted the charges made against him by Vichy. Like Daladier and Blum four years earlier, he turned the tables on his erstwhile accusers – arguing that if France had started rearming in 1934 instead of 1936 her prospects would have been far brighter in 1940. In the end, Gamelin found plenty of other people and other institutions besides himself and the army to share the blame: the institutions of the Third Republic; the fragmentation of the party system; the unnamed conspirators "whose subterranean actions only became apparent when the earth caved in under our feet";[26] above all, Weygand and Pétain.

In equally voluminous and continually retouched narratives, Reynaud provided an interpretation of the defeat that alternated between incriminating the whole nation[27] and incriminating the accusers of Riom.[28] Lebrun and others took a similar tack, presenting a detailed historical narrative to contextualise their pre-defeat choices in the most favourable possible light. More subtle and perhaps more effective as self-justification was the diary genre used by Baudouin. A day-by-day account of pre- and post-armistice events, purported to have been written at the time, Baudouin's testimony had the aura of an unfiltered primary text. The subtext that the author surely intended but was too clever to state was expressed in Malcolm Muggeridge's foreword to the English translation (also published in 1948). "Subsequent events and enthusiasms have inevitably altered the attitude of many Frenchmen to the events of 1940 and induced much convenient forgetfulness. It would have been easy for M. Baudouin similarly to adapt his narrative. That he has not done so may have increased the difficulties of his own present situation but will surely be a source of thankfulness to all who want to know what actually happened in France."

Evidently, the chief purpose of these authors was to prove that whoever had been responsible for the critical mistakes or the criminal actions, it was not they. Thus, for example, Reynaud kept up a long-running polemic with Weygand, denying the latter's allegation that Reynaud had been the first to utter the dreaded word armistice and asserting, to the contrary, that Weygand himself (and Pétain) had first proposed it. And Gamelin defended his major strategic decisions and denied that he had underestimated German capabilities or failed to appreciate the potential of *blitzkrieg*. In this trial-by-memoir, there were scores of accusations and no confessions, continual invocations to the higher justice of history and the patriotic imperative of truth-telling alongside flagrantly self-interested justifications and rationalisations. In sum, a fitting end to the fiasco of Riom.

The defeat in Liberation politics

While memories of 1940 reverberated through court proceedings and in postwar memoirs, they were rarely discussed in such detail in political settings. Occasionally, though less often than one might have expected, the defeat was invoked in critical post-Liberation debates over reconstruction. At the end of 1945, for instance, a frustrated General de Gaulle, increasingly at odds with the majority in the Constituent Assembly, appealed pointedly to the lessons of 1940: "We have begun to reconstruct the Republic. You will continue to do so. However you do it . . . if you do it without taking into account the lessons of our political history over the past fifty years and, in particular, the lessons of what transpired in 1940, if you do not take into account the absolute necessity of authority, dignity and accountability on the part of the government, you will reach a situation where . . . you will bitterly regret having taken the path you have taken."[29] In the very same debate, the memory of 1940 was employed against de Gaulle by members of the Constituent Assembly who criticised his preference for short-term defence expenditure over longer-term industrial reconstruction.[30] These economic modernisers argued that the defeat had happened because for decades the nation had neglected her industrial infrastructure.

In general, however, the leaders who emerged after 1944 based their rhetoric and self-identity much more on the Resistance experience than on the lessons of 1940. The touchstone of Resistance reconstruction thinking was the Common Programme of the CNR (March 1944). This programme, to which Liberation politicians continually referred, scarcely mentioned the defeat. The closest it came was a reference to building new democratic institutions with "the efficiency that had been lost as a result of the corruption and betrayals that preceded capitulation". Moreover, the political eclipse of the "old guard" was justified primarily in terms of what they had done after the defeat, not before. Members of the prewar parliament who were declared ineligible to hold office after the Liberation were being punished for their vote on July 10, 1940, or for their subsequent association with Vichy. It was their actions after the armistice that got Third Republic politicians into trouble (or extricated them from trouble in the case of those who were relieved of ineligibility by virtue of Resistance heroism), not their actions during the phony war.

Even though most members of the new political elite were truly new (85% of the members of the Constituent Assembly elected in 1945 had had no experience in prewar legislatures) and were almost unanimous in ruling out the possibility of resurrecting the Third Republic, they were uninterested in founding their legitimacy on the lessons of 1940. None of the three leading parties (the Communist party, the Socialist party and the Christian Democratic MRP) placed a high priority on holding a national inquest into the defeat. Very few of their leaders acknowledged 1940 as a transformative moment for themselves or for their parties. The non-Communist left linked its anti-Vichy or anti-Nazi resistance to prewar anti-fascism. The MRP's founders, Catholics who had disobeyed the Church hierarchy's strictures against resistance and come to national prominence through clandestine action, portrayed their wartime activism either as an extension of their prewar experience in a range of social Catholic organisations and causes or simply as a product of their religious principles. Still more striking was the reticence of both the Communist party, which emerged from the occupation as *the* party of resistance, and General de Gaulle, the symbol of resistance who presided over the Liberation government until January 1946.

The Communist view of 1940 was shaped by the party's need to deal with the awkward memory of the non-aggression pact that Stalin had signed with Hitler in August 1939 – a pact which had kept the party out of organised resistance to Germany until the German invasion of the USSR in June 1941. In order to vindicate its stance in 1939–41 and rebut charges of slavish adherence to Moscow, the party had to establish a retrospective continuity between its Popular Front strategy of the mid-1930s, the disengaged strategy of August 1939 to June 1941, and its Resistance strategy after June 1941. This required the Communists to posit a single consistent enemy (fascism and the capitalist "trusts"), against which they had been fighting the entire time. The fascist leagues of the mid-1930s, the Daladier reaction in 1938–40, and the Vichy reaction in 1940–44 thus became different manifestations of the same basic phenomenon. Communist rhetoric focused not on the defeat, but on a long-term process of capitalist betrayal, which party spokesmen traced back to the anti-republican riots of February 1934: "This decade of history is the history of the decadence, bankruptcy and treachery of the old ruling class, the decadence, bankruptcy and treachery of large capital, that is to say the trusts. And this decade of history marks the rise, uneven but indisputable, of the new national forces which are today united on a common programme and fighting against the forces of the past. . . ."[31] Consistent with this view of the past were the public celebrations that the Communist party sponsored in the wake of Liberation – for example, a February 1945 commemoration of the General Strike of February 1934 or an October 1944 commemoration of the martyrdom of Communist hostages shot in 1941.[32]

In these months immediately after Liberation, when the Communist movement was so closely identified with national resistance and the Soviet Union enjoyed unprecedented popularity, the party did not face much hostile scrutiny of its record in 1939–40. Anti-Communism did not take

long to reappear, however. During the almost perpetual electoral cam-
paigning between October 1945 and November 1946, the PCF had to
parry increasingly open attacks on its record in the late 1930s. In response,
it threw up what one historian called "a smokescreen of outraged patriotism
and perfervid purging zeal".[33] Prime targets of this rhetoric were the remnants of the Third Republic leadership – especially Daladier and Reynaud,
the men who were most closely associated with the anti-Communist repression of 1939–40. In October 1945, Daladier stood for election in the
Vaucluse (unsuccessfully, as it transpired), and his campaign was subjected
to violent attacks from the PCF.[34] Seven months later, in elections for the
Second Constituent Assembly, he ran again and was elected. In July 1946,
the PCF tried to invalidate both his and Reynaud's election. The parliamentary party accused Reynaud of having delivered France to the Fifth
Column in 1940 by promoting Pétain, Baudouin and Bouthillier into his
government. They attacked Daladier for sabotaging a possible Anglo-French-
Soviet alliance in August 1939. In a rephrasing of the pre-defeat charge
against the French right (that they had preferred Hitler to the Popular
Front), both Reynaud and Daladier were accused of having been more
interested in crushing the working class and the Communist party than in
prosecuting the war against the national enemy.[35]

For quite different motives, de Gaulle was also concerned to view the
defeat within a longer context. As head of the provisional government in
1944–46, he articulated a version of recent events designed to restore
national unity by placing the entire Vichy episode in parentheses and cred-
iting Liberation to the uninterrupted resistance of the nation since 1940.
This version denied all legitimacy to the transformation of July 1940, and
since (in de Gaulle's words) the Republic had never ceased to exist, it also
contested the Resistance's claim to embody a whole new order. Like the
Communists, de Gaulle chose to embed the defeat in a longer narrative,
but one beginning in 1914, not in 1934. In speeches and ceremonies
in 1944 and 1945, the General repeatedly advanced his view of the two
world wars as forming a single "thirty years' war". As Henry Rousso has
observed, the effect of combining the two wars into a single phenomenon
was to "divert attention from unique aspects of World War II" (aspects such
as "the role of irregular partisans, ideological conflict and the genocide")
and to link "France's internecine struggles" to foreign invasion.[36] It also
reduced the defeat of 1940 to a temporary setback in a conflict that had
begun a quarter-century before and ended in victory five years later. This
was precisely the view of the defeat which de Gaulle had been expressing
since June 1940, when he had assured the few officers who had rallied to
London that they were "the vanguard of the France which is continuing a
thirty years' war begun in 1914".[37]

Wartime Gaullism had represented a denial of defeat. From the outset, de Gaulle had argued that the underlying geopolitical realities (Britain's island geography, Germany's antipathy towards Soviet Russia, Japan's antipathy towards the United States) had made both globalisation of the conflict and Allied victory inevitable. Vichy's fundamental crime, therefore, had been its acceptance of a premature armistice. The gradual revelation of de Gaulle's foresight and Vichy's miscalculation had contributed crucially to the mystique and political influence of Gaullism. But once the revelation was complete, once the war was clearly won, there was little for de Gaulle or his supporters to gain by revisiting Vichy's miscalculation. As the Pétain trial showed, this memory tended, in retrospect, either to rehabilitate the Third Republic leadership via the fiction that Reynaud, Daladier and the rest had been victims of a premeditated plot, or to inculpate the vast majority not just of the political class but of the general public, who had shared Pétain's belief in the unavoidability of an armistice. Neither of these outcomes was appealing to de Gaulle. On the one hand, the General had no desire to remind the nation of just how universal the feelings of relief had been in July 1940, since that was a fact which starkly contradicted the Gaullist myth of a nation-in-resistance. On the other hand, he did in fact believe that the weakness of the political system had contributed to the disaster. As he later wrote, in a letter to his one-time patron and then political opponent, Paul Reynaud: "In my view, France's misfortune was that . . . in the moment of extreme peril its political regime proved incapable of fulfilling its most basic duty, namely to defend the country. It was this regime (non-existent head of state, discontinuity in government, confusion in Parliament, political games and rivalries) that in large measure paralysed you."[38]

But these were the words of a politician out of office. As head of the provisional government, de Gaulle had been rather circumspect on the issue, and most of the Liberation elite had followed his lead. It was not until 1947, after the departure of de Gaulle from office and on the eve of the Communists' departure, that a systematic parliamentary post-mortem on the defeat was launched.

The commission of enquiry

The history of the commission of enquiry that conducted this post-mortem only confirms the low profile of the defeat by the late 1940s. Composed of parliamentarians from all the main parties and a number of non-parliamentary members representing Resistance groups, the commission received a vast and sweeping charge – to investigate "all the political, economic, diplomatic, and military events which, between 1933 and 1945, preceded, accompanied and followed the armistice, so as to determine the responsibilities incurred and, if need be, to propose political and judicial sanctions". In more than one hundred hearings between 1947 and 1951 the commission heard testimony from most of the key French participants (political, diplomatic and military) in the events leading up to the armistice. In the end, its labours, though abbreviated by the calling of a general election in 1951, yielded nine volumes of testimony and two volumes of report.

And yet this protracted and dutiful enquiry was, in many respects, a non-event. The commission had been created in August 1946 in the waning days of the wartime Resistance coalition of Communists, Socialists and Christian Democrats. By the time the hearings began in 1947, international and domestic tensions associated with the onset of the Cold War had broken up this coalition. Within the commission a dispute over the chairman-ship prompted the resignation of its Communist members, and they were soon followed by the representatives of the CNR. (This walk-out had been foreshadowed the summer before by a similar Communist walk-out from the High Court.[39]) Inevitably, critics suggested that the investigation's purpose was to construct an "official" history in line with the interests of the so-called "Third Force", the anti-Communist, anti-Gaullist coalition which took control of the Fourth Republic's first legislature. General de Gaulle said as much in November 1947, when he declined to appear before the commission. "No-one can be both a party to proceedings and a judge at the same time. Clearly I am an interested party. So, equally, is the commission, since it is composed of men who have been delegated to it by the political parties. However fine may be their intentions, such a situation makes it impossible for them to consider impartially recent events . . . for which they themselves, or at least the organisations that have appointed them, were, to a large degree, responsible."[40]

There were indeed insuperable problems with the process. Many of the key witnesses were giving sworn testimony for the third or fourth time. A number of them had testified in Riom and in one or more of the postwar trials. Several had also published detailed accounts of their actions in 1940. Consequently, the purpose of much of the testimony that the commission received was to demonstrate consistency with prior testimony or to justify claims and assertions that had already been made. Over the many months of hearings, commission members developed an impressive grasp of the minutiae of the historical record, but they never became especially adroit at penetrating these layers of carefully crafted memory. They tended to ask witnesses questions that were so specific and that required such a pre-cise memory of events ten or more years in the past that they invited the regurgitation of previously stated positions. The ex-Vichy minister Yves

Bouthillier said more than he intended when he was pressed on contradictions between his testimony and that of other witnesses and responded: "my recollection accords with what I wrote in my book".[41]

The history of the commission bore out at least some of de Gaulle's suspicions. If commission members did not seek actively to exonerate the party organisations to which they belonged, their work certainly had the effect of redirecting blame elsewhere. It was not insignificant that the armistice, rather than the defeat itself, was identified as the central event to be investigated. The armistice was a political decision made by Pétain. Focusing on that decision made the machinations of Vichyites-to-be (before June 1940) and actual Vichyites (after June 1940) critical. It allowed the commission to construct a narrative not so different from the one that the PCF had popularised in 1944–45, linking pre-1940 anti-republicanism, exemplified by the anti-parliamentary riot of February 6, 1934, to the treachery of June 1940 and the collaboration of 1940–44.

The commission presented the armistice as a step that need not have been taken. Their case for its avoidability focused on the other options that Reynaud and members of his government explored in the crucial weeks of early June, in particular the Breton "redoubt" and the withdrawal to North Africa. To some members of the commission, the most plausible reason that these paths were not taken was sabotage by military commanders (especially Weygand) and by politicians around the then Vice-Premier Pétain. The motives adduced to explain this sabotage were various – to ensure that the Republic would go down with the army, to forestall social disorders, or to advance personal interests.[42] From the moment that defeat seemed likely, Weygand and Pétain had been determined to convert it into a change of regime. In the words of a former Third Republic minister, Landry, "France was the victim of a treasonous plot in which many soldiers and civilians participated."[43] Had Reynaud attempted to hold on to power or replace Weygand, commission members alleged, there would have been an outright coup.[44]

The commission probed, albeit in a somewhat unsystematic way, the pre-armistice relationships of those who later came to prominence in Vichy. Its purpose, clearly, was to uncover evidence of a conspiracy and of preparations for a coup. Commission members showed great interest, for example, in a meeting that took place at Paul Baudouin's residence in Bordeaux on June 15, 1940 – a meeting held in the absence of the Prime Minister but attended by Pétain, Weygand, Darlan, Bouthillier and Baudouin. Was this the occasion, one commission member speculated, when the advocates of an armistice orchestrated their strategy for overturning Reynaud and ending the fight?[45] This was impossible to verify, but it was apparently what commission members wanted to believe.

For the republican establishment of the late 1940s, the defeat itself was a more politically sensitive issue than the armistice. The commission ran out of time (perhaps thankfully) before it could fully marshal its thoughts on that issue. But the documentation that it gathered suggests that its strategy would have been to highlight the side of the story that Vichy had repressed at Riom – the fatal stagnation, mental as much as organisational, that had overcome the French army after the First World War. Whereas Vichy had emphasised the Republic's failure to prepare adequately for war, the commission emphasised the grave responsibilities of the military establishment. It documented the interwar army's refusal to move with the times or to develop new technologies and techniques of aerial and motorised warfare. It exposed classic instances of Luddite thinking (by Pétain, Weygand and a host of others), quoting generals who championed the horse over the motorised vehicle or insisted on the limited offensive capabilities of tanks. And it publicised warnings that had been raised and ignored by the High Command (for example, a March 1940 report by a member of parliament detailing the weak defences around Sedan, precisely where the panzers broke through two months later).[46]

When it came to assessing the responsibility of the Republic, the commission was more magnanimous and less pointed. The interwar nation, it suggested, had placed too much trust in the League of Nations. It had failed to develop the rich possibilities of the Empire or to keep up with the industrialisation of its rivals. This stagnation was certainly the fault of the political and economic elites, but the commission's indictment was delivered more in sorrow than in anger: "What had become of the ardent public-spiritedness of our forefathers a hundred years after the Three Glorious Days [of 1830] and a hundred and fifty years after 1789? Scepticism replaced faith. The Republic had been drained of its spiritual content, its creative dynamism."[47]

While the commission of enquiry laboured to shift responsibility a few degrees in this direction or that, there is no sign that the rest of French society cared much about what it was doing. The press coverage was desultory. Apart from one cloak-and-dagger episode (a secret visit to interview Pétain in his prison cell in 1947), the commission's work attracted little public attention. The issue of 1940 had become a footnote in French politics. Perhaps, as Robert Young has suggested, this was precisely what the postwar regime required: "[W]hat was paramount in the late 1940s was the need for some form of national reconciliation under the new Fourth Republic. That goal would not be met by further revisitations to the most painful period in modern French history, by fresh recriminations against or apologies for the buried Third Republic. Accordingly, the blurred but powerful impression left by the [commission of enquiry] report itself was that responsibility for the collapse was so widespread as to be indeterminate."[48]

The defeat in Fourth Republic politics

By the 1950s, as Henry Rousso has shown in his influential study of the "Vichy syndrome", the memory of the Resistance had become infinitely malleable and was being manipulated in order to serve a variety of political purposes. Rousso's argument about the memory of the Resistance applies also to the memory of defeat. Over the course of the Fourth Republic era (1946–58), interest in any serious investigation of the defeat's causes waned. Instead, 1940 became largely a debating point, evoked from time to time, but rarely confronted as an issue in its own right.

Naturally, evocations of this supreme disaster tended to cluster at moments of renewed international or internal tension. One such moment was the autumn of 1950 when the National Assembly debated first a proposal to grant amnesty to wartime collaborators and then the intensifying war against the Vietminh in French Indochina. The amnesty debate reopened the issue of Vichy's legality and the degree of culpability involved in following the orders of a duly constituted legal authority. François Quilici, a prominent figure in the wartime Gaullist movement, now suggested that the thesis of Vichy's illegality had been a necessary fiction invented in London by a tiny dissident movement that needed to establish a legal basis for itself and could do so only by denying one to Vichy.[49] Pétainist sympathisers seized the opportunity to re-emphasise the embarrassing truth that almost all the politicians in Vichy in early July 1940 – even those who had tried to amend the motion voted on July 10 – had agreed on the principle of giving Pétain extended powers.[50]

In the Indochina debate a fortnight later, parliamentarians drew analogies with what had preceded defeat in 1940 rather than with its aftermath. A prominent right-winger alleged that there was a Communist Fifth Column in the army, actively sabotaging the military effort against the Vietminh.[51] The Radical party veteran Maurice Viollette, a former Governor-General of Algeria and member of the 1936 Popular Front government, termed critics of the French war effort in Indochina "defeatists" and compared them to those who had refused to "die for Danzig" in 1939 and had (in his view) fatally undermined the country's will to fight the following year.[52] Speakers in this debate essentially defined the nation's options in terms of the options of 1940, amended only to amalgamate Indochinese Communists and German Nazis into the single category of "totalitarians".

For example, the MRP notable Paul Coste-Floret dismissed the idea of nego-
tiating with the Vietminh thus: "In 1940, in a moment of temporary defeat,
we heard a voice inciting us to stop fighting against totalitarianism, and
we know full well how that would have ended without the marvellous outburst of French resistance."[53] To submit again would be, in the hyperbolic
words of one right-wing deputy, "a new June 1940 worse than the original
because it would be cowardly as well as dishonourable".[54]

When this defeat materialised, with the humiliating surrender at Dien
Bien Phu in May 1954, again the echoes of 1940 could not be contained.
"Strange defeat", commented *Esprit*, quoting Bloch's observation that "the
fate of France no longer depends upon the French" and commenting on
the depressing similarities between these "successive defeats".[55] To some,
Dien Bien Phu was a repeat of 1940 – French commanders surprised by
the enemy's capabilities when they had no right to be surprised; a civilian
nation unwilling to make the hard sacrifices necessary for victory; allies let-
ting France down at the critical moment; another manifestation of a long-
term decline in national power. To others, Dien Bien Phu was a product of
1940, of the displacement of French influence in Asia that had occurred
during the war and had never been restored.[56]

The political parties which were identified with the Fourth Republic
(ranging all the way from the Socialists on the left to the MRP and the
Radicals in the centre and a variety of independents and conservatives on
the right) had little incentive to dwell on this analogy. A decade after the
Liberation, voters were increasingly disenchanted with the Republic, critical of its operation and bitter about the unfulfilled ambitions of 1944.[57] The
mere mention of 1940 reminded voters of the high-minded pledges never to
repeat the errors of the past that so many of the Fourth Republic's founders
had made in 1944–46. Amid fresh defeats, with the need for constitutional
reform as pressing in 1955 as in 1939, it was hardly politic for the mainstream parties to summon up the broken promises of "never again 1940".
Only political forces that were anti-system, like the anti-tax protest movement led by Pierre Poujade, had an interest in recalling those promises. In
a television broadcast during the general election campaign of December
1955–January 1956, Poujade exploited one of the defeat's main symbols
(the POWs) with a directness that his more respectable rivals could not
possibly risk: "Thousands of Frenchmen were taken prisoner in 1940 . . .
During their long captivity, they thought a lot about the country and its
rebirth . . . Since the war, in the more than ten years that they have been
paying taxes, what has become of their hopes? What was the point, what
is the point, of their sacrifice?"[58]

A similar pattern – unease in the mainstream, while anti-system forces
exploited the memories of 1940 – recurred four years later in the Republic's

final crisis. Many aspects of the regime's agony compelled comparison with the agony of its predecessor in 1940. One was the pusillanimity of the republican leadership, or rather its combination of verbal defiance and behind-the-scenes concessions. Just as Reynaud's radio heroics had masked the gradual transfer of power to the defeatists, so in May 1958 the Prime Minister, Pierre Pflimlin, and the majority in the National Assembly expressed a hard line against the military and civilian insurgents in Algeria, while manifestly failing to stand up to the army leadership. The reemergence of de Gaulle as a central political figure also, of course, recalled June 1940. The General himself saw that: his May 15 press statement marking his reentry into the political fray based his legitimacy squarely on 1940: "Not so long ago, the country, in its depths, trusted me to lead it in its entirety to salvation. Today, amid the trials that face it once again, let it know that I stand ready to assume the powers of the Republic." The day after his statement, a group of prominent civilian and military figures publicly urged the President of the Republic to take up de Gaulle's offer. They termed the nation's predicament "comparable to that of 1917 or 1940 in many respects, more serious still in other respects".[59] Anti-Gaullists saw the analogy in a more complex and sinister light. In the debate in the second chamber (the *Conseil de la République*), de Gaulle's statement was compared to Pétain's *actes constitutionnels* in 1940, while critics in the French and foreign press overtly likened de Gaulle's role to the Marshal's in the midst of defeat.[60]

In the last weeks of May, as the rift between the army in Algeria and the government in Paris widened and as parliament was forced to move towards the de Gaulle option, the ghosts of 1940 became ever more visible. The Communists, who were the most outspoken opponents of the recourse to de Gaulle, were quite explicit. "A new Vichy is being prepared", warned their chief parliamentary spokesman, Jacques Duclos, on May 27.[61] According to Duclos, the army in Algeria was now playing the role that Weygand's "legions" had played in 1940 – coercing a fearful assembly into a supposedly legal abdication. Pierre Cot, the prewar Air Minister and postwar Communist fellow-traveller, made a similar point in more coded language, when he warned the government: "When your house is on fire, you don't waste your time making plans for how to arrange the fixtures; you make a chain to fight the fire."[62] The irony of hearing this wartime Gaullist cliché dusted off and used against de Gaulle was surely not lost on Cot's audience. Indeed, plenty of non-Communist republicans shared these apprehensions. Among the 224 deputies who opposed de Gaulle's investiture on June 1 were a considerable number of Socialists and Mendésistes and even a couple of Christian Democrats. The arguments of these opponents unmistakably echoed those of the eighty Noes of July 10, 1940. Thus Pierre Mendès-France: "I cannot agree to cast a vote coerced by insurrection and the threat of a military coup. For the decision that the Assembly is going to make – each of us here knows full well – is not a freely made decision; the consent that will be given is tainted";[63] and the Christian Democrat François de Menthon (like Mendès-France, a minister in de Gaulle's Liberation government): "General de Gaulle is coming to power, imposed on the nation's representatives by the threat of secession, more precisely by the threat of a military coup. The National Assembly is no longer fully free to choose."[64] In the *Conseil de la République*, one of the eighty, Marcel Plaisant, was there to re-enact his stand of 18 years before. "Experience does not always prevent the repetition of mistakes. Nevertheless, there are some remarks which remain engraved in the memory. Those who aim for absolute power always protest the legitimacy of their intentions and the purity of their designs . . . The next day, however, one wakes up to learn of their usurpation."[65]

These echoes of 1940 were amplified by the intellectual left. In *Esprit*, Jean-Marie Domenach likened the students and workers who demonstrated on behalf of the Republic at the end of May to the generation of the *exode*. "On the faces of these kids, I see the reflection of our hope and anger when we were fleeing southwards in June '40, convinced that we were going to make a stand with Reynaud or Weygand or whomever. . . ."[66] In *Les Temps Modernes*, an editorial by Marcel Péju noted the irony that the man who had personified resistance to the forces of submission in 1940 had now become "like Pétain, the product of abdication, the representative of a people discharging the weight of its history into his hands".[67] But probing beyond this apparent irony, in a direction reminiscent of that adopted by Vichy's defenders in the amnesty debates, Péju suggested that the Third Republic had in fact been dead long before the Germans arrived and that Vichy had been legal both in the strict constitutional sense and in the looser sense that it had represented public opinion in the wake of defeat. De Gaulle's historic role in 1940–44 had been to thwart the true revolution that the Resistance wanted, "to hide the vacancy of power behind the fiction of an essential France, embodied by him, betrayed by Pétain and in the end restored". 1958 was the same story: de Gaulle was personifying a pseudo-rupture in order to forestall a genuine revolution.

For neo-Vichyites, too, de Gaulle's challenge to the Fourth Republic was more than just an irony. From their perspective, it was also a fresh vindication of Pétain's challenge to the Third Republic. Not that all neo-Vichyites supported de Gaulle's investiture in June 1958; some did and some did not.[68] But they had fewest inhibitions about confronting the analogy with 1940. Thus, for example, Jean Le Cour Grandmaison in June 1958: "I will say that the reasons that determine my attitude towards General de Gaulle today are precisely the same ones that led me in July 1940 to hand over the powers of the failing Third Republic to Marshal Pétain."[69] In the parliamentary debates of June 1 and 2, only Tixier-Vignancour, an unrepentant ex-Vichy minister, addressed the precedent of July 10 head-on. In order to explain why he could not vote de Gaulle full powers even though he had supported his investiture the day before, Tixier recalled the wartime commission that de Gaulle had created in Algiers to judge those who had voted Pétain full powers in 1940. "This commission announced to us – by which I mean to those Third Republic deputies and senators who on July 10, 1940 had voted a motion specifying that the government was to write a new constitution, to be ratified by the nation and applied by such assemblies as it might create – that we had no right to delegate that constitution-making authority and that we 580 deputies and senators had thereby committed a serious offence . . . You will pardon me for thinking that I could never have imagined that twice in my lifetime I would be asked to delegate the fraction of constitution-making authority that I possessed and – what is more – that the second time I would be asked to do so by the same man who had punished me for having agreed to delegate it the first time."[70] To insist, as Tixier did, that the circumstances in 1958 were the same as in 1940 was to say that Pétain's actions had been no more reproachable then than de Gaulle's were now. Gaullists in the assembly loudly protested, while those who had voted for de Gaulle denied that their vote was equivalent to a Yes on July 10. Nonetheless, Tixier's provocation exposed the republican establishment's continuing unease with the memory of July 10.

Within the longer span of postwar history, May–June 1958 was atypical. Rarely, if at all, over the preceding fourteen years had the precedent of 1940 held such political relevance – in spite of a series of military and diplomatic reverses, each of which amplified the sense of impotence and humiliation associated with 1940; in spite of the reemergence of a West German state and the resurfacing of the issue of German rearmament; in spite of a persistent current of Germanophobia within French public opinion.[71] 1940 remained peripheral because the problems and crises of the postwar era were too different from those of the 1930s to invite analogising. To see how things could easily have been otherwise, one need only consider the protracted parliamentary debates over the European Defence Community (a European army including German forces) in 1953 and 1954. The Germanophobia expressed in these debates, particularly but not exclusively by the far right and the far left, demonstrated a continuing inclination to view Germany as the main threat to national security. Had the occasion arisen, this fear and hostility could quickly have brought 1940 and its lessons back to centre stage.

As it was, the German threat did not become a burning issue. The entire configuration of the international order had changed since the late 1930s.

On none of the major questions confronting Fourth Republic governments
– Indochina, Algeria, decolonisation, economic modernisation, Cold War
rivalry, even European integration – was the record of 1940 essential to
defining policy or crystallising political alignments. Take, for example, the
contest between Communism and anti-Communism, in many respects *the*
defining issue of the Fourth Republic. Because the Communist party had
been proscribed at the beginning of the phony war, it had been absent from
the debates in Vichy in July 1940. Insofar as it had not been implicated in
the vote of July 10 and indeed had been victimised by the parliamentary
majority that voted in favour of full powers, the immediate memory was
not an embarrassing one. On the other hand, the Communists' absence
meant that they could claim no special badge of honour, as the 80 who
voted against full powers could; and the fact that defeat came in the midst
of a singularly difficult period for the party, when it was being compelled
to adhere to Stalin's 1939 pact with Hitler, meant that in general this was
not a year on which the party liked to dwell. Conversely, the absence of
Communists in July 1940 reduced the salience of that period for anti-
Communists. The latter could and did allege that Communist subversion
had contributed to the defeat. But it was implausible to suggest that Communist subversion was sufficient to explain the débâcle. Any political points
that were scored against the PCF by recollecting the party's accommodation to the Nazi–Soviet pact were more than offset by the embarrassment
certain to be caused to conservative or centrist politicians who had voted
Pétain full powers or flirted with Vichy before entering the anti-Communist
consensus of the Cold War. The memory of the defeat was an issue that
was always likely to divide anti-Communists and, thus, had a limited utility
in an era when fear of the PCF and the Soviet Union was of paramount
concern.

Similarly, the memory of defeat had little relevance to the politics of
decolonisation. Certainly, one context for the laborious postwar reformulation of the Empire as *"Union Française"* and for the desperate rearguard
action to hold it together was a sensation of national decline. This sensation
was amplified by the defeat in 1940. Each colonial setback in the late 1940s
and 1950s was attended by a rhetoric that recalled that of 1940 (Vichy-
or London-style), stressing the fundamental loyalty of the Empire and its
indispensability to national power and prestige. But except on a purely
rhetorical plane, the "lessons" of 1940 were barely applicable to conflicts
such as those in Indochina and North Africa. These were different kinds of
wars, fought against a different kind of enemy (notwithstanding the total-
itarian label), in a fundamentally different world. Moreover, every major
party (with the partial exception of the PCF) was divided against itself
on Indochina and Algeria. The painful memory of 1940 could only have

exacerbated these divisions, without holding out the prospect of any advant-ageous realignments.

To go back to Rousso's argument about the manipulation of wartime memory, it may be necessary to draw a distinction between two parts of this memory: the part pertaining to the phony war and the defeat and the part pertaining to the Occupation. Whereas memories of what had followed defeat did continue to shape understanding of the political problems and dilemmas that the nation confronted in the 1950s, memories of what had preceded it played a much less important role. As we have seen, this reflected the greater salience of Occupation issues to the problems of the 1950s. Perhaps it may also be explained by the essential character of the memories. Memories of the Occupation, whether of collaboration or re-sistance, were memories of actions, accommodations and choices – good or bad, heroic or unheroic, patriotic or partisan. In other words, they were memories of things that French men and women *did*. The memory of defeat, however, involved victimisation, loss of control, suffering – in short, it was too essentially passive to make for good politics.

Notes and references

1 *The Flanders Road* (London: John Calder, 1985), p. 172.

2 J. Kayser, *Un Journaliste sur le front de Normandie. Carnet de route, juillet–août 1944* (Paris: Arléa, 1991), p. 128.

3 *La France et les Français de la Libération, 1944–1945* (Paris: Musée des Deux Guerres Mondiales, 1984), pp. 27, 29. One of the first people to express this sentiment was Churchill, in the wake of the Allied landings in North Africa in November 1942. In his famous "end of the beginning" speech, Churchill commented on reports of the German retreat in North Africa: "I could not but remember those roads of France and Flanders, crowded, not with fighting men, but with helpless refugees – women and children – fleeing with their pitiful barrows and household goods, upon whom such merciless havoc was wreaked . . . I could not help feeling that what was happening, however griev-ous, was only justice grimly reclaiming her rights." Quoted in M. Gilbert, *Winston S. Churchill*, 8 vols (Boston, Massachusetts: Houghton Mifflin, 1966–88), vol. 7, p. 254.

4 A. Brossat, *Libération, fête folle* (Paris: Éditions Autrement, 1994), p. 38.

5 A. Jacques, *Journal d'une Française* (Paris: Seuil, 1946), p. 98.

6 M. Rouchaud, *Journal d'une petite fille, 1940–1944* (Paris: Gallimard, 1945), pp. 254–5.

7   P. Maillaud, *Over to France* (London: Oxford University Press, 1946), p. 91.

8   A. Desile, *Des sombres années de l'occupation aux chemins de l'été 1944* (Coutances: Editions OCEP, 1983), p. 86.

9   M.-L. Osmont, *The Normandy Diary of Marie-Louise Osmont, 1940–1944* (New York: Random House, 1994), p. 69.

10 C. Lewin, *Le Retour des prisonniers de guerre français* (Paris: Publications de la Sorbonne, 1986), pp. 88–91.

11 P. Novick, *The Resistance versus Vichy* (New York: Columbia University Press, 1968), p. 58.

12 Y.-F. Jaffré, *Les Tribunaux d'exception, 1940–1962* (Paris: Nouvelles Editions Latines, 1962), p. 108.

13 This story, which was published by de Monzie, was first raised at Pétain's trial by Paul Reynaud: *Procès du Maréchal Pétain* (Paris: Imprimerie des Journaux Officiels, 1945), p. 22.

14 *Procès du Maréchal Pétain*, pp. 42–3.

15 L. Noguères, *La Haute cour de la Libération (1944–1949)* (Paris: Les Editions de Minuit, 1965), pp. 90–2.

16 R. Aron, "Après l'événement, avant l'histoire", *Les Temps modernes*, 1: 1 (1945), pp. 155–6.

17 29 July 1945.

18 11 August 1945.

19 3 August 1945.

20 *Combat*, 2 August 1945.

21 *Le Procès Laval* (Paris: A. Michel, 1946), pp. 52, 60.

22 *Le Procès Laval*, p. 51.

23 *Les Evénements survenus en France de 1933 à 1945. Témoignages*, 9 vols (Paris: PUF, 1951–52), vol. 1, pp. 118–19.

24 *Les Evénements . . . Témoignages*, vol. 2, p. 526.

25 See, for example, M. Gamelin, *Servir*, 3 vols (Paris: Plon, 1946–47); P. Reynaud, *La France a sauvé l'Europe*, 2 vols (Paris: Flammarion, 1947); P. Baudouin, *Neuf mois au gouvernement (Avril–Décembre 1940)* (Paris: La Table Ronde, 1948); P.-E. Flandin, *Politique française, 1919–1940* (Paris: Les Editions Nouvelles, 1947); F. Charles-Roux, *Cinq mois tragiques aux affaires étrangères* (Paris: Plon, 1949); A. Lebrun, *Témoignage* (Paris: Plon, 1945); G. Bonnet, *Défense de la paix*, 2 vols (Geneva: Editions du Cheval Ailé, 1946–48); and M. Weygand, *Rappelé au service* (Paris: Flammarion, 1950).

26 Gamelin, *Servir*, vol. 1, p. 368.

27 Reynaud, *La France*, vol. 1, p. 33.

28 *La France*, vol. 2, pp. 72–3.

29 *Journal Officiel* (hereafter *JO*). Débats de l'Assemblée nationale constituante, 31 Dec. 1945, pp. 731–2. This Constituent Assembly was the successor to the Consultative Assembly (1943–45). It was constituted by the first postwar national elections (October 1945), and its main responsibility was to draft a constitution for the Fourth Republic. The draft that it approved was rejected in a national referendum in May 1946, and a second Constituent Assembly had to be elected in June 1946. It was this body that drafted the Fourth Republic's constitution, narrowly approved in another referendum on October 13, 1946.

30 R. Frank, *La Hantise du déclin. Le rang de la France en Europe, 1920–1960: finances, défense et identité nationale* (Paris: Belin, 1994), pp. 110–11.

31 G. Monmousseau, *Cahiers du Communisme*, nos 8–9 (1945), p. 13.

32 G. Namer, *Batailles pour la mémoire* (Paris: Papyrus, 1983), pp. 14–19, 50.

33 Novick, *Resistance versus Vichy*, p. 182.

34 E. du Réau, *Edouard Daladier, 1884–1970* (Paris: Fayard, 1993), p. 446.

35 *JO*, Débats, 6 July 1946, p. 2621.

36 H. Rousso, *The Vichy Syndrome* (Cambridge, Massachusetts: Harvard University Press, 1991), p. 17.

37 André Dewavrin (Colonel Passy) in O. Wieviorka, *Nous entrerons dans la carrière* (Paris: Seuil, 1994), p. 437.

38 C. de Gaulle, *Lettres, notes et carnets*, 12 vols (Paris: Plon, 1980–88), vol. 7, p. 60.

39 Novick, *Resistance versus Vichy*, pp. 182–3.

40 *Rapport fait au nom de la commission chargée d'enquêter sur les événements survenus en France de 1933 à 1945*, 2 vols (Paris: PUF, 1952), vol. 2, p. 545.

41 *Les Evénements . . . Témoignages*, vol. 8, p. 2477.

42 See especially volume 6 of the testimony, which contains numerous testy and often harsh exchanges between General Weygand and members of the commission.

43 *Les Evénements . . . Témoignages*, vol. 8, p. 2435.

44 See, for example, the exchange between a former minister in the Reynaud government, Louis Rollin, and Michel Clemenceau, a member of the commission: *Les Evénements . . . Témoignages*, vol. 5, p. 1395.

45 *Les Evénements . . . Témoignages*, vol. 7, pp. 2064–5; vol. 8, pp. 2468–72.

46 *Rapport*, vol. 2, pp. 359–60.

47 *Rapport*, vol. 1, p. 85.

48 R. Young, *France and the Origins of the Second World War* (New York: St Martin's Press, 1996), p. 41.

49 Quilici's comments (4 Nov. 1950, *JO*, Débats, pp. 7454–6) must be seen in the context of a controversy known as the Rémy affair. In April 1950, Colonel Rémy, one of the most famous of Gaullist wartime operatives, published an article alleging that de Gaulle had told him in 1946: "Remember that France had two strings in its bow. In June 1940 it needed the Pétain 'string' as much as the de Gaulle 'string'." Rémy's version was denied by de Gaulle (not altogether convincingly) and unleashed a storm of protest from the left, which believed that the Gaullists were trying to reach out to former Vichyites in order to pursue their attack on the Republic. For a penetrating analysis of the Rémy affair, see Rousso, *Vichy Syndrome*, pp. 32–40.

50 *JO*, Débats, Assemblée Nationale, 4 Nov. 1950, pp. 7454–6, 7471–2.

51 *JO*, Débats, Assemblée Nationale, 22 Nov. 1950, p. 8007.

52 *Idem*, pp. 8031–2.

53 *Idem*, p. 8024.

54 *Idem*, p. 8052 (M. Jean Legendre).

55 *Esprit*, June 1954, pp. 982–4.

56 See the National Assembly debate of 1–9 June 1954.

57 The growing divorce between public opinion and the regime is particularly well treated in J.-P. Rioux, *The Fourth Republic, 1944–1958* (Cambridge: Cambridge University Press, 1987).

58 M. Duverger *et al.* (eds), *Les Elections du 2 janvier 1956* (Paris: Armand Colin, 1956), p. 176.

59 *Le Monde*, 17 May 1958, p. 4.

60 *Le Monde*, 18–19 May, 21 May 1958.

61 *JO*, Débats, Assemblée Nationale, 27 May 1958, p. 2533, 2538.

62 *Idem*, p. 2540.

63 *JO*, Débats, Assemblée Nationale, 1 June 1958, p. 2577.

64 *Idem*, p. 2591.

65 *JO*, Débats, Conseil de la République, 16 May 1958, p. 870.

66 *Esprit*, July–Aug. 1958, p. 129.

67 *Les Temps modernes*, 153–154 (Nov.–Dec. 1958).

68 Rousso, *Vichy Syndrome*, p. 77.

69 Quoted in *Esprit*, July–Aug. 1958, p. 134.

70 *JO*, Débats, Assemblée Nationale, 2 June 1958, pp. 2618–19.

71 D. Lerner and R. Aron (eds), *France Defeats EDC* (New York: Praeger, 1957), pp. 74, 89.

PART TWO

The Defeat in History

Thus far, the analysis has adopted the perspective of the generation of
1940, examining how they reacted to defeat and how they integrated it
into their politics. Part Two, by contrast, approaches the defeat's impact
from the perspective of history. The following chapters do not offer an
historiographical review (since that has been well done by others[1]) nor do
they attempt a single retrospective interpretation of 1940's significance.
Rather, their purpose is to present three alternative ways of viewing the
defeat as a turning point, each assuming a different set of chronological
parameters and leading to a different conception of the defeat's significance. The key to any interpretation of a turning point is the "before" and
the "after" that one posits. If one adopts a short-term perspective, compar-
ing France's situation in June 1940 with that in June 1939 or June 1941,
one confronts a distinctive set of issues: abrupt transformations in personal
circumstances as well as in the circumstances of institutions and social
organisations; attempts to parry or absorb or exploit these transformations;
more or less gradual, more or less successful adaptations to the new status
quo. These issues are quite different from those that arise if one compares
the decade after defeat with the decade before. The massive but short-term
disruptions of the Occupation are less relevant to that kind of comparison
than the trajectories interrupted by defeat or the trajectories that resumed
in the postwar era. And the issues are different again if one views these six
weeks, embedded in a six-year war and a decade of crisis, within the still
larger context of a century of transformation.

Terrifying and destructive as the experiences of war and Occupation undoubtedly were, some scholars have questioned whether terror and
destruction in the short term need necessarily produce profound change
in the long term. This scepticism has been expressed, for example, by the

distinguished medieval historian Jacques Le Goff, reflecting on his personal experience during the war: "The temporary phenomena of restriction or degradation, even ruin, connected with the war did not seem to me to have the same significance, from the point of view of the course of history, as the inventions that I had seen change daily life in the previous decade or as the outline of a new society associated with the Popular Front."[2] Le Goff's conclusion, informed by his desire to distinguish a history of events from the deeper history of the *longue durée*, is that "wars, even world wars, do not drive history".[3] My bias would run in the opposite direction. There is ample evidence (some of which will be discussed in Chapters Six and Seven) to suggest that in the late industrial era of the twentieth-century global conflicts have had profound and long-lasting effects. More to the point, it is surely still premature to make dogmatic assertions about the deeper historical meaning of a century that is just ending. The aim of the rest of this study is not to privilege the short term over the longer term or vice versa, but to explore the impact of defeat in various contexts, recognising that we still have only part of the story.

Notes and references

1   See, for example, the work of Robert Young: *France and the Origins of the Second World War* (New York: St Martin's Press, 1996).

2   Pierre Nora (ed.), *Essais d'ego-histoire* (Paris: Gallimard, 1987), p. 206.

3   *Idem.*

CHAPTER FIVE

The short term: aftermath

From now on, it can be said that plague was the concern of all of us. Hitherto, surprised as he may have been by the strange things happening around him, each individual citizen had gone about his business as usual, so far as this was possible. And no doubt he would have continued doing so. But once the town gates were shut, every one of us realised that all, the narrator included, were, so to speak, in the same boat, and each would have to adapt himself to the new conditions of life.

Albert Camus, *La Peste* (1947)[1]

On February 24, 1943, the poet Maurice Blanchard noted in his diary: "Thirty-two months today".[2] This recalls the way that the Free French broadcaster Jacques Duchesne marked the passing of the Occupation from London; each evening on the BBC, Duchesne reminded his listeners that it was the *n*th day of "the French people's struggle for liberation".[3] Whether the memory was a stimulus to resist (in the next breath Blanchard daydreamed about killing a German) or a pretext for submission (as we have noted, Pétain also reminded himself every day of what had happened in 1940), it is incontestable that May–June 1940 remained a looming presence so long as the German occupiers were present. The concept of defeat as a collective turning point had an immediacy and concreteness in those years that it lost as soon as the Occupation ended.

But to acknowledge that defeat was omnipresent in those years is not to argue that it was the only reality or that it was an unchanging and undifferentiated reality. In fact, even when viewed from this short-term perspective, the defeat's impact appears shifting and incomplete. To describe these shifts and variations comprehensively would require a far fuller analysis of the Occupation than is feasible here. Instead, this chapter will make three broad points. The first is to note the disconcerting combination of continuity and discontinuity that characterised occupied France. The second is to observe how certain of the most significant discontinuities were, as it were, absorbed even before the end of the Occupation. In other words, in some respects, the nation moved beyond defeat before the defeat was finally undone. And the third point is the obvious but essential one – that some individuals and groups suffered directly and personally as a result of the defeat while others did not, or at least not to the same extent. Furthermore, the defeat's impact on individuals, like its impact on the collectivity, revealed itself gradually over the course of the Occupation.

Continuity and change under the Occupation

In his remarkable memoir of life in Auschwitz, Primo Levi wrote that "Sooner or later in life everyone discovers that perfect happiness is unrealizable, but there are few who pause to consider the antithesis: that perfect unhappiness is equally unattainable."[4] Levi suggested that certain of the prisoners' hardships – their uncertain knowledge of the future, their fatalism about imminent death, their ever-present material cares – blocked out, as much as intensified, the agony of their condition. It goes without saying that to be a "prisoner" in occupied France was a quite different situation from being imprisoned in a concentration camp (relatively few French men and women faced "the certainty of death" in the same terms as Levi and his fellow prisoners). But Levi's observation about the unattainability of perfect unhappiness is relevant to the French experience of occupation, in the sense that there too a fundamental misery was partially overshadowed by subsidiary woes (such as the grind of day-to-day survival) and by the unpredictability of the war's course and the nation's future. The feeling of total defeat that Léon Werth had expressed in June 1940 (see p. 18 above) could not persist for long. Life resumed and, as it did so, the radical simplification of June – one side embodying nothing but defeat, the other nothing but victory – yielded to more complex relationships (between occupiers and occupied, between past and present, between one French man or woman and another).

Unlike much of Eastern Europe, occupied France was not subjected to forced migrations on a mass scale or to wholesale assault on the national culture. Paris was not Warsaw; lives proceeded, by and large, in the same places and in the same company as before the defeat. Most people kept the same jobs; most students and schoolchildren continued their studies as before. But this facade of normality only heightened a sensation of unreality because, in fact, life *had* changed. The suitcases that passengers carried in trains were as likely to contain potatoes as clothes. Neighbours or acquaintances could suddenly "become" something different – Gaullists or deportees or "collabos". With the partial exception of the Catholic and Protestant churches, most of the major social institutions of prewar France had been disrupted or disbanded. In a postwar essay, Jean-Paul Sartre used shop windows as emblems of this disjuncture between appearance and reality: "Thousands of times in the course of those four years, French people saw bottles of Saint-Emilion or Meursault displayed in rows in grocer's shop windows. Intrigued, they would come over to take a look, only to read a sign that said: 'display only'. So it was with Paris: display only. Everything was hollow and empty: the Louvre without paintings, the Chamber without deputies, the Senate without senators. . . ."[5]

Political life, as Sartre suggests, was as much affected as anything else. On one level, politics continued: that was the fundamental choice that Vichy made in 1940. As we have seen, the architects of the National Revolution saw the defeat not as a reason to suspend politics but as the occasion to implement long-held political agendas, even if they preferred to characterise these agendas as apolitical. The persistence of a French State also ensured the appearance of a certain continuity, especially in the southern zone before November 1942. The main administrative units, the ministries, remained largely the same as in 1939, sometimes even headed by men who had been fixtures in political life before the war (Flandin and Laval, for example) and for the most part staffed by the same bureaucrats. Cynics noted that ministerial reshuffles (for example, eight Ministers for Information in four years) were as frequent under the new authoritarian regime as under the old republic – as though some political mores were too deep-rooted to be affected by a change of regime.

And yet this familiar carousel was turning under conditions that were changed beyond all recognition. The political centre had been relocated to a provincial backwater that was the very antithesis of Paris. A radical transformation in the political elite had taken place. Few of Vichy's luminaries were new to power, but most were new to political power: this was notoriously a regime in which generals and admirals, inspectors of finance and businessmen, journalists and intellectuals found their way into government. At least as remarkable as the turnover in Vichy was the transformation represented by de Gaulle's emergence in London. Not a single prominent Third Republic politician rallied to London in June 1940. In the fortnight after June 18, the British government tried hard to find such a person to lead the London dissidents, and was unable to do so. In later years, it is true, various members of the prewar republican elite found their way to London or to North Africa and attained prominence within de Gaulle's movement. But this did not alter the fact that in 1940 no one but a junior minister who had never been elected to any office was willing to take up the mantle of Free France. In London, as in Vichy, the leading figures were rarely nonentities, but they had little or no experience of high government office.

This change of personnel was associated with major structural changes in political life – the arrival of Occupation authorities, the formation of an authoritarian French regime, the dismantling of representative institutions (with parliament cast into abeyance after the vote of July 10 and political parties abolished shortly thereafter). It was also associated with a larger fragmentation of the national community in the wake of the phony war and the defeat.

A nation fragmented and reconstituted

Every indication suggests that in 1939, after more than five years of intense political turmoil, France was already a badly divided society. The outbreak of war papered over some of these divisions, as left and right rallied to the cause of national defence. But it also created new or deeper divisions. In the wake of the Nazi–Soviet pact of August 1939, a wave of intense anti-communism swept over the public and the republican establishment. Daladier's government launched a sweeping political and judicial campaign against the PCF: it dissolved the party organisation, closed party offices, impounded party assets, arrested party deputies and officials, interned party activists. The anti-Communist campaign fed on and encouraged fears of subversion from within – fears which could be directed at other groups, such as foreign refugees or even French citizens evacuated from the border regions in the northeast and east. Relations between the latter (many of whom were German-speaking) and their hosts were intermittently tense.[6] So, too, were relations between rural and urban populations, with the former feeling that once again their sons were being forced to bear a dispropor-tionate share of the burden of military service. There was widespread grumbling at the government's decision to return urban workers from the front to essential work in the factories.

Such latent tensions were exacerbated by the defeat. The issue of blame was inherently divisive, and Vichy's sectarianism made it more so. The differential impact of occupation was also inherently divisive – not just as between north and south or town and country, but as between neighbour and neighbour. Notwithstanding the social levelling allegedly induced by the *exode*, the immediate effect of defeat was to increase inequality, even more the perception of inequality. Emblematic was the ever-widening gulf in a black-market economy between the rich or well connected who could maintain their prewar living standard and the majority who became progressively hungrier and shabbier. To be able to eat well in circumstances such as these gave one a rare sense of power, as the German Ernst Jünger observed;[7] and, conversely, it excited strong resentment.

In a quite tangible way, the armistice institutionalised the fragmentation of French society. For all Vichy's claim to sovereignty, the demarcation of occupied and unoccupied zones created what often felt like two different countries. In the south until late 1942 there were few of the sights and sounds of defeat that made such an impression in the north. A Scottish woman living in the unoccupied zone until late 1942 did not see a Nazi flag until she travelled to Paris to join her husband.[8] Heading in the opposite direction about the same time, a Jewish schoolteacher and his wife were struck by the relative freedom of the south, symbolised for them by Swiss newspapers and American films.[9] The main way in which defeat impinged on life in the south was through food shortages and rationing. In August 1940 the newspaper *L'Eclaireur de Nice et du Sud-Est* commented that "Rationing shows us the face of defeat. We must pay, we must show our solidarity with the whole French people."[10] The fact that one had to show one's solidarity demonstrated how different life in the two zones was.

Travel or communication between occupied and unoccupied zones or between the *zone interdite* (prohibited zone) and other regions was extremely difficult. In August 1940 the German authorities suspended mail operations between the zones. The following month, they introduced special interzone postcards intended for the transmission of messages to family members. The impersonal "telegramese" of the postcards (the sender had to choose the appropriate category – "in good health", "sick", "wounded", "killed" – and was unable to add personal comments) dramatised the loss of intimacy that those separated by defeat had suffered. Refugees wishing to return to the north had to gain German authorisation to cross the line and could only do so at a handful of transit points. Those who had come from the sixteen departments in the *zone interdite* were forbidden to return. Securing a pass required an acceptable reason for travel (personal reasons did not pass muster) and often a great deal of perseverance. Not surprisingly, people soon tried to circumvent the regulations by smuggling themselves across the line. One of the familiar set-pieces of the wartime memoir is the story of the illegal night-time crossing – fraught with alarms and with the suggestion that the local guides ("*passeurs*") made a handsome profit out of the passage.

Those most directly affected by the demarcation line were the people living in communities divided by it. In many departments, the line disrupted traditional economic arrangements by separating villages from their market towns or by cutting across direct routes. Individual farms or villages or towns were themselves split up by the line, which often followed the path of a river or a stream. In Abbeville, for example, a bridge across the Somme formed the boundary between the *zone interdite* and the occupied zone: to cross from one part of the city to the other, local residents had to show an identity card and a special local pass. In Vierzon, which was one of the three main transit points to the north, the Cher was the dividing line. The left bank was in the free zone, the right bank occupied, and since most of the shops as well as the railway station happened to be on the right bank, residents were forced to present themselves to the German authorities on a daily basis.[11] The superimposing of this new geography on existing communities and traditional boundaries was a powerful symbol of German domination and of the fragmentation of the national community.

The domination, of course, lasted as long as the Occupation lasted, but over the course of four years the fragmentation was partially offset by the emergence of new institutions and new forms of association. The first such institutions were created by Vichy in order to advance the cause of the National Revolution and to fill the void left by the dismantling of prewar institutions such as unions and political parties. In this category, one might put the numerous professional associations that benefited from Vichy's corporatist vision, the rural camps (*chantiers de la jeunesse*) that were set up to provide wholesome national service for young men, the leadership schools established to train new elites, the *Légion Française des Combattants* for veterans. Most of these institutions failed in their self-appointed mission and declined in membership after 1942. But especially in 1940 and 1941 some provided a framework for collective action and for self-conscious attempts to fashion new kinds of community. The famous "leadership school" at Uriage was the classic case: it defined itself as a new order – part monastic, part chivalric.[12]

The northern zone counterparts to these Vichy organisations were the collaborationist parties and movements fostered by the Occupation authorities. These organisations may have been on the political fringes, but they were sizeable in terms of membership, in spite of Vichy's attempts to block their operation in the south. Each of the two major parties – Déat's *Rassemblement National Populaire* and Doriot's *Parti Populaire Français* – had at its peak (in 1942) 30,000 members or more.[13] Their meetings attracted very substantial audiences, as did the collaborationist press (the anti-semitic *Au Pilori*, for example, had a circulation of more than 50,000). This collaborationist sub-culture served a variety of purposes. For the hard core of activists, it was a vehicle for the expression of ideological commitments or the pursuit of political ambitions. For others, membership was a pragmatic choice, made to establish useful connections or in the hope of gaining a relative's release from a POW camp. At the other end of the spectrum, many of those who attended the rallies, no doubt, did so out of curiosity or in search of excitement amid the notorious greyness of occupied life. Clearly, the group aspect to these organisations – manifested in the wearing of uniforms and in the public demonstrations of allegiance (the only such demonstrations that the occupiers allowed) – was not insignific-ant. Collaborationism was capable of fostering intense camaraderie among its participants. This camaraderie, in fact, probably intensified as collab-oration became a lost cause. In the first two years of the Occupation, active supporters of collaboration tended to be male, urban, middle-aged and middle class; in the second two years, while still largely urban and male, they were increasingly youthful, less well educated and lower in social stand-ing.[14] The more prudential collaborators, in other words, jumped off the bandwagon, leaving more of the thrill-seekers, crusaders and zealots.

Resistance proved another countervailing force to fragmentation – and ultimately the most important one. It recreated a sense of community on two levels. On one level, the Resistance viewed itself as the embodiment of the nation. Gaullists, in particular, claimed that a vast, unarticulated com-plicity existed between an activist minority and the silent majority. Here was the left-wing Gaullist Pierre Brossolette speaking on the BBC in Sep-tember 1942: "It has seemed to me that through the painful and heroic trials of the Resistance, a . . . profound and . . . magnificent solidarity . . . has been forged among the entire French people."[15] In the same month, Brossolette published a much-remarked newspaper article, arguing that the defeat and occupation had replaced the old political landscape with an entirely new one, composed only of resisters and collaborators. All the prewar political divisions and hatreds, he claimed, had disappeared.[16] That concept of the Resistance as an agent of rediscovered national solidarity, transcending divisions of class and faith and basing itself on shared values, was a potent ideal, and one that gained in force as the Occupation pro-gressed. It was not, however, the reality. In 1940–42 the Resistance was a heterogeneous collection of relatively small-scale networks and move-ments, concentrated in urban areas. Certain social categories (young men, workers, "*classes moyennes*") were over-represented in these networks and movements; others (including peasants, women, and the elderly) were under-represented. Overall, the composition of the early Resistance did not reflect the larger society.[17]

On another level, Resistance movements themselves represented new forms of communal organisation and action. Resistance, it may be said, began in the encounter of individual with like-minded individual and in the liberating realisation that one was not alone.[18] Undoubtedly, prior associa-tions – familial, occupational, political or social – played a major role in determining where, when and among whom such encounters took place.

But though prewar relationships influenced recruitment, the organisations themselves were very different from prewar organisations because of the unprecedented circumstances under which they operated and their need to improvise clandestine identities and structures. Interestingly, resisters often delved far back into national or regional history for identities that seemed appropriate to their situation: Protestant resisters in the Cévennes, for example, identified with eighteenth-century Protestant revolts against the royal government and the Catholic Church, while urban resisters adopted the language and symbolism of the 1790s to express their patriotic and republican ardour.[19] As Olivier Wieviorka has remarked, this recourse to the deep past was not purely rhetorical:[20] it reflected the reality that prewar forms of political action – structured around political parties and legally sanctioned organisations, articulated in a more or less free press – were irrelevant under conditions of occupation.

The form that these improvised communities took depended on a number of factors: the timing and circumstances of their formation and recruitment, their leadership, their size and scope, their geographic location, the nature of their activities. The final factor was particularly crucial. The functions that a movement performed shaped the organisation that developed to perform them. The tracts and newspapers that Resistance movements printed and circulated, for example, necessitated particular kinds of network – among those who did the writing and printing and copying, among those who distributed the copies, among the readers. Likewise, groups that rescued and hid prisoners on the run required a chain of safe houses, forgers or civil servants to secure identification papers and ration cards, guides to cross the demarcation line or the border. The only generalisation that one could make about Resistance *qua* community is that the high level of risk and heavy dependence on group loyalty produced intense and inwardly focused bonds.

Early Resistance groups tend to be viewed primarily as pioneers of the larger-scale Resistance of the later years. They should also be seen as one of a number of new social phenomena emerging after the firestorm of 1940. Radio broadcasting, particularly French language broadcasting from London, stimulated another such phenomenon, the circle of listeners around a wireless set. Within a few months of the armistice, both German and Vichy authorities were reporting a widespread preference for BBC broadcasts over Vichy or Paris radio.[21] One listener from the southwest who contacted the BBC in September 1940 described how "the whole village gathers each evening in the five or six houses with wireless sets powerful enough to pick you up on short wave".[22] In an evocative memoir of rural life in the unoccupied zone, a young peasant from Ussel recalled that his household had only a home-made wireless set which could pick up Radio Paris but not London. Once or twice a week after supper, his family would go to a friend's house to listen to "Les Français parlent aux Français" (from London), with the doors locked and the shutters closed.[23] Vichy could prohibit people from listening to foreign radio stations in public (as it did in November 1940) but it was impossible to enforce a subsequent prohibition on listening in their homes (an October 1941 ordinance made this punishable by two years' imprisonment).[24]

The radio encouraged a withdrawal from public places into familial or other close circles. This was neither a uniquely French development nor peculiar to the Occupation. The German historian Detlev Peukert commented on a comparable development in Germany, where the mass production of cheap wireless sets produced "a pronounced shift whereby people found their daily (or rather, evening) leisure entertainment within the family".[25] The extent of this withdrawal into an "individualised private sphere" is impossible to evaluate, but it seems at least conceivable that the political conditions, as well as the living conditions, of Occupation gave it an added significance. Contemporaries certainly claimed that while the demarcation lines and prison camps split up family members and friends, the conditions of Occupation drew them together. In the words of one Parisian: "People want to be with their own kind, they stay at home rather than have to sit beside a *boche* at the cinema or the theatre . . . For the vast majority, the best entertainment in the occupied zone is to listen to the French radio from London."[26] In terms of organised resistance, however, one could also argue (as Peukert did in the German case) that retreat into the private sphere – however much it occurred – weakened the potential for collective action and encouraged self-absorption and a sense of self-sufficiency.

Contributing to the inward inclination of families were the inexorable constraints of daily life after defeat – the curfew, the rationing and the shortages. Fuel shortages encouraged family members to congregate in the warmest rooms, often (it seems from wartime diaries) the kitchen. And shopping became such a time-consuming and gruelling business (involving queuing not just for food, but for requisite coupons, passes, etc.) that family members often divided up the queuing responsibilities. The queue itself evolved into a kind of extended family, "the preeminent site of a new sociability".[27] Since the very reason for the queue was a shortage which was associated with German presence in France, it was both a daily manifestation of the nation's plight and a logical place to express a sense of grievance – at the Germans or at the authorities in general. Such grumbling falls into a different category from resistance, although it could obviously have the effect of fostering a shared identity among those standing in line.

The hallmark of all these forms of association was their localised, as opposed to national, scale. That began to change in 1942. In June of that year Laval, who had recently been brought back by Pétain to head the government, introduced the *Relève*, whose purpose was to lure volunteers into working in Germany in exchange for the release of French prisoners of war. Well before Laval converted this programme into a compulsory labour draft (the *Service du Travail Obligatoire* of February 1943), the voluntary aspect of it had been exposed as a fiction. The threat of deportation led hundreds of thousands of young men to abscond, many joining rural outlaw bands known as *maquis*. For the first time, much of southern society was drawn into a posture of collective disobedience.

Amplifying this change in the south was the sudden German invasion of the unoccupied zone following American landings in French North Africa in November 1942. This instantly reduced the significance of the demarcation line (not all bad because it also eased travel between different regions of the country), ended the special status of the south, and destroyed the illusions of privileged groups that the Vichy regime could protect them from the worst ravages of occupation. In short, the German action restored the geographic unity of the country. It may also have contributed to social unity. If, as has often been asserted, the direct German presence had made society more unified in the north than in the south, Hitler's invasion extended this inadvertent benefit to the whole country. Vichy officials certainly detected signs to that effect. In December 1942, for example, the prefect in the department of Loiret reported that, over the preceding weeks, peasants, workers and bourgeois in his region had achieved "a veritable sacred union" against the occupation forces ("*union sacrée*" being the term that had been used to denote the broad patriotic consensus of the First World War).[28]

To some extent, it is possible to talk about a reconstitution of the national community during the final stages of the Occupation after 1942, even though that period was marked by progressively bitter and violent conflict between opposing elements within French society and by ever more direct and deadly victimisation of individuals. This reunification can be viewed as a product of both negative and positive developments. The negative one was the declining threat that collaboration posed to national unity. While the majority of the population had always rejected collaboration (instantaneously in the *zone interdite*, quickly in the occupied zone and by mid-1941 even in the unoccupied zone), a not insignificant minority had favoured it. One recent and authoritative study has estimated support as late as 1942 at 20–25% of the unoccupied zone and 15–20% of the population as a whole. Pockets of support existed particularly within the bourgeoisie and *classes moyennes* and among the families of prisoners of war and former prisoners ("*rapatriés*").[29] The rifts that were thereby opened up within French society were significant in 1940 and 1941. After 1942, however, collaboration became a more marginalised and unpopular position. The radicalisation of collaborationist France, symbolised by the deadly war that the Vichy *Milice* waged against resisters in the winter and spring of 1944, reflected this gulf between an increasingly alienated society and an increasingly repressive state. As Stanley Hoffmann was one of the first to note, the radicalisation and marginalisation of Vichy "brought together people and groups that had remained separated both in prewar France and in the period of Vichy which preceded Laval's return to power [i.e. mid-1942]".[30]

In a positive sense, the Resistance itself was an agent of national reunification. Between the rural *maquis* that emerged in 1943 and the surrounding population in the south, there was a more active complicity than had existed in the earlier, urban-based Resistance. The emergence of the *maquis* also stimulated more connections between this urban Resistance and a rural population that it had hitherto ignored (or criticised for profiteering or pro-Vichyism). Resistance newspapers which had barely mentioned the peasantry before 1943 increasingly addressed themselves to that audience.[31] At the same time, at the leadership level these decentralised movements were increasingly brought into alignment under de Gaulle's auspices. A gradual process of amalgamation culminated in May 1943 with the creation of the *Conseil National de la Résistance*, in which all the major movements (Communist and non-Communist) were represented. The CNR promptly recognised de Gaulle as head of France's provisional government. By the end of 1943, with de Gaulle's provisional government established on French soil (in Algeria) and increasingly large-scale coordinated resistance inside France, Brossolette's claim of a national solidarity seemed more realistic.

Even then, the reemerging national community was expressed less in organisational form (since the majority of the population did not participate actively in the Resistance and those who did participate did so primarily at a local level) than in a broad consensus not unlike the anti-republican reaction which had supported Vichy in 1940. This, again, was a negative solidarity – against the policy of collaboration, against the depredations of the occupiers, against the privations that the nation had been forced to suffer in common since 1940.

A future lost and regained

The reformulation of the national community accompanied the reemergence of a long-term future. In 1940–42 Vichy had insisted that France had a future – as a morally purified, politically and socially reconstructed nation in partnership with a victorious Germany. But this vision had had a very limited appeal, and such acceptance as it achieved was based on the widespread belief in 1940 that German victory was unavoidable. For most people, the defeat represented a closing down of horizons. To those still in Paris in mid-June 1940, the thick pall of black smoke hanging over the capital (the consequence of huge petrol fires outside the city) seemed a perfect symbol for the nation's situation. "This utter darkness is the defeat", noted one observer.[32] A government official in the occupied zone, Bernard Lecornu, described the almost physical sensation of defeat settling in. "Up to that point, I had attended to the most urgent tasks, as they presented themselves: the refugees, then the prisoners, the food supply, the locals to be extricated from their many conflicts with the occupiers . . . Then one day the first trainload of prisoners left the station at Châteaubriant for the *stalags* and the *oflags*. The dejected faces behind the windows of the wooden carriages wrung my heart; the period of the provisional was ending, with all the hopes or simply illusions that it could permit; the war was entering its winter quarters, settling down, digging in. This convoy bound for Germany materialised our defeat."[33] When the convoy pulled out, what was left behind was a society caught in a static present. In his essay on Paris under occupation, Jean-Paul Sartre explained how the utter helplessness of the French situation took away their future. Unable to project what would happen the following week or the following month, the population largely gave up thinking about the future and absorbed themselves in the banal task of daily survival – the only task that still lay within their power to carry out.[34] Sartre described Paris as a phantom city – an image extended by the economist Charles Rist to the entire society: "Here, in the powerless state that we are in, we have the impression of being no more than phantoms. We come, we go, we are busy with work, but in a world that is no longer the real world. From all that really lives, thinks, hopes, stirs with normal human feelings, we are cut off. Our world is covered by a lid. . . ."[35]

This claustrophobia began to dissipate before the end of the Occupation. In a variety of ways, the population adapted to the shortages and the rationing – by recourse to black markets (which were abundant by the end of 1940) and "grey markets" (i.e. unofficial arrangements whereby people bought or bartered for produce directly from producers); by forging and trading rationing cards, pilfering, recycling (pullovers out of human hair!), substituting (tea leaves for tobacco, ground chestnuts for coffee, dental crowns made out of steel). Not that it became any less of a struggle, but the more experienced in this struggle people became, the less helpless in a certain sense they felt. Finding ways to get by (the famous "*système D*"[36]) restored at least a partial sense of control.

More important still was the growing realisation that the Occupation was not likely to last for ever. Of course, different people emerged from the static present at different times. Perhaps the first to recover a future were the activists, of either resistance or collaboration, who insisted on the possibility of shaking France out of its rut. But they were small minorities. In early 1942, after the widening of the war to include the United States, the hypothesis of German defeat began to gain wider credence. "The final outcome is not in doubt", wrote a Jewish author from Alsace in February 1942. The question, he went on to say, was *when* would Germany be defeated?[37] Already as early as mid-1942 there were rumours in Paris of a forthcoming Allied invasion of France.[38] Six months later, the successful American landings in French North Africa and the reports of the German defeat at Stalingrad made Allied invasion seem a realistic prospect. The rumours intensified, often with a specificity ("the next full moon") that recalled the rumours of May–June 1940. "1918!" read graffiti in Marseilles and Paris at the end of 1942.[39] For those in gravest danger, such analogising was an important way of keeping up morale (as it was in the ghettos in Poland, where the analogy with 1918 also flourished around the same time).[40] By early 1943, however, there was a general expectation that an Allied invasion would occur in the near future. Thereafter, the progression towards optimism was not uninterrupted. Good news such as that which came in July 1943, with the Allied landings in Sicily and the fall of Mussolini, encouraged hopes of Liberation by Christmas. But the fact that no Allied invasion materialised produced a backlash by the end of the year, especially as Allied air raids caused mounting French casualties. In early 1944, as Kedward has noted, "*Le débarquement* became a term used to indicate the future that never comes."[41] Still, the impatience of 1943 and 1944 was a quite different phenomenon from the hopelessness of 1940. It was the temporary deferral of a future which was bound to come eventually. Yet another winter under occupation was a depressing thought, but it was widely assumed that this winter would be the last.[42]

The reemergence of a future for France had particular implications for two elements within the population. For collaborators, the developments in North Africa and the USSR raised the possibility that the New European Order might collapse even before it had been completed. On the day in November 1942 that US forces landed in North Africa, the fascist intellectual Drieu la Rochelle wrote: "I am done for. Germany is done for."[43] This was a time when some collaborators began to look for ways to extricate themselves from their commitments, while others plunged still deeper into collaboration in an attempt to consolidate the new fascist order in Europe before it was swept away by the monstrous combination of Anglo-American capitalism and Soviet bolshevism.

On the other hand, for those who were targeted by the Occupation authorities – be it for deportation to the death camps or for labour service –

the encouraging trend in the larger war coincided with increasing personal danger. Of course, this coincidence was no accident: the more Germany was forced on to the defensive, the more pressing was its need to exploit the resources of occupied territories and the more imperative it became, in the eyes of Hitler and the Nazi leadership, to press ahead with the Third Reich's historic mission, in particular its annihilation of European Jews. For Jews in France, the resumption of a national future in 1942 set in motion a race between two futures. Would the collective liberation that many could now foresee come before the victimisation that was bearing down on them as individuals? To quote an observer in the unoccupied zone in July 1942, the challenge was to outlast the Terror: "we are in 1793, it's a question of making it to 1794."[44]

The victims of defeat

From the very outset, the defeat had had more direct and dangerous consequences for Jews than for non-Jews. "No oil and potatoes in the markets, that's what the defeat means for the *hoi polloi*", wrote one leader of the French Jewish community in 1940, bitterly reflecting on the far greater sacrifices imposed specifically on Jews by Vichy's *statut des juifs*. "Racism has become the law of the new state."[45] The first two years of occupation saw a steady escalation in anti-Jewish persecution. It came both from the various German authorities and from Vichy and was spurred on by a kind of infernal competition between the two, as Vichy tried to maintain control over anti-Jewish policy by emulating or even outdoing German initiatives. The first steps involved an assault on the civic rights of Jews and restrictions on their professional activity, access to education and economic assets. Among the provisions of the October 1940 *statut des juifs* was an order permitting the internment of non-French Jews (an order extended in 1941 to cover all Jews), and in following months the French authorities arrested thousands of individuals. In the north, the Germans also ordered mass internments (though most of the actual round-ups were conducted by French police). In May 1941, for example, 4,000 Polish, Czech and Austrian Jews were detained in Paris and interned in French-run camps at Pithiviers and Beaune-la-Rolande. 1941 and 1942 also saw a steady drumbeat of regulation (both German and French) designed to identify and classify the Jewish population, segregate them, limit their mobility and cut them off from the conveniences of normal life. The culmination of this segregation was a German order in June 1942 requiring all Jews in the occupied zone to wear a yellow star on their clothing. Shortly thereafter, on July 16–17, 1942, came the largest round-up ("*rafle*") to date, again conducted by French police. More than 12,000 men, women and children were arrested in Paris. Families were detained in a sports stadium on the outskirts of the capital (the Vélodrome d'Hiver or "Vel d'Hiv"), while single people and couples without children were sent to an improvised internment camp at Drancy, which was to become the "antechamber to Auschwitz".[46] The Vel d'Hiv operation was the first in a series of mass arrests in both occupied and unoccupied zones. It thus marked a critical escalation in anti-Jewish policy, leading ultimately to the deportation and death of more than 75,000 people, perhaps a third of whom were French citizens.

To describe the defeat's impact in terms of its victims is not unproblematic. Virtually everyone felt victimised by the defeat one way or another. Food shortages may not seem so awful to those threatened with social ostracism, imprisonment or death. But one's own privations inevitably loom larger than the unseen sufferings of others, and most people certainly felt that they suffered through the Occupation. There were other groups besides Jews who saw themselves as special victims in relation to the general population – inhabitants of the *zone interdite*, northerners who had to live with the German presence, prisoners of war who had borne the immediate brunt of defeat, workers who endured the bourgeois *revanche* for 1936, and so forth. It is an instructive irony that the more than 600,000 workers who went to Germany (most of whom returned safely at the end of the war) were seen as the "real" deportees,[47] while there was far less public concern about Jewish deportees, only 3% of whom survived deportation.

Applying the category of victim may also distinguish the experience of different groups with false clarity, implying that this experience was wholly distinct and recognised as such from the outset. As we have noted, the application of anti-Jewish policies was incremental, just as the German conception of the Final Solution evolved in 1940 and 1941. In June 1940, whatever they knew of the treatment that Nazis had meted out to Jews elsewhere, few Jews in France had any inkling of what the defeat would lead to. To quote the historian Jacques Adler: "No effort of imagination, however pessimistic, could conceive of [what had happened in Germany] happening in France."[48] An even more monstrous leap of imagination would have been needed to conceive of Hitler's ultimate plans. That many Jews would lose their livelihood quickly became clear. It was also soon evident that collectively they would be made to suffer all manner of humiliations and that individually they would be in constant danger of arrest or internment. Still, these were threats that could, theoretically at least, be parried. The gradual escalation of anti-Jewish measures, the fact that they came from two different sources (Paris and Vichy) and applied differently in the two zones, encouraged the persistence of an illusion of adaptation, the illusion that while the consequences of defeat would be far more onerous and dangerous for Jews than for non-Jews, they would not be entirely and fundamentally different.

Finally, the category of victim homogenises people who did not always perceive themselves to be a homogeneous group. A basic division separated native-born Jews from immigrants. In certain respects French authorities treated the two groups differently (for example, they sometimes exempted Jewish war veterans from discriminatory measures). But the distinction held more significance for Jews themselves than for the anti-semites in Vichy, most of whom, in the end, believed that all Jews were alien and expendable. Leaders of French Judaism sought to escape the victim category by distancing themselves from the immigrants and reaching an accommodation with Vichy that would preserve French Jews' rights. Immigrants, on the other hand, tended to have fewer illusions about the government's intentions, both because of their own past experiences and because they were the first ones targeted by Vichy's anti-semitic initiatives.[49]

Notwithstanding all these limitations of the terminology, the simple and important fact remains that defeat had quite different consequences for different people. For some, it even presented opportunity. By the end of 1941, 7,000 French businesses were benefiting from orders placed by German civilian or military authorities.[50] When Jewish-owned businesses were "Aryanised", that is, confiscated and turned over to non-Jewish administrators, there was no shortage of French volunteers to take them over. Numerous individuals wrote unsolicited letters to the *Commissariat Général aux Questions Juives*, enquiring as to the availability of Jewish businesses, sometimes expressing specific preferences, sometimes willing to take anything.[51] For others, no doubt the majority, defeat was somewhere between an inconvenience and a trauma, closer to one or the other as one's own circumstances and those of one's family dictated. But for certain people, above all Jews, the arrival of the Nazi occupation and the formation of the Vichy government constituted a mortal threat. To quote Lucien Lazare: "The only non-Jewish Frenchmen to be persecuted were those who rebelled, resisted, or violated the laws of the occupier or of the Vichy regime. By contrast, all the Jews – men, women, and children, even invalids and helpless patients in the hospitals – were first subjected to a discriminatory and humiliating regime and then marked out for deportation and death."[52]

In one sense, Liberation marked the end of a phase that might be termed the aftermath of defeat. In another sense, of course, there was an aftermath to the aftermath. Part of that was the "Vichy syndrome" – the selective remembering and forgetting of the crimes of the Occupation era, the memorialisation of a certain version of it and then, in later decades, its reopening as a political issue and cultural preoccupation. Less politically divisive but equally central to the stories that postwar French society told about itself was the memory of wartime deprivation. The material hardship of the Occupation became after 1945 a stimulus to modernisation and a reason to make peace with a consumer society that in the past had often been stigmatised as un-French. A recent cultural history of French modernisation has aptly noted the prevalence of a "biological metaphor" in postwar discourse. The cliché was that a "hungry, deprived France . . . now . . . could eat its fill", both literally in terms of food, but more generally in terms of consumption.[53]

Almost as prevalent as this metaphor of wartime hunger/postwar consumption was the psychological metaphor of a humiliated nation "driven" to recover its self-esteem. The humiliation of 1940, which was still being exposed at war's end by the dismissive attitudes of at least some Allied leaders and by France's exclusion from major inter-Allied conferences, was often invoked after 1945 to justify or to explain a reassertion of French power. This reassertion was evident, for example, in the development of an atomic energy programme in the late 1940s, succeeded in the 1950s and 1960s by the development of a French atomic bomb. It was evident also in the protracted attempt to retain an empire and in the ambitious and independent-minded foreign policy pursued by de Gaulle in the 1960s and often emulated thereafter.

If we are to say something useful about such large claims about the long-term impact of defeat, we must look beyond the concept of aftermath that has informed this chapter. Simply put, too much intervenes between 1940 and the postwar period for us to be able to relate postwar developments directly to 1940, except in the most general terms. To understand the defeat's more enduring reverberations, we need to ask different questions – not "What did defeat precipitate?" but "What did it interrupt and what did it perpetuate?" It is to those questions that we will turn next.

Notes and references

1 *The Plague* (New York: Vintage, 1991), p. 67.

2 M. Blanchard, *Danser sur la corde. Journal 1942–1946* (Toulouse: P. Thierry, 1994), p. 187.

3 J.-L. Crémieux-Brilhac, *La France Libre* (Paris: Gallimard, 1996), p. 221.

4 *Survival in Auschwitz* (New York: Collier, 1961), p. 13.

5 J.-P. Sartre, *Situations III* (Paris: Gallimard, 1949), p. 27.

6 More than half a million inhabitants of Alsace and Lorraine were evacuated in September 1939, most to rural departments in central and southern France. For an excellent analysis of the sometimes hostile reaction they received there, see L. Boswell, "Franco-Alsatian conflict and the crisis of national sentiment during the phoney war", *Journal of Modern History*, 71: 3 (1999), 552–84.

7 H. Le Boterf, *La Vie parisienne sous l'occupation*, 2 vols (Paris: France-Empire, 1974–75), vol. 1, p. 24.

8 J. Teissier du Cros, *Divided Loyalties* (London: Hamish Hamilton, 1962), p. 233.

9 R. Nordmann, *Le Bain* (Paris: La Porte Etroite, 1946), p. 169.

10 Quoted in D. Veillon, *Vivre et survivre en France 1939–1947* (Paris: Payot, 1995), p. 90.

11 BBC Written Archive Centre, Caversham, Reading: Anonymous Letters from France, 1940–1945, no. 158 (31 Dec. 1940). I am grateful to Ms Ellen Leb for drawing my attention to this source.

12 J. Hellman, *The Knight-Monks of Vichy France* (Montreal: McGill-Queen's University Press, 1993), pp. 61–6.

13 B. Gordon, *Collaborationism in France during the Second World War* (Ithaca, New York: Cornell University Press, 1980), pp. 119, 145. Philippe Burrin estimates the PPF's membership at 40,000–50,000, in *La France à l'heure allemande* (Paris: Seuil, 1995), p. 422.

14 Burrin, *La France*, pp. 433–7.

15 Quoted in L. Douzou, "L'entrée en résistance", in A. Prost (ed.), *La Résistance, une histoire sociale* (Paris: Les Editions de l'Atelier, 1997), p. 14.

16 "Renouveau politique en France", *La Marseillaise*, 27 Sept. 1942, reprinted in G. Brossolette, *Il s'appelait Pierre Brossolette* (Paris: A. Michel, 1976), pp. 269–73.

17 O. Wieviorka, "Structurations, modes d'intervention et prises de décision", in Prost (ed.), *Résistance, une histoire sociale*, pp. 55–68.

18 For a vivid example of one such encounter, see L. Douzou, *La Désobéissance. Histoire du mouvement Libération-Sud (1940–1944)* (Paris: Odile Jacob, 1995), pp. 40–2. See also the testimony of one of the founders of the Franc-Tireur movement, Jean-Pierre Levy: *Mémoires d'un franc-tireur. Itinéraire d'un résistant (1940–1944)* (Brussels: Editions Complexe, 1998), pp. 39–40.

19 For such themes, see especially the work of H. R. Kedward: *Resistance in Vichy France* (Oxford: Oxford University Press, 1978); and *In Search of the Maquis* (Oxford: Oxford University Press, 1993).

20 Wieviorka, "Structurations", p. 60.

21 J. Sweets, *Choices in Vichy France* (New York: Oxford University Press, 1986), pp. 144–5.

22 BBC: letters from France, no. 168 (15 Sept. 1940).

23 R. Limouzin, *Le Temps des J3* (Treignac: Les Monédières, 1983), pp. 88–9.

24 A more effective counter-strategy was to offer programming that listeners wanted to listen to. In the final period of the Occupation, Vichy found in Philippe Henriot a propagandist of the requisite talent: Henriot's broadcasts attacking the Resistance as a communist Fifth Column attracted much of the audience that listened to "Les Français parlent aux Français". See H. R. Kedward, "The Vichy of the other Philippe", in G. Hirschfeld and P. Marsh (eds), *Collaboration in France. Politics and culture during the Nazi Occupation, 1940–1944* (Oxford: Berg, 1989), pp. 32–46.

25 D. Peukert, *Inside Nazi Germany: Conformity, Opposition, and Racism in Everyday Life* (New Haven, Connecticut: Yale University Press, 1987), p. 78.

26 P. Corday, *J'ai vécu dans Paris occupé* (Montreal: L'Arbre, 1943), p. 129.

27 Veillon, *Vivre et survivre*, p. 128.

28 Quoted by J.-M. Flonneau, in J.-P. Azéma and F. Bédarida (eds), *Le Régime de Vichy et les Français* (Paris: Fayard, 1992), p. 515. See also Kedward, *In Search of the Maquis*, pp. 7–8.

29 Burrin, *La France*, pp. 187–93.

30 S. Hoffmann, *In Search of France* (New York: Harper and Row, 1965), p. 35.

31 F. Marcot, "Pour une sociologie de la Résistance: intentionnalité et fonctionnalité", in Prost (ed.), *Résistance, une histoire sociale*, p. 26.

32 R.-R. Lambert, *Carnet d'un témoin (1940–1943)* (Paris: Fayard, 1985), p. 68. As Douzou has observed, the metaphor of defeat plunging the nation into darkness has been a commonly used one, not least by resisters who represented their actions as helping to bring France back into the light: *La Désobéissance*, p. 31.

33 B. Lecornu, *Un Préfet sous l'occupation allemande* (Paris: France-Empire, 1984), p. 36.

34 Sartre, *Situations III*, pp. 28–9, 39.

35 C. Rist, *Une Saison gâtée* (Paris: Fayard, 1983), p. 154.

36 "D" for "la débrouillardise" (resourcefulness).

37 R. Brivet, *Carnets de guerre 1940–1945* (Paris: La Pensée Universelle, 1978), p. 101.

38 B. Pierquin, *Journal d'un étudiant parisien sous l'occupation* (n.p., 1983), p. 79 (entry of 14 June 1942).

39 Lambert, *Carnet*, p. 199; J. Biélinky, *Journal 1940–1942* (Paris: Cerf, 1992), p. 271.

40 For example, E. Ringelblum, *Notes from the Warsaw Ghetto* (New York: Schocken Books, 1974), pp. 261, 299; A. Lewin, *A Cup of Tears. A diary of the Warsaw Ghetto* (Oxford: Blackwell, 1988), pp. 98–9.

41 Kedward, *In Search of the Maquis*, p. 74.

42 See, for example, Pierquin, *Journal*, p. 107.

43 P. Drieu la Rochelle, *Journal 1939–1945* (Paris: Gallimard, 1992), pp. 301–2.

44 Brivet, *Carnets*, p. 115.

45 Lambert, *Carnet*, pp. 84–5.

46 R. Paxton and M. Marrus, *Vichy France and the Jews* (New York: Schocken Books, 1983), p. 252.

47 Paxton and Marrus, *Vichy France*, p. 219.

48 J. Adler, *The Jews of Paris and the Final Solution* (New York: Oxford University Press, 1987), p. 50.

49 Adler, *Jews of Paris*, pp. 223–7. For a critique of too straightforward a distinction between French and foreign Jews, see V. Caron, *Uneasy Asylum. France and the Jewish refugee crisis, 1933–1942* (Stanford, California: Stanford University Press, 1999), pp. 360–1.

50 Burrin, *La France*, p. 250.

51 R. Poznanski, *Etre juif en France pendant la seconde guerre mondiale* (Paris: Hachette, 1994), pp. 111, 187–8.

52 L. Lazare, *Rescue as Resistance* (New York: Columbia University Press, 1996), p. 28.

53 K. Ross, *Fast Cars, Clean Bodies. Decolonization and the reordering of French culture* (Cambridge, Massachusetts: MIT Press, 1995), pp. 71–2.

CHAPTER SIX

The medium term: transitions

... under the shock of defeat and occupation, concern for the future
took precedence over allegiance to the past. Not to repudiate this
allegiance: refusal to change would have meant certain decline and
betrayal of the heritage.

René Rémond, "Le contemporain du contemporain" (1987)[1]

In the late 1950s and 1960s, indeed around the same time as the nuclear
tests in the Sahara, the signs of a profound transformation in France's
internal and external situation reached critical mass. For a number of years
before de Gaulle's return to office, there had been unmistakable evidence
of a vigorous economic and demographic revitalisation. But the succes-
sion of colonial crises and the persistence of an ineffectual and, to its
critics, outmoded political system diminished the impact of these economic achievements. Analyses written in the 1950s more often than not
portrayed the irrefutable postwar successes within a framework of continuing overall decline.[2] This changed after 1958, partly as a result of the
accumulation of good economic news (in the early Fifth Republic accel-
erating growth rates were accompanied by expanding foreign trade,
especially with European Economic Community partners, and rising
investment rates), partly as a result of the successful transition to a more
presidential style of government, and partly because of the gradual resolu-
tion of colonial problems. The whole bias of interpretation switched in
these years. Instead of diagnosing malaise, observers were now chiefly concerned with explaining a postwar miracle, or rather two miracles. One was
the emergence of a more industrialised and urbanised, more growth- and
consumption-orientated, more efficiently governed, in short more modern,

nation. The other was an external miracle, involving reconciliation with Germany and Italy, liberation from ever-present anxieties about attack from across the Rhine and from the self-imposed burden of colonial myths, and revitalisation of the nation's military capacities and international prestige.

Subsequent generations of historians have added shade to this black and white view prevalent in the first flush of modernisation. Economic historians, for example, have challenged the dichotomy between an "old" and a "new" France by showing that nineteenth- and early twentieth-century French entrepreneurship was not inherently inferior to that of competitors and by highlighting evidence of modernisation and technological innovation before the war.[3] And, as de Gaulle's ambitious and contentious foreign policy in the 1960s showed, the Fifth Republic was far from definitively reconciled to a realistic view of France's role in a superpower world. Still, even though much did not change, it is hard to cast the French experience between the 1930s and 1960s except in terms of a "second French revolution", in which the balance between the forces of change and continuity shifted in favour of the former.

Few authors, if any, have suggested that 1940 alone had a determining effect on this transformation. The lag time between the defeat and the full flowering of the new France (even allowing for the fact that the Fourth Republic contributed more to the miracle than was credited at the time) makes this argument hard to sustain. Furthermore, the defeat itself has always been heavily contextualised in France, viewed not as a discrete catastrophe but as the culmination of a long-standing and systemic national crisis — in the words of Henri Michel, "the outcome of a long process of disintegration affecting all the activities of the French nation".[4] While some military and diplomatic historians have questioned the explanatory force of this "decadence" model,[5] the reality of a pre-existing malaise can hardly be denied. This greatest of disasters neither inaugurated the crisis of the old France nor (given the mixed record of the Occupation and Fourth Republic periods) resolved the crisis.

So what did it do? This question proves to be anything but straightforward. In most other countries, the war had the effect either of legitimising or (more commonly) of discrediting prewar elites, institutions and regimes. In France, the war did neither or, rather, it did both — discrediting in the short term, but in the longer run partially relegitimising. Instead of bringing about an abrupt and complete rupture, it generated a profusion of continuities, which were frequently in contradiction with one another and which cumulatively complicated rather than simplified the course of French political history.[6]

Roads to 1945: France and Britain compared

Since 1940 was also a particularly significant year in British history, it may be of more than passing interest for French historians to consider how British historians have dealt with the issue of 1940's impact. One of the most influential interventions in that debate was made more than two decades ago by Paul Addison's book, *The Road to 1945*. Addison argued that the events of 1940 played a critical role in shifting British politics to the left and laying the foundations for a postwar consensus in favour of social security, family allowances, a nationalised health service, a Keynesian approach to economic management, and full employment. Central to Addison's argument was an interpretation of prewar politics: he suggested that before 1940 the Labour party had been on the verge of electoral defeat and that the "progressive centre", where so many of the guiding principles of the postwar consensus originated, had been a marginalised minority. Without the shocks of 1940 (the creation of Churchill's coalition government, Dunkirk, the Fall of France, the Battle of Britain), the pessimists/realists who had governed Britain in the 1930s and who doubted the State's capacity to guide economic growth, provide for comprehensive social welfare or win another war against Germany could not have been displaced.[7]

Applying this logic to the French case, one might argue that there, too, the impact of 1940 cannot be fully understood without taking prewar trajectories into account. Such arguments are necessarily speculative. Even if one identifies significant discontinuities between pre- and postwar eras, how can one be sure that they were necessarily the consequence of the disasters of 1940? Who is to say that the changes would not have happened anyway, as a result of the intense pressures of fighting a total war? (The similarities between the postwar records of European nations with very different wartime experiences might suggest precisely that.) And the argument also assumes (or at any rate implies) that the issues determining policy before May 1940 were essentially different from those in the post-defeat era. In point of fact, the course of French politics had been affected by the looming possibility of war long before the German attack was launched. As Robert Frank's studies of rearmament have demonstrated, from the mid-1930s onwards the challenge of resisting Hitler and Nazism had exacted major political as well as financial costs.[8]

Notwithstanding these qualifications, Addison's approach offers a useful way of exploring the defeat's longer-term consequences. And at first glance there are clear substantive parallels between the two experiences.[9] In France, as in Britain, the end of the war produced a dramatic realignment in domestic politics. As we have already noted, a large majority of the men and women elected to the Constituent Assembly in 1945 were new to national politics. The centrist and conservative parties which had been in the ascendant in the Daladier/Reynaud years found their support sharply curtailed at Liberation. The right's share of the general election vote fell from 42% in 1936 to just 15% in 1945. Daladier's Radical party suffered an equivalent decline. The new parliamentary elite of 1945 was dominated by three parties of the left – the Communist party, the Socialist party, and the Christian Democratic MRP. None of these parties could be identified with the governments of the late Third Republic: the PCF had been dissolved by those governments, the Socialist party had been forced into opposition to them, and the MRP had not even existed in May 1940. All three parties, however, were closely identified with the Resistance and drew much of their popularity and credibility from that association.[10] The Resistance experience had both shifted the political balance to the left and reinvented the parties that benefited from the shift.

Each of the major political actors at the Liberation (not just the parties mentioned above but also de Gaulle and the remnants of the Resistance movements) was committed to a radical overhaul of political, economic and social institutions. Admittedly, overhaul should not be confused with re-volution: in the autumn of 1944, there were localised attempts on the part of resisters to revolutionise economic and political institutions at the grass roots, and these impulses were quickly suppressed by de Gaulle's govern-ment, with the active complicity of the Communist party, following Stalin's orders. But the government's blocking of a complete rupture with liberal capitalism and parliamentary democracy did not mean a return to the prewar status quo. While facing a variety of pressing problems inherited from the Occupation, successive Liberation governments instituted a series of reforms that were, by any standards, radical and far-reaching. Between 1944 and 1947, they enfranchised French women, expanded and over-hauled the social welfare system, took major industrial sectors into public ownership, established a mechanism for channelling investment into mod-ernisation of the nation's industrial infrastructure (the planning system), founded the Ecole Nationale d'Administration (ENA), and implemented a scheme for worker participation via *comités d'entreprise*. The great failure of the Liberation elite lay in the constitutional realm, where it was not able to convert the broad consensus in favour of change (in October 1945, 96% of voters rejected the option of reinstating the Third Republic) into a sig-nificantly altered system. Even there, it was evident that the necessity of reforming republican institutions was more urgently felt and more widely acknowledged than in 1939, just as was the necessity of recasting France's relationship to the Empire.[11]

Another form of renewal occurred within the State's administrative elite. After the Liberation, a new generation of civil servants rose to positions of authority – men such as Hervé Alphand in the Foreign Ministry, Guillaume Guindey, Olivier Wormser and François Bloch-Lainé in the Ministry of Finance, and Robert Marjolin and others in Monnet's planning commissariat. This new elite did not subscribe to all of the Resistance's priorities, but they shared its enthusiasm for modernisation and played an important role in the French government's "mental conversion" in favour of policies stressing growth and higher productivity.[12]

In many cases (as was true in Britain), the blueprints for this postwar reformism had been drawn up in the 1930s in response to the protracted economic depression and to the internal and international crises of that decade. Most of the schemes for rationalising and managing capitalism, for example, had been proposed before the war. But in the 1930s these had been the ideas of a "non-conformist" minority (to borrow an adjective from a well-known intellectual history of this issue[13]), not of the political–administrative establishment. As Richard Kuisel has noted, "the planners of the 1930s, like the corporatists, lacked a political or social base".[14] Even the Popular Front government of 1936–37 had kept its distance from the non-conformist programme and limited its structural reform to nationalisation of certain armaments manufacturers and reorganisation of the Bank of France.[15]

After the break-up of the Popular Front coalition, political trends had pointed in a direction diametrically opposed to that of 1944. After April 1938, the month in which Daladier became Prime Minister, the bulk of his Radical party parted ways from their erstwhile Popular Front allies and moved towards a new coalition with the centre-right. The evidence of by-elections and opinion polls in the late 1930s does not suggest a dramatic swing in public opinion away from the marxist parties, but it does indicate a significant realignment of centrist opinion in the direction of Daladier's conservative coalition.[16] The popularity and political success of this coalition have often been overlooked because of the long shadow cast over them retrospectively by the defeat. At the time, however, this consolidation of opinion behind Daladier seemed a highly significant development.

The clearest indicator of the change in political climate under Daladier was the official attitude towards the working class. In 1938 the class which was to be lauded six years later as the moral and political backbone of the nation was harshly criticised for rising above its station and for claiming privileges that it did not deserve or that the nation could not afford. Although Daladier's main priority was to speed up French rearmament, not to settle scores with the Popular Front (of which, of course, he had been a member), he quickly drifted into a policy of confrontation with labour.

In August 1938 he decided that he could not reach an agreement with the trade unions to modify the forty-hour work week – to Daladier a prerequisite for speeding up rearmament, for the unions an assault on the most symbolically important achievement of 1936. So the Prime Minister opted to act unilaterally. When his policy provoked a general strike at the end of November, Daladier took strong measures to ensure that the strike failed. In its wake the government collaborated with management in a vigorous repression: strike leaders and "trouble-makers" were fired and in some cases fined or imprisoned; blacklists were drawn up and circulated; the unions lost members and influence; strikes dried up; and low overtime pay rates benefited employers more than workers. When war broke out, the political and social balance clearly favoured the *patronat*, inter-class relations were strained, and there was little interest in collaborative arrangements such as the experiments in industrial democracy that were beginning to take shape in Britain (and that were to be so marked a feature of the Liberation era in France).[17]

Another element in the "reaction" of the Daladier years was its appeal to the confidence of capital – an appeal symbolised by the person of the Finance Minister after November 1938, Paul Reynaud. Though the government's pressing rearmament needs prevented it from undoing the nationalisations that the Popular Front had implemented (indeed, it took advantage of the leverage that the nationalisations gave the State),[18] the Daladier/Reynaud policy as a whole represented an unabashed reversion to liberal tenets, remarkable in light of the international circumstances of the time. Until war actually broke out, Reynaud fought shy of full-scale industrial mobilisation. To quote a recent authoritative work on this subject, "[B]y 1939, with Reynaud's market economics in the ascendant, the acceleration of arms output became treated like any other economic objective. In this way no different from porcelain or perfume production, the munitions manufactures so essential to the safety of France became treated like any civilian consumable, to be a function of private business decisions, which the government would push only by the most general and traditional capitalist mechanisms of constraining state indebtedness and encouraging lower interest rates."[19] The prestige of liberalism was as high in 1939 as it had been for a decade. It was also higher than it was to be again for another decade. During the Occupation, resisters ceaselessly criticised the liberal dogmas of balanced budgets and financial orthodoxy, and suggested that these dogmas had contributed to France's unpreparedness in 1940. By the time of the Liberation, even liberals felt compelled to criticise "anarchic" prewar liberalism and recommend more systematic management of the economy, either through direct State management or through some form of organised collaboration among State, business and labour.[20]

The twin vogues for planning and corporatism, which had been building since the onset of the Depression in the 1930s, crested in the mid-1940s.

In short, the late 1930s saw the pendulum of French politics swing back to the centre-right and away from left-leaning reformism. Away, too, from the extreme anti-republican right, which had gained prominence in the mid-1930s by exploiting bourgeois fears of social disorder and which was to come back into its own after the defeat. If anything, Daladier's government defused the appeal of these groups, by demonstrating that strong authority was compatible with the Republic, by shattering the Popular Front coalition and easing anxieties about social disorder.[21] Many of Daladier's policies (for example, his tough policies towards foreign immigrants, his crackdown on the Communist party and his highly publicised attempt to tackle France's demographic woes via a comprehensive *code de la famille*) stole the far right's thunder. Though a disaster for French diplomacy, the Nazi–Soviet non-aggression pact of August 1939 helped to consolidate Daladier's position internally, by making the Communist/non-Communist polarity the central one in wartime politics.

It would be a mistake to read too much into this rightward shift: not just because (as already observed) the parties of the left lost relatively little ground, but also because what happened in 1938–39 was replicating a long-established pattern. Twice since 1919 left-centre election victories had been followed by rightward adjustments midway through the ensuing legislatures (in 1926 and 1934). Even without the looming presence of war, it was likely that the failures and disappointed hopes of the Popular Front would have worked to the advantage of conservatives. Still, it is undeniable that the political balance immediately before defeat was strikingly different from that immediately after Liberation, and that, as in Britain, the events of 1940 played a crucial role in discrediting a politically conservative, economically orthodox consensus and opening the way to a more optimistic view of the State's capacity to promote economic modernisation and social welfare.

Complexities of the French transition

The critical word here, however, is the qualifier "immediately". This points up the essential difference between British and French experience. In the former case, one can speak of a prewar consensus yielding to a postwar consensus, with the wartime coalition paving the way for this transition. In the French case, the transformation was far less clear-cut. Three main factors explain the greater complexity of the French experience.

First, in France the pessimist/realist consensus had been challenged before the war to a degree that had not occurred in Britain. The Liberation's anti-pessimism had clearly been prefigured by the anti-fascist Popular Front of the mid-1930s. This alliance of political parties of the left and centre and of non-party organisations, including the main trade union confederation, the *Confédération Générale du Travail* (CGT), had come to power facing an array of foreign and domestic challenges comparable to those of 1944. And like the Liberation coalition, the Popular Front had struggled to keep a disparate political alliance together while both exploiting and containing a great and spontaneous popular *élan*. In the Popular Front's responses to these challenges more than in the actual programme which brought it to power, historians have detected various impulses that were to reemerge a decade later. One was a modernising impulse, which aimed not at the destruction of the capitalist system (still the left's theoretical objective) but at preserving what could be preserved through enlightened State intervention. Several of the most prominent innovations of the Liberation (the nationalisations, the Ministry of National Economy, the *Ecole Nationale d'Administration*) had been pioneered in 1936. So too the impulse to integrate workers more fully into the national community, by guaranteeing them a more secure existence and giving them greater control over their lives inside and outside the workplace, clearly united 1936 and 1944. In both years an outburst of social and cultural "effervescence"[22] from below prompted decisive intervention from above.

It should also be noted that even within the pessimist/realist camp, there were signs of a significant evolution well before the outbreak of war. The quintessential realists in France were men such as the former Prime Minister, Pierre-Etienne Flandin, and Daladier's Foreign Minister, Georges Bonnet. Their attitudes were quite different from those of Reynaud, who as Finance Minister was in a position to challenge them effectively in the months before and after September 1939. Reynaud, whom one British diplomat described in November 1938 as "something of a French Winston",[23] had made his reputation by championing a series of anti-establishment political causes (most recently in favour of de Gaulle's schemes to create a mechanised, professionalised army). This background marked him out as anything but a defeatist. Though his approach to industrial mobilisation was, as we have seen, resolutely pro-business and exploited the right's hostility towards the Popular Front, Reynaud did not share the Bonnet/Flandin view that, as a result of the Popular Front, victory was beyond France's capabilities. And whereas Churchill had to wait until September 1939 to reenter government, Reynaud had become a minister in April 1938 and a central figure in the ministry from November of that year.

Even Daladier, whose attitudes are notoriously hard to read (in part because they changed during his time in office), did not entirely fit the profile of a pessimist/realist. Around the time of the Munich crisis, he had been painfully aware of France's military shortcomings, particularly in the air, and of the nation's dependence upon its British ally. But his vigorous and combative policies after Munich suggested a far less fatalistic attitude than that of his foreign minister Bonnet. The success of his government's economic policies encouraged Daladier's belief that France could yet make up for its belated rearmament. In his mind, the key was to postpone the actual fighting for the year or two that it would take to prepare France's industrial infrastructure for war. The strategy did not work, but unlike the strategy of appeasement it aimed to win, rather than merely avoid, a war.[24]

A second source of complexity was introduced by the chaos of the war years in France. The Resistance, which was bound to play a central role in the definition of any postwar consensus, had been born under conditions that precluded straightforward reliance on prewar models of organisation or reform. As the previous chapter noted, resisters often looked to a much deeper past for an identity appropriate to their circumstances. Though they certainly did articulate ideas that had been circulating before the war (and spawned committees and think-tanks comparable to those in Britain), the movements themselves were the very antithesis of the government-appointed commissions that laid the foundations for the British postwar consensus. By definition, they were fighting the State, contesting the legitimacy of the established authorities, appealing to a higher law. As a result, their language and self-identity (for example, their claims to transcend partisan interests and to embody patriotism) were difficult to reconcile with the norms of pluralistic democracy. Hence their often frustrating transition to peacetime republicanism after 1944.

On the other side, too, the progression from pre-defeat to post-defeat politics was sinuous in the extreme. As has been said many times, Vichy was a schizophrenic regime: it drew both on deep-rooted archaisms (royalism, integral nationalism, corporatism, regionalism) and on a variety of modernist tendencies (fascism, technocracy, social catholicism, pacifism). Less often remarked than either its archaism or its modernism but equally important for our purposes were Vichy's affinities with the eleventh-hour reformism of the regime that it replaced and despised. The miraculous recovery ("*redressement*") achieved under Daladier rallied much of the same conservative opinion that rallied to Vichy the following year. Daladier's achievement, in the eyes of the bourgeoisie, was to restore a sense of social order and patriotic purpose. In the spring of 1939, French cardinals praised his work in terms that were to become all too familiar after defeat: "The grave dangers that threaten the country from outside, the social upheavals that have so deeply disturbed us in recent years, have compelled all French-men seriously to examine their consciences. And at last all have realised the abyss into which the country was heading. Thanks to God, once again France showed that in the critical hours of her history . . . she was capable of mending her ways."[25]

The "stability" of Daladier's rule reflected the unacknowledged demise of parliamentary government. Daladier governed largely through a system of "decree-laws", whereby parliament delegated authority to the govern-ment for a specified period of time in a specific area of policy. Daladier was by no means the first Prime Minister to receive such powers, but he expanded their use in significant respects, receiving decree-law power for longer periods and less narrowly defined purposes. For months on end during his period in office parliament was reduced to a state of "*demi-chômage*" (semi-unemployment).[26] Even among republican supporters, there was a growing sense in 1939 that the Third Republic was in a state of ter-minal collapse. This disintegration from within may be said, in retrospect, to have facilitated the effective dissolution of the Republic in July 1940, just as the personalisation of power under Daladier and the public's appetite for a strong authority anticipated Pétain's rule.

There are also parallels between the repressive policies directed particu-larly against Communists and foreigners under Daladier and the full-scale repression mounted under Vichy. The anti-Communist hysteria sparked by the announcement of the Nazi–Soviet pact set much of the peculiar tone of the phony war – peculiar in the sense that France was at war with Ger-many, not the Soviet Union, and yet in official circles anti-Sovietism seemed much more intense than anti-Nazism. As one Communist ruefully noted, it was entirely legal to buy and read *Mein Kampf*, but being caught with a pamphlet about cotton-growing in Azerbaidjan meant a five-year prison sentence.[27] The emergency measures taken against the PCF may not have had the scope of Vichy's subsequent repression, but some of the policing mechanisms that the Daladier government put in place were taken over by Vichy. And the almost daily attacks – both verbal and legal – inured French citizens to a level of virulence in official discourse and illiberalism in official actions, which may well have had the effect, after defeat, of easing the accom-modation to still more extreme attacks.

If demonisation of Communists helped to hold together the alliance of centre and right in September 1939 as in July 1940, so in both cases did demonisation of immigrants and Jews. What is striking about anti-immigrant feeling and anti-semitism in the late 1930s is how respectable it had become. Its acceptance into the political mainstream was exemplified by the introduction of the writer Jean Giraudoux into the government. Just weeks before Daladier made him Minister of Information, Giraudoux had published, to considerable fanfare, a book filled with anti-semitism and lurid xenophobia.[28] Depicting immigrants as pests and criminals, Giraudoux had suggested that France needed a special minister to safeguard the French race.

A related fear to this racial one was the anxiety that immigrants constituted a potential Fifth Column, which might sabotage national defence in the event of war. During the Munich crisis there had been disturbing reports of Polish immigrants in the north and east proclaiming their preference for a German victory and shouting "Heil Hitler" and of Italian immigrants dressed in fascist uniform.[29] When Daladier's government tightened restrictions on immigrants in 1938, instituting wide-scale internments, "forced residence" and deportations, the measures were generally very well received, on the left as well as the right.[30]

Clearly, there was an element of continuity between this concern with surveillance and purging before mid-1940 and Vichy policies after that date.[31] That is not to label Daladier's France "pre-Vichy": in the absence of the abrupt discontinuity of May–June 1940, there is no reason to assume that the one would have led to the other.[32] Still, it is important to note the prevalence of a rhetoric of mounting distrust and polarisation in the period immediately before defeat. The rhetoric was hardly new: French society had been polarised throughout the 1930s. But the "other" that defined politics in the late 1930s was no longer (as in 1934–36) fascism; increasingly, it was communism (or the figure of the immigrant or the Jew). It is also striking to observe how far republican governments were willing and able to go in order to combat these internal threats. Without overtly overturning the principles of parliamentary government and the rule of law, the ministries of Daladier and Reynaud showed a willingness to jettison liberal values and to conflate fear of foreign governments with hostility towards those inside France whom they associated with foreign interests.

Finally, a third complicating issue in the French case, present perhaps but not to the same degree in Britain, was the evanescence of the new consensus of the Liberation. While British history of the late 1940s and the 1950s was marked by a convergence around the consensus of 1945 (the so-called "Butskellite" phenomenon[33]), in France there was a concerted reaction against Liberation politics. Though few of the major Liberation-era reforms were undone, the coalition that was chiefly responsible for them soon fell apart. In 1947 the PCF ministers were forced out of the government, and shortly thereafter the party assumed a militantly anti-regime, confrontational strategy that isolated it from non-Communist opinion. In succeeding years a "Third Force" defining itself negatively as both anti-Communist and anti-Gaullist, clung on to power. Within this Third Force, the centre of gravity shifted progressively to the right: the MRP and the

Socialists continued to participate in ministerial coalitions, but lost ground in relation to a resurgent Radical party and a revived centre-right. In the general elections of 1951, the parties of the right, which had been decimated in 1945–46, reclaimed a significant representation, and the following year a conservative politician heavily implicated in Vichy (Antoine Pinay) became Prime Minister.

Meanwhile, this parliamentary trend was replicated in other areas of public life. One, recently highlighted by Henry Rousso, was the gradual legal and political rehabilitation of Vichy. With increasing success, neo-Vichyites campaigned to exonerate the wartime regime, arguing variously that Pétain's motives had been unimpeachable, that he had had no choice but to sign the armistice and accept German demands, and that the regime's servants had been victimised unfairly at the Liberation. The marginalisation of the Communist party and the break-up of the Liberation coalition assisted the neo-Vichyites. It had always been essential to their case to associate the Resistance with communism and thereby to challenge the Resistance's monopoly on patriotism. The more threatening the Soviet Union became and the more faithfully the PCF appeared to follow the Soviet line, the more convincing this association became to moderate and conservative republicans. The logic of the Cold War encouraged reconciliation between the latter and fellow anti-Communists who had been on the other side of the fence during the Occupation. In the early 1950s, the centrists and conservatives who increasingly controlled French politics passed two sweeping amnesty laws. By 1952, only 1,570 of the 40,000 collaborators jailed in 1945 were still in prison.[34]

The history of the press offers a similar story.[35] This was an area where the Liberation had brought about a huge transformation. The defenders of Vichy had been purged and a mass of new publications infused with the spirit of the Resistance had emerged. The contrast with the prewar press was striking: in 1939, conservative and Radical party papers (representing, broadly speaking, the constituency supporting Daladier and Reynaud) had controlled 46.2% of newspaper circulation; in 1944 they controlled just 12.7%. However, the new, mostly left-wing, newspapers quickly ran into difficulties, and the old proprietors counter-attacked, fighting to recover confiscated assets and to regain readers. By 1947, in terms of readership and resources, much of the Liberation transformation had been reversed. The demise of the new press (to which *Le Monde*'s success was the most notable exception) was characteristic of a broader pattern. Partly it reflected a rapidly reduced will on the part of the State to purge and renew French institutions (a reduced will also evident in the failure of constitutional reform). Partly, it reflected divisions within the Resistance and the naïvety of Resistance aspirations to "moralise" national life. And finally it also reflected

the reemergence of market realities and the vigorous reassertion of bourgeois interests.

This rapid disintegration of the Liberation consensus sets up yet another
set of continuities between the prewar and postwar eras. In the late 1940s
and 1950s, as in 1938–39, anti-communism mobilised a broad spectrum of
French opinion, ranging from elements of the left (the Socialist party being
a prime target of Communist invective) to moderates and conservatives.
The suspicion of communism which had cemented Daladier's support after
the announcement of the Nazi–Soviet pact was more than ever a factor in
the early years of the Cold War, as French Communists organised massive
strikes at home and defended Soviet aggression in Eastern and Central
Europe. In a sense, the international structure of the late 1940s gave bourgeois interests the conflict that they would have preferred to have in 1939–40,
the "right-wing war" (in Sartre's words[36]) combining assertiveness against
the Soviet Union with an internal war against Communist organisations
inside France.

In both periods, anti-communism went along with a revival of economic
liberalism (reflecting the conservative interests that were advantaged by
anti-communism), but a liberalism that was sometimes more uncompromis-
ing in rhetoric than in practice. Facing urgent tasks (rearmament in one
case, reconstruction in the other), the authorities re-emphasised the role of
the free market and of competition, while continuing to orient the overall
direction of economic development. During the phony war, for example,
Daladier's Minister of Munitions, Raoul Dautry, had stressed the need for
investment in modern plant and equipment and had tried to use State
power to energise private enterprise rather than to bury it under bureaucratic regulation – an approach akin to the kind of "indicative" planning that
Jean Monnet championed after 1945. The team that Dautry assembled in
his ministry itself came to symbolise the continuities in economic policy-
making and innovation from the 1930s to the 1950s. It was drawn from the
ranks of the prewar technocratic avant-garde (groups such as, *Redressement
Français*, *X-Crise*, *Nouveaux Cahiers*) and supplied many of the technocrats
who tested the waters in Vichy and dominated reconstruction policy after
the Liberation.[37]

Just as we should be cautious about viewing the Daladier/Reynaud era
as "pre-Vichy", so we should be cautious about labelling it "pre-Monnet". It
is important to emphasise that in 1940 the traditional financial orthodoxies
still governed French economic policy. Daladier and Reynaud prepared
France's defences "in a consciously chosen regime of limited sacrifices, limited efforts".[38] Without the disaster of 1940 it is entirely possible that Dautry's
wartime experiments, as well as other earlier forerunners of Monnet's
modernisation commissions,[39] would have had no postwar future.

At most one can say that the trend just before the war and during its early months was towards belated and limited adjustments. With the anti-immigrant measures came a group of reforms to encourage population growth. With the extension of decree-law powers came a protracted debate about parliamentary and electoral reform, culminating in a vote in the Chamber of Deputies in June 1939 in favour of proportional representation. At the time, with the Daladier government about to announce that general elections were being postponed for two years because of the international crisis, this vote had little immediate impact. But, like the *code de la famille* and the neo-liberalism of Dautry, proportional representation was a concept to which postwar leaders returned. In short, the record of the late 1930s suggested a regime rather less stagnant and immobile than has often been portrayed. On the eve of defeat, French democracy, like French capitalism, seemed to have weathered the storms of the 1930s, to have changed less than critics or reformers would have liked and less than might have been predicted three or four years before, but to have changed nonetheless.

1938–1948: full cycle?

A decade later, one could say essentially the same. After all the traumas of defeat and occupation and the euphoria of liberation, the Fourth Republic seemed uncannily reminiscent of the late Third Republic. The new regime had adopted proportional representation with the expectation that it would help to organise parliament around disciplined parties rather than informal and shifting alliances of deputies, but it was still struggling, without notable success, to find a constitutional/electoral formula that would foster strong and stable yet accountable government. In spite of elaborate safeguards introduced in 1946 to insulate the Prime Minister from parliamentary intrigue, the regime's practices tended to revert to traditional ones, with premiers preferring to resign rather than provoke a dissolution of parliament and new elections. This propensity was encouraged by the transformation of the political landscape after 1947 – the breakdown of the tripartite Liberation coalition that had designed the constitution, the isolation of the Communist party, and the emergence of a potent Gaullist threat to the Republic. The last of these developments was critical. In 1947, de Gaulle created a mass movement, the *Rassemblement du Peuple Français* (RPF), to press for a new constitution and for the General's return to the helm. The RPF's staunch anti-communism and virulent hostility towards the republican leadership attracted many former Vichyites to its ranks, while its cult of personality, confrontational rhetoric and mass rallies aroused republican fears of a return to the politics of the interwar leagues. With constitutional reform thus associated with the RPF and with the Republic facing a simultaneous challenge from the extreme left, the republican parties had no incentive to risk early elections via dissolution or to introduce any reforms that might threaten a very precarious equilibrium. The possibility (conceivable in 1944 and realised after 1958) that de Gaulle could be the agent of a consensual constitutional modernisation seemed increasingly remote in the late 1940s. It became still more remote after the RPF failed to make a decisive breakthrough in the elections of 1951.

This reconstituted Republic clung more tightly than ever to the colonial myths that in 1938–39 had compensated for anxieties in Europe. Defeat and occupation had only increased the need for a compensating myth. At the end of the war, French international prestige had sunk far below prewar levels. The dismissiveness of Allied leaders was particularly striking. Roosevelt did not expect France to recover great power status for at least 25 years and opposed France's claim to resume colonial rule.[40] Rejecting French requests to participate in the Yalta conference, Churchill told the British Foreign Secretary, Anthony Eden, that Canada had more right than France to be considered the "Fourth Power".[41] Churchill's friend, General Smuts of South Africa, openly predicted a generation or longer in the international wilderness: "We may talk about [France] as a Great Power, but talking will not help her much. We are dealing with one of the greatest and most far-reaching catastrophes in history, the like of which I have not read of. The upward climb will be a bitter and a long one."[42] Stalin had been more willing than his Western partners to recognise the legitimacy of the wartime Gaullist government, and after the Liberation he met with de Gaulle in Moscow. But he was no more impressed by de Gaulle's pretensions than was Roosevelt. Certainly one could find less damning assessments of France's status; Smuts's comments, for example, were deplored by some members of the House of Commons. But the larger fact – inconceivable in 1939 – was that the French government's participation was no longer considered indispensable at major inter-Allied conferences such as those at Dumbarton Oaks (1944), and Yalta, San Francisco and Potsdam (1945). Even the French Foreign Minister Bidault privately admitted that France was "a defeated country", whose "dream of restoring her power and glory at this juncture [February 1947] seems far from reality".[43] Where France regained the trappings of great power status (for example, in securing a seat in the United Nations Security Council and in sharing in the occupation of Germany), it owed its promotion to the intervention of its more powerful allies.

In these circumstances, the loyalty that various parts of the Empire had shown to de Gaulle's movement during the war appeared a critical asset. In

1945–46 it was commonly said, both in the press and by government officials, that only the Empire stood between France and irreversible decline.[44]
Wrote one postwar Minister of Colonies *à propos* his government's plans to
create the French Union, "at stake is France's chance to exert worldwide
influence".[45] This unchanging belief in the Empire's compensatory value
was bolstered, somewhat paradoxically, by an equally widespread belief in
the demise of the "old imperialism" of the prewar years. The architects of
the French Union freely acknowledged that a transformation had taken
place as a result of the defeat. To quote a key colonial official: "The
populations of the Empire . . . have sized up the decline in France's physical
and moral strength and it is absolutely certain that under no circumstances
can they think of their subordination again as they did in 1938. In 1938
that subordination was accepted as a lasting state of affairs, one that had no
earthly reason to end, whereas today it is compared to France's weakened
state and viewed accordingly as something that can be reconsidered."[46] The
assumption of Liberation reformers that only an updated Empire *could*
survive evolved into an assumption that because the Empire had been
updated (via the French Union and a variety of government-sponsored
reforms) it *would* survive. The Fourth Republic's rearguard action in the
Empire was a strategy conceived by people who believed that they had
understood the lessons of defeat.

At the same time, the last-minute realisation of 1938–39 that a modern
army could only be as effective as the industrial infrastructure that sus-
tained it was more prevalent than ever a decade later. After Liberation,
parliamentarians from across the political spectrum challenged de Gaulle's
insistence on maintaining high military expenditures. Important budget
debates in 1945–46 clarified that the new regime would place a higher
priority on reconstruction than on national defence. To quote Robert Frank's
gloss on the new policy: "Modernise the economy first. Military power will
come afterwards, as a natural consequence, and all the more certainly."[47]
In a sense, the modernisation strategy of the postwar years – accepting a
certain degree of financial dependence on the United States in return for
the opportunity to modernise the industrial infrastructure and build a basis
for longer-term independence – was first cousin to that which Daladier and
Reynaud had hoped to use to thwart Hitler. There was an obvious tension
between this long-term strategy and the colonial strategy which drew France
into overseas wars and required massive military expenditures (exactly the
kind of short-term, non-remunerative investment that the record of the
1930s had discredited).[48] The heightened sense of national weakness
that flowed from defeat led simultaneously in both directions – down the
cul-de-sac of the French Union and towards a concept of national power
based on technology and economic modernisation.

All this is to suggest a modest view of the defeat's impact. In spite of the rhetoric of revelation and revolution, the defeat set the nation back into a cycle that it had just passed through between 1934 and 1938. The cycle began again with a crisis of republicanism – obviously a far more catastrophic crisis in 1940 than in 1934. The triumph of reaction, like its spectre in the mid-1930s, in turn, prompted a reassertion of republican values and the emergence of a broad-based reformist coalition of the left and centre-left, the Resistance in ideological terms replicating the history of the Popular Front. When this coalition gained power, it was able to accomplish a significant legislative agenda, while disappointing the more millenarian hopes of its rank and file. Eventually, the coalition splintered and power shifted back to more centrist and conservative elites, who disassociated themselves from the overtly ideological projects of their Popular Front/ Liberation predecessors while pragmatically retaining many of the governmental structures that their predecessors had put in place. In 1948, as in 1938, this "revival of bourgeois fortunes" (to use Richard Vinen's term[49]) involved bitter confrontation with elements of the working class and harsh repression of strikers.

In substance, neither the reformist rhetoric of the Liberation nor the neo-liberal rhetoric of the late 1940s was particularly novel. If one looks back to the late 1930s, for example, one finds Daladier and others voicing many of the platitudes that were later attributed to the revelation of defeat. At the Radical party congress in October 1938, the Prime Minister declared that France could not resign itself to becoming "a third-rank nation", that it had to choose between bold action and becoming "a country which drapes itself in its historical memories".[50] A few months earlier, he had told the nation in a radio broadcast that "We must put France back to work ... France's economic strength is an essential element in its prestige and power."[51] The necessity of modernising the industrial infrastructure was widely acknowledged in 1938–39. To quote another prominent Radical, the President of the Chamber of Deputies Edouard Herriot, "A country's military strength – and this is what is so serious about our situation in relation to Germany – is a function of its industrial strength."[52]

This did not mean that by the late 1940s the nation was back where it began. At the level of individuals, there had been a significant turnover in the nation's political leadership. For this largely new elite, the feeling of having had new truths revealed to them was undoubtedly strong; the spectre of third-rank status had become less of a rhetorical flourish and the choice between modernisation and decline more real-seeming. On a collective level, the reformist energy of 1944, fuelled by the extremism of the preceding reaction, had taken the nation far beyond the hesitant improvisations of the Popular Front. Few of the institutional innovations of the Liberation were undone by the increasingly conservative coalitions of the post-1947 years. And the second economic miracle was more long-lasting than the Reynaud/Daladier miracle had had a chance to be: the index of industrial production (1938 = 100) had fallen to 50 by 1945, but recovered to 113 in 1948, 143 in 1951 and 213 in 1958.[53]

Where the language of revelation may be misleading is in a selective remembering of the past. To focus only on those revealed truths that were acted upon in the postwar era (for example, the truths about the need for economic modernisation) is to distort the actual experience of 1940. The defeat produced many other "revelations" – about the inherent inefficiency of democratic governments, the inherent effectiveness of authoritarian rule, the inability of states to cooperate except under conditions of coercion, the wastefulness and irrationality of free markets, the loyalty of the Empire. These revelations were shown, in the long term, to be premature or erroneous. The postwar renewal of France and of Western Europe was only possible because these other "lessons of 1940" proved misguided. After 1945, the spell of authoritarian government was broken, the deathwatch at the bed of liberal capitalism was lifted, the empires rapidly declined, and new forms of freely consented international cooperation, both among Europeans and between Europe and the United States, emerged. Much of what 1940 had seemed to mean at the time turned out to be profoundly irrelevant to the transformations of the later twentieth century.

Notes and references

1 P. Nora (ed.), *Essais d'ego-histoire* (Paris: Gallimard, 1987), p. 304.

2 See, for example, W. Baum, *The French Economy and the State* (Princeton, New Jersey: Princeton University Press, 1958); H. Lüthy, *France against Herself* (New York: Praeger, 1955); J. Chardonnet, *L'Economie française, étude géographique d'une décadence et des possibilités de redressement*, 2 vols (Paris: Dalloz, 1958–59); and M. Laure, *Révolution, dernière chance de la France* (Paris: PUF, 1954). Chardonnet praised the economic plans, acknowledged great improvements in industrial output but still portrayed the postwar record as a failure. Similar ambivalence was expressed by J.-M. Jeanneney, *Forces et faiblesses de l'économie française, 1945–1956* (Paris: A. Colin, 1956).

3 See the discussion of this literature in J. Bouvier, "Libres propos autour d'une démarche révisionniste", in P. Fridenson and A. Straus (eds), *Le Capitalisme français 19e–20e siècle* (Paris: Fayard, 1987), pp. 11–27.

4 H. Michel, *La Défaite de la France* (Paris: PUF, 1980), p. 4.

5 See the excellent comments in R. Young, *France and the Origins of the Second World War* (New York: St Martin's Press, 1996), pp. 37–59.

6 R. Vinen, *Bourgeois Politics in France, 1945–1951* (Cambridge: Cambridge University Press, 1995), p. 25.

7 P. Addison, *The Road to 1945* (London: Quartet Books, 1977), pp. 15–21.

8 R. Frank, *La Hantise du déclin. Le rang de la France en Europe, 1920–1960: finances, défense et identité nationale* (Paris: Belin, 1994); R. Frank(enstein), *Le Prix du réarmement français* (Paris: Publications de la Sorbonne, 1982).

9 Addison's argument resembles the influential thesis of Stanley Hoffmann, which presents the war as the moment when the critics and outcasts of the prewar status quo "pushed France out of the drydock in which she had been waiting for permanently postponed repairs". See S. Hoffmann *et al.*, *In Search of France* (New York: Harper and Row, 1965), p. 33.

10 O. Wieviorka, "Structurations, modes d'intervention et prises de décision", in A. Prost (ed.), *La Résistance, une histoire sociale* (Paris: Les Editions de l'Atelier, 1997), pp. 55–68. This identification with the Resistance was as strong among the conservative minority in 1945–46 as among the leftist majority; indeed, it has been suggested, the very rarity of Resistance credentials on the right made them all the more valuable to those few who possessed them. See Vinen, *Bourgeois Politics*, pp. 267–8.

11 A. Shennan, *Rethinking France: Plans for Renewal, 1940–1946* (Oxford: Oxford University Press, 1989), pp. 106–68.

12 W. Hitchcock, *France Restored: Cold War Diplomacy and the Quest for Leadership in Europe, 1944–1954* (Chapel Hill, North Carolina: University of North Carolina Press, 1998), p. 38.

13 J.-L. Loubet del Bayle, *Les Non-conformistes des années 30* (Paris: Seuil, 1969).

14 *Capitalism and the State in Modern France* (Cambridge: Cambridge University Press, 1981), p. 118.

15 Kuisel, *Capitalism and the State*, pp. 119–25.

16 F. Goguel, "Les élections législatives et sénatoriales partielles", in *Edouard Daladier, Chef de Gouvernement* (Paris: Presses de la FNSP, 1977), pp. 45–54; C. Peyrefitte, "Les premiers sondages d'opinion", in *ibid*, pp. 276–7.

17 J.-L. Crémieux-Brilhac, *Les Français de l'an 40*, 2 vols (Paris: Gallimard, 1990), vol. 2, pp. 256–7.

18 Frank(enstein), *Prix du réarmement*, pp. 271–88.

19 M. Alexander, *The Republic in Danger: General Maurice Gamelin and the Politics of French Defence, 1933–1940* (Cambridge: Cambridge University Press, 1992), p. 139.

20 See Kuisel, *Capitalism and the State*, pp. 157ff; Shennan, *Rethinking France*, pp. 224–86.

21 K. Passmore, *From Liberalism to Fascism. The Right in a French province, 1928–1939* (Cambridge: Cambridge University Press, 1997), pp. 295–7.

22 J. Jackson, *The Popular Front in France: Defending Democracy, 1934–38* (Cambridge: Cambridge University Press, 1988), p. 289.

23 J. Harvey (ed.), *The Diplomatic Diaries of Oliver Harvey, 1937–1940* (London: Collins, 1970), p. 219.

24 For a more critical view of Daladier and Reynaud, suggesting that they were, in their own way, defeatist, see R. Girault, "Les décideurs français et la puissance française en 1938–1939", in R. Girault and R. Frank (eds), *La Puissance en Europe, 1938–1940* (Paris: Publications de la Sorbonne, 1984), pp. 38–9.

25 Quoted by J.-M. Mayeur, in *Edouard Daladier, Chef de Gouvernment*, p. 246.

26 G. Le Béguec, "L'évolution de la politique gouvernementale et les problèmes institutionnels", in *Edouard Daladier, Chef de Gouvernement*, pp. 55–74.

27 G. Sadoul, *Journal de guerre* (Paris: Les Editeurs Français Réunis, 1977), p. 62 (22 Oct. 1939).

28 *Pleins pouvoirs* (Paris: Gallimard, 1939). See M. Marrus and R. Paxton, *Vichy France and the Jews* (New York: Schocken Books, 1983), pp. 52–3.

29 R. Schor, *L'Opinion française et les étrangers en France* (Paris: Publications de la Sorbonne, 1985), p. 704.

30 Schor, *L'Opinion*, pp. 666–70.

31 Marrus and Paxton, *Vichy France*, pp. 55–8, 64–5, 71.

32 Vicki Caron has demonstrated that the Daladier government was not so blinded by xenophobia and anti-semitism as to overlook the contribution that foreigners could make to the war effort. In 1939–40 the government emptied the internment camps to recruit troops and included immigrant-owned businesses in the economic mobilisation effort. Such steps, Caron concludes, "would not have been proffered by a more conservative administration". *Uneasy Asylum. France and the Jewish refugee crisis, 1933–1942* (Stanford, California: Stanford University Press, 1999), p. 358. F. Muel-Dreyfus has sounded a comparable note of caution in her study of Vichy familialism: *Vichy et l'éternel féminin* (Paris: Seuil, 1996), pp. 191–2, 220–1. While many of the pro-family spokesmen and organisations that had spurred Daladier to action in 1938 reappeared in Vichy, the latter's family policy was more ideologically charged and militant.

33 The term is an amalgam of R. A. Butler, the Conservative Chancellor of the Exchequer in the early 1950s, and his Labour party counterpart, Hugh Gaitskell.

34 H. Rousso, *The Vichy Syndrome* (Cambridge, Massachusetts: Harvard University Press, 1991), pp. 53–4.

35 O. Wieviorka, "La presse", in P. Buton and J.-M. Guillon (eds), *Les Pouvoirs en France à la Libération* (Paris: Belin, 1994), pp. 140–58.

36 *Les Carnets de la drôle de guerre* (Paris: Gallimard, 1983), pp. 375–6 (8 Mar. 1940).

37 Crémieux-Brilhac, *Les Français*, vol. 2, pp. 108–9.

38 Alexander, *Republic in Danger*, p. 138.

39 On one such important forerunner, the 1937 *Comité d'Enquête sur la Production*, see M. Margairaz, *L'Etat, les finances et l'économie. Histoire d'une conversion, 1932–1952*, 2 vols (Paris: Comité pour l'Histoire Economique et Financière de la France, 1991), vol. 1, pp. 394ff.

40 W. Kimball (ed.), *Churchill and Roosevelt: the Complete Correspondence*, 3 vols (Princeton, New Jersey: Princeton University Press, 1984), vol. 2, p. 607.

41 M. Gilbert, *Winston S. Churchill*, 8 vols (Boston: Houghton Mifflin, 1966–88), vol. 7, p. 1155.

42 See Smuts's speech to the Empire Parliamentary Association in London, 25 November 1943: J. Van der Poel (ed.), *Selections from the Smuts Papers, December 1934–August 1945* (Cambridge: Cambridge University Press, 1973), pp. 456–69. The quotation here is from p. 461.

43 Quoted in Hitchcock, *France Restored*, p. 72.

44 For example, see articles in *Le Monde*, 14 June 1945, 18 May 1946.

45 Letter of P. Giacobbi to the Governor General of French West Africa, 21 June 1945, in *Archives Nationales Section Outre Mer, Affaires Politiques*, 214.

46 "Conférence par M. le Gouverneur Laurentie", 25 June 1945, in *Archives Nationales Section Outre-Mer, Affaires Politiques*, 214.

47 Frank, *Hantise du déclin*, p. 111.

48 Frank, *Hantise du déclin*, pp. 111–13.

49 Vinen, *Bourgeois Politics*, p. 1.

50 Quoted in E. du Réau, *Edouard Daladier 1884–1970* (Paris: Fayard, 1993), p. 304.

51 Quoted in du Réau, *Daladier*, p. 232.

52 Quoted by S. Berstein, in Girault and Frank (eds), *La Puissance en Europe*, p. 292.

53 J.-P. Rioux, *The Fourth Republic, 1944–1958* (Cambridge: Cambridge University Press, 1987), p. 177.

CHAPTER SEVEN

The long term: legacies

Rivers knew only too well how often the early stages of change or cure may mimic deterioration. Cut a chrysalis open, and you will find a rotting caterpillar. What you will never find is that mythical creature, half caterpillar, half butterfly. . . . No, the process of transformation consists almost entirely of decay.

Pat Barker, *Regeneration* (1993)[1]

1940 eclipsed: the national view

Within two decades of 1940 the events of that spring already seemed to belong to another era.[2] This last bout in a decades-long European conflict was separated from the postwar era by the global conflagration of 1941–45 and by the Cold War confrontation of two vast superpowers, each of which overshadowed the participants in the "last European war" (to borrow the title of John Lukacs' history of it[3]). By the end of the 1950s, with Germany divided between East and West and with West Germany and France firmly engaged on the path of reconciliation and cooperation, the likelihood of renewed conflict between these historic enemies had receded.

Developments in succeeding decades only accentuated this impression of the datedness of the brief war of 1939–40. The modernisation of French society encouraged the perception of a fundamental divide between the nation of the *exode*, with its wheelbarrows and horse-drawn carts, and the ultra-modern France of nuclear energy and nuclear weapons, high-speed trains and televisions. In addition, de Gaulle's successful break with a style of politics so closely associated with the defeat and so seemingly replicated under the Fourth Republic allowed the French to view the paralysis of 1940 as part of their past rather than their present. The soundness of such a view was confirmed in the 1980s, when the Fifth Republic was consolidated and legitimised by the transition to a Socialist president and left-wing governments. At the same time, in the 1980s and 1990s the rapid acceleration in the progress towards European integration and the absorption of a reunified Germany into the new Europe removed lingering anxieties that a post-Cold War Western Europe might lapse back into its pre-1940 state (as has unfortunately happened in the Balkan region). In short, the trend of France's – and of Europe's – recent history has tended to submerge the memory of 1940, even as this same history has refocused the nation's attention on other aspects of its wartime experience (as we will argue below).

The memory of the defeat has been eclipsed both by consoling and by painful memories. The chief consolation has been provided by the Gaullist epic. De Gaulle's 1958 reenactment of his wartime "assumption" of France settled once and for all the retrospective primacy of June 18 over the weeks preceding it. After 1958, the memory of the defeat was wrapped up in the memory of its Gaullist antidote. This remained so even after the General's death in 1970. During the fortieth anniversary commemorations in 1980, the writer Max Gallo noted how much the monumental figure of de Gaulle had come to obscure the defeat.[4] Opinion polls in the early 1980s found that the French viewed the Liberation as a more important event than the defeat or the armistice; this suggested a popular desire to stress the uplifting end of the story rather than the depressing prologue.[5] In 1990 – a year that marked not just the fiftieth anniversary of the defeat and de Gaulle's *appel*, but the centenary of the General's birth and the twentieth anniversary of his death – the tendency to focus on the General himself rather than on the disastrous circumstances that prompted his emergence was even more marked. Amid the lavish memorialisation of de Gaulle, little attention was paid to what the historian Jacques Duquesne termed "the forgotten truths of the summer of '40".[6]

Meanwhile, in a different way, the defeat has also been eclipsed, especially since the 1960s, by the memory of the dark years that followed it. While the public's interest and the media's attention have continued to be focused on the Occupation (as a result of long-delayed trials of prominent collaborators, high-profile academic or legal disputes over Holocaust denial, and revelations about the wartime record of prominent public figures),[7] the defeat has been a much less controversial or prominent issue. The recent revelations about President Mitterrand's wartime record provide an instructive example in this respect. When Mitterrand's political skeletons (his prewar affiliation with far right organisations, his devotion to the National Revolution, his friendship with notorious collaborators and anti-semites) were exposed in 1994, the revelations also compelled a reassessment of his experiences during and immediately after the campaign of 1940.[8] Most notably, they undermined Mitterrand's own previous accounts of a straightforward transition from defeat and captivity to resistance: in fact, he had been as attached to a certain brand of anti-republican, Catholic nationalism before the war as he remained in 1941 or 1942. And yet, if 1940 had not produced the ideological metamorphosis that he later claimed, the new information confirmed the centrality of this trauma to his subsequent career. For example, it was during his absence in a German prisoner-of-war camp that his fiancée decided to break off their engagement.[9] This personal hurt fused with a generalised resentment (dating back to the outbreak of war) at the unique sacrifice that he felt his generation was being forced to make. Mitterrand returned to France in late 1941 with an attitude towards the defeat that combined indignation, self-righteousness, and perhaps a certain self-pity. It was an attitude that stayed with him for the rest of his life.[10]

For present purposes, however, the essential point is that what caught the eye of the media and the public in this *affaire*, as in most others, was Mitterrand's record in Vichy and his relationship to Vichyites rather than his experiences in 1939–41. We may explain this in a number of ways. One explanation, already alluded to, is the perceived irrelevance of the war of 1939–40 to the issues of the 1980s and 1990s – both because the war was fought against an enemy who is no longer a conceivable enemy and because it is seen as a kind of pre-modern conflict (it is striking how often contemporary media use the image of the horse to portray the French war effort, even though the Allies possessed at least as many tanks as the Germans). By contrast, many of the most controversial aspects of the Vichy record (for example, its racial prejudices, its hostility to immigrants, its coldly bureaucratic approach to tragic human situations) retain an obvious relevance to the politics of the 1980s and 1990s, marked as they have been by the revival of the far right, by anti-immigrant feeling, and by the persistence of Holocaust denial. No contemporary phenomenon has kept the memory of 1940 alive as Jean-Marie Le Pen and the *Front National* (or for that matter "ethnic cleansing" in the Balkans) have kept the issues of 1940–44 alive.

In addition, in critical respects the memory of the defeat has been inherently unproblematic, at least in comparison with the memory of the Occupation years. To judge again by public opinion surveys (admittedly a crude instrument), by the 1980s a consensus had formed about the defeat, a depoliticised consensus acknowledging the necessity of the armistice, blaming both the Third Republic and the generals for the defeat, and discounting overtly partisan explanations for the disaster (such as those which blamed it on the Popular Front). In Henry Rousso's words, "The French are no longer divided about the defeat of 1940."[11] More important still, the defeat does not appear to raise for the French the searching moral and political dilemmas that are posed by the Occupation. The key is that the defeat has always been viewed as the outcome of a prolonged national decadence. As a result, there is no "what if?" question hanging over its memory. Great defeats may evoke rich nostalgia (take the case of the American South), but only in circumstances where an alternative to defeat strikes a deep chord, that is where nostalgia is possible. This is not the case with the later Third Republic (perhaps somewhat unfairly, as the previous chapter argued). If there were any sense that France did not need a disaster of this magnitude to renew itself, then the work of historians who have laboured to question the inevitability of the collapse would have had far more resonance and generated much more controversy than they have. But the assumption is that, if it had not been this disaster, it would have been another one, so dysfunctional had become the political system and so divided and resistant to change had become French society.

With the Occupation, however, there have always been hypothetical alternatives to fuel the debate about the choices that Vichy or the Resistance made. What if the Vichy government had stuck to the letter of the armistice or had not pursued the mirage of collaboration? What if French bureaucrats and policemen had sabotaged rather than facilitated German plans to round up Jews? What if Vichy's patriotism had not been subordinated to narrow partisanship? What if the Resistance had survived into the postwar era as a coherent movement? What if de Gaulle and Moulin had not sanctified the reconstitution of the political parties in 1943? For each of these questions, plausible counterfactual scenarios can be imagined. The sense that the French had real choices to make in 1940–44 keeps the history of that period alive and controversial.

And, finally (and not insignificantly in a country as thoughtful and self-conscious about its past as France) there is the inherent difficulty of commemorating a defeat of this kind. Certainly it is possible to commemorate a defeat where the defeated exhibited great courage or fought against overwhelming odds (as the memorialisation of Resistance heroism in 1944 demonstrates) or where a defeat can be remembered as the first step towards ultimate victory. But the French débâcle in 1940 hardly fits into either category. It was marked at least as much by incompetence and cowardice as by their opposites. And even the tremendous sacrifices that French soldiers and civilians made, even the remarkable courage that many displayed in the face of defeat, served no larger good. They were, to use a harsh word, futile. As the writer Saint-Exupéry noted in his recollections of his service as a reconnaissance pilot: "Sacrifice loses all nobility if it is

159

nothing but a parody or suicide. It is a fine thing to sacrifice oneself: some die in order that others may be saved. One clears the ground to prevent the conflagration from spreading. One fights to the death, in the entrenched camp, to give the rescuers time. Yes, but whatever one does, the fire will engulf everything, there is no camp on which to fall back, there are no rescuers to be hoped for."[12] The problems of commemorating this sacrifice were then compounded by Vichy's determination to frame the defeat's memory in a blatantly partisan way. By blaming the defeat both on selectively chosen individuals and on entire classes of people, Vichy made any subsequent attempt to confront the memory politically suspect. As Stanley Hoffmann has put it, "The slide from self-examination to denunciation, starting in June '40, then the oft-repeated hunt for scapegoats throughout the black years and after the Liberation . . . can help explain a certain vacuum or a relative silence surrounding the disaster."[13]

Such are at least some of the reasons for what Hoffmann has called the "stunning contrast between the proportions of the May–June 1940 catastrophe and the role it plays in the country's intellectual production".[14] Some scholars have wondered whether this relative neglect of the large questions about the defeat's causation that Bloch posed in *Strange Defeat* reflects historians' unease with what they might find. Omer Bartov has suggested that "Historians' unwillingness to undertake an analysis of interwar France with an eye to the deep roots of the collapse was, and still is, probably mainly due to the discomfort of discovering in a post-1945 world that fear of war could lead to collaboration in atrocity, that anti-militarism can bring about fascism, and that lack of a certain ruthlessness in policy-making can easily allow for much greater abuse by others."[15] This perhaps implies a more gaping hole in the historiography of the 1920s and 30s than in fact exists. It is certainly true that Bloch's important questions about the non-military causes of defeat were not tackled comprehensively until Jean-Louis Crémieux-Brilhac did so in 1990 (and, like Bloch, Crémieux-Brilhac was a participant in these events struggling to come to grips with his personal feelings of shame and anger).[16] But many other aspects of the defeat's causation have been studied quite intensively over the years, as Robert Young has recently shown.[17] If there is a gap in the historical literature, it exists less in relation to the long-term roots of the defeat than to its immediate context, the late 1930s and the phony war. The latter periods are much less thoroughly studied than the crisis years before 1938 or the dark years after defeat. Witness a recent, massively authoritative study of economic and financial policy-making from 1932 to 1952 – 1,350 pages, of which just six deal with the months between September 1939 and May 1940.[18]

One could make a similar claim about the place of the defeat in contemporary culture. The experience of May and June has inspired a steady flow

160

of personal narratives (for which, again, *Strange Defeat* was an influential prototype). Most such autobiographical works were written and published in the two decades after 1940, although others continue to this day to be extricated from desk drawers and family archives and to find their way into print. 1940 has also frequently found its way into literary fiction and cinema, with the decade or so after Liberation again the high point. Novels such as the final volume of Sartre's *Les Chemins de la Liberté* (1949) and films such as René Clément's *Les Jeux Interdits* (1952), were influential in shaping retrospective views of the débâcle in the early postwar years. Thereafter, however, the defeat has never stimulated a body of creative work comparable to that stimulated by the Occupation – whether because the themes raised by the latter were more interesting or more profound or of more enduring resonance, or perhaps simply because there was more to the protracted experience of occupation than to the intense but transitory sensation of defeat. In any event, it is hard to see how a case for 1940's long-term significance could be based on its cultural impact or on its prominence within the collective memory.

"Fulcrum of the twentieth century": an international view

An alternative way of conceptualising a long-term legacy is by reintegrating the defeat into the vast conflict of which it was just one episode. Inasmuch as the defeat constituted a turning point in the world war, it could be said to have helped to precipitate the global and local transformations associated with the war's later stages and aftermath. That logic inspired one of the more expansive expressions of 1940's significance. In a book published in the 1960s, General André Beaufre described the French army's collapse as "the most important event of the twentieth century".[19] By removing the main western counterweight to German power, Beaufre suggested, the fall destroyed the balance of power in Europe. The full significance of this was masked temporarily by the brief hegemony of Germany, but once that hegemony had been destroyed the real meaning of 1940 emerged: "The destruction of Germany . . . left in place of the traditional Europe only a zone of weakness, while the USA and the USSR, now overwhelming powers, disputed between themselves the dominance of the world which Europe had lost, and which led inevitably to the fashion for decolonization."

Tinged though it may be by Gallocentrism, this claim about the defeat's longer-term impact has much to recommend it. The defeat precipitated major shifts in policy on the part of other key states. As a consequence of the collapse, France's main ally and Germany's sole remaining foe, Great Britain, redirected its energy and attention towards Washington. The Churchill government's search for a "special relationship" with the United States reversed the current of interwar relations and opened the way to the Anglo-American collaboration of 1941–45 and beyond. The evolution of British policy was matched by an evolution of American priorities. The Roosevelt administration was as shocked by France's defeat as anyone, and responded to it by hasty rearmament and by steadily intensified support for Britain. While there was, of course, a vast difference between offering Britain material support via Lend-Lease (approved by Congress in March 1941) and actually entering the war, the trend of American policy as a result of France's fall was clearly towards closer engagement with Britain. That was also clearly Hitler's view of the situation – a view which influenced his aggressive strategy at the end of 1941.

Within Europe, the trend of Hitler's thinking after June 1940 was in favour of turning to the East and fighting the war against "Judeo-Bolshevism" that had been his enduring obsession. Even as German forces prepared to mount their unsuccessful invasion of Britain in the summer and autumn of 1940, Hitler's thoughts were increasingly focused on when and how to launch his attack against Russia. A number of contingencies (such as the unexpectedly resourceful resistance of the British and the Soviet government's continuing willingness to provide Germany with the food and raw materials it needed) affected the timing of the war's extension in the East. Hypothetically, a more cautious German regime might have settled for what it had already gained by the end of 1940, in which case the war might have entered a kind of stasis, with neither side able to achieve a break-through victory against the other, and the future superpowers confining themselves to the margins.[20] But this hypothesis runs counter to all that we know about the dynamics of the Nazi regime and the nature of Hitler's leadership. Taking the longer view, Beaufre's logic – that the fall of France encouraged Nazi Germany to embark on a globalisation of the war that ultimately proved its undoing – is highly persuasive.

From that first step one may reach a number of further conclusions about the legacies of 1940. A leading historian of Anglo-American rela-tions, David Reynolds, has suggested three such legacies.[21] The first was the postwar confrontation between the superpowers. Like Beaufre, Reynolds argues that the collapse of France created the conditions both for the accelerated emergence of the two superpowers (as the two states best equip-ped to mobilise the vast industrial and human potential necessary to win a globalised war) and for an eventual vacuum in Europe after Germany's inevitable defeat. The combination of a devastated continent and two preeminent powers with quite distinct political and economic systems created the precondition for the postwar division of Europe into West and East. Could France and Britain have prevented their eclipse and the shifting of the international centre of gravity away from Europe? Perhaps not in the longer term, but in the short term a stalemate in Western Europe would have extended the life of a "multipolar" system and forestalled the stark confrontation between superpowers that emerged in the later 1940s.

A second legacy was the stimulus for all West Europeans, but particularly the French, to pursue cooperative arrangements with neighbouring nation-states. The lesson that the French learned – Reynolds, of course, acknowledges that it was only learned after France's initial postwar strategy of dismantling Germany and taking control of its economic resources had been overruled by the United States – was that "France could not live with the more powerful Germany as a rival nation-state, so both must sacrifice some elements of national sovereignty to ensure peaceful coexistence."[22] By contrast, what the British learned in 1940 was to rely on the support of the United States rather than alliance with France or other European states – a lesson that explains a good deal about the British ambivalence towards European institutions in the decades after 1950.

Finally, a third legacy concerned areas outside Europe. This was the staggering blow to European power in Asia and Africa. Less important than the short-term loss of control over territories or assets (losses that were, in most cases, made good at the end of the war) was the shattering of the imperialists' aura of invincibility. To quote Beaufre again, "Our prestige was shattered: Allah was no longer with us."[23] The eclipse of British and French power after June 1940 encouraged the development of anti-colonial movements within the empires and, in the longer term, shifted the global balance of power in favour of the two superpowers, each of which had both ideological and self-interested reasons to undermine the European empires.

In Reynolds' analysis, the crucial events of May–June 1940 took place on both sides of the Channel. The legacies of France's defeat are equally the legacies of the British decision to carry on the war. Underlying his interpretation of these legacies is a sense of irony where the British experience is concerned: Britain's "finest hour", like France's darkest hour, led ultimately to relative decline. The rise of the superpowers and the decline of empire affected the defeated and undefeated alike, while the movement towards European integration benefited the defeated French more than the victorious British. As a result of their wartime experience, the British became so preoccupied with their American connection that they found it impossible to commit unequivocally to Europe – a textbook example of the long-term perils of military/political success. Some British historians have pushed this sense of irony much further, suggesting that the government should have explored a diplomatic solution after the fall of France and that Churchill's policy of "no surrender", based on the hope of American assistance, led eventually to a fatal weakening of the British Empire and the supplanting of Britain's power by the United States.[24] Certainly such revisionism has had its counterpart in France, going all the way back to Vichy (many of whose supporters believed that France should have pursued negotiation with Hitler before May 1940). But in France the revisionist view of 1940 has never progressed very far because there really is no golden age myth to demolish. Not only was the collapse itself unarguably disastrous, but the prevailing view has always been that France was ripe for disaster, indeed had been moving inexorably towards that disaster since the too-great exertions of the First World War. That view, originating in the summer of 1940, has persisted to the present.

The fable of defeat and renewal

For the French, the long-term issue raised by these mid-century shifts in the international order was not whether they could have been avoided (to many, they were already inevitable in the 1930s, and the defeat and the dwarfing of European power by the superpowers made them unarguable), but how they could be adjusted to and compensated for. The declinist angst that the nation had passed through in the interwar years (and that the British were to experience after 1945) was no longer relevant. Defeat, unlike victory, made for realistic self-assessment and grim determination to renew. This, in essence, is the story that the French have told about the long-term legacy of 1940. To quote the words of the historian Yves Durand: "The shock of the defeat convinced the majority of the French people once and for all that they were no longer a dominant power. The 1940s will probably have been for them what the great inflation of 1923 was for the Germans: a catastrophe creating a point of no return and the feeling that the best way of recovering stability was to prepare for the future rather than to go back to 'the old days'."[25]

The ultimate legacy of defeat thus becomes postwar renewal. The psychological appeal of this view, which was widely expressed once it was possible to see that France *had* been renewed, is not hard to appreciate. It restores a sense of agency to the national experience in this century, by constructing 1940 as a conscious turning point and postwar policies as deliberate adaptations to defeat. It contrasts an interwar era characterised by a sense of helplessness and drift with a postwar era marked by purposefulness (even if the purpose was misguided at times). In that sense, it redeems the defeat itself, not in the short term perhaps, but in the longer perspective. Would an undefeated society have summoned up the energy to modernise or an undefeated state have found the mechanisms to promote such modernisation? Would an undefeated Republic have produced a de Gaulle or given him enough legitimacy to reconstruct republicanism? Would an undefeated France have had the wisdom to appreciate how European cooperation might advance national interests as well as international peace and security?

As I noted at the outset of this study, these claims are impossible to verify, hard even to substantiate. On certain issues, especially relating to national security, the painful memory of 1940 was from time to time directly invoked, and such invocations give us explicit evidence of a link between the memory of the past and the postwar determination to renew. In the 1950s, for example, the pioneers of France's atomic *force de frappe* (strike force) often referred back to the war for inspiration. As one of them later recollected, after noting that he had spent time in Buchenwald: "If France had some nuclear weapons and the means to launch them, it would be protected from a repetition of its terrible experiences in 1914 and 1940."[26] When de Gaulle's government finally exploded a bomb in February 1960, it portrayed the test as an atonement for 1940 and a guarantee that it would never happen again.[27] The constitution of the Fifth Republic was itself clearly influenced by de Gaulle's recollections of 1940. Michel Debré, the constitution's main architect, has recalled how de Gaulle insisted on the inclusion of what became Article 16 (giving the President of the Republic emergency powers in a crisis): "The President's right to assume the powers of the Republic in an emergency appeared a necessity to the General. He emphasised to us repeatedly that if the laws of 1875 had provided for this right, President Lebrun would have decided to transfer the government to North Africa in June 1940 and France's situation would have been entirely different."[28]

On the other hand, if there really is truth in this notion of a collective conversion, instances such as these, in which direct allusions are made to 1940, must be the tip of the iceberg. The presumption is that the trauma of 1940 created personal memories of embarrassment, loss or disgust, which millions of individuals carried around with them for the rest of their lives and which shaped their choices, both in private and in public spheres. René Rémond, one of the nation's most eminent contemporary historians, has written quite movingly of this private experience of a collective failure: "There is probably no more terrible a trial for a people than the defeat of its armies: in the scale of crises, this is the supreme catastrophe. It scarcely matters whether one was formerly a pacifist or a militarist, whether one hated war or resigned oneself to it . . . defeat creates a deep and lasting traumatism in everyone. It wounds something essential in each of us: a certain confidence in life, a pride in oneself and in the group to which one belongs, an indispensable self-respect."[29] This is to restate a very old view of war's impact – defeat's impact, in particular. After France's defeat at the hands of Prussia in 1870, the philosopher Ernest Renan had described war as "one of the conditions of progress, the lashing that prevents a country from falling asleep, by forcing self-satisfied mediocrity out of its apathy".[30]

That the 1940s constituted a turning point in French history seems, from the perspective of the year 2000, impossible to deny. The defeat stands at the beginning not just of a short-term nightmare but of a long-term metamorphosis that has radically altered most aspects of France's political, cultural, social and economic life. What appeared ambiguous in 1950 or even in 1960 is now unarguable. On the other hand, as every logician knows, *post hoc* is not necessarily *propter hoc*. It is possible to take a less voluntarist view of France's postwar recovery than the generation of 1940 has sometimes done. 1940 should be viewed primarily in terms of a process of decay, not so much the decay of prewar society (since much of what appeared as decay in 1940 was destined to thrive after 1945), but the decay of an international system. One way of appreciating this is to ponder the dead end that France had reached in June 1940. For years, it had been confronted by the spectre of another terrible war, a war that it did not want but increasingly felt it could not avoid. The conflict with Germany seemed destined to persist indefinitely. The international economy had collapsed amid industrial and agricultural depression and resurgent nationalism. The idealistic hopes of 1919 or of the mid–late 1920s had vanished. Europeans were at one another's throats again, and there seemed no plausible reason to predict improvement. Faced with the necessity of choosing among only unsatisfactory outcomes (rearmament at ruinous cost, peace at ruinous cost, war at ruinous cost), it was scarcely surprising that people clung to fantasies about avoiding war or winning war without fighting it or fighting against people (at home or abroad) who were not in fact the enemy.

The fantasies and illusions, in other words, were not symptoms of collective complacency that the French could simply shake off, once stunned back to reality by defeat. They were the absurd products of an absurd world, adaptations to a vast crisis in economic and political relations. It was only when that crisis was resolved, as it was as a result of the war (not as a result of the defeat), that the fantasies and illusions could be jettisoned. If France had not been defeated in the first phase of the war, it is possible that the illusions would have persisted longer than they did. But if the war had not led to the replacement of the international system that had brought Europe to this dead end, the illusions might not have been jettisoned at all.

Notes and references

1 (New York: Plume, 1993), p. 184.

2 John C. Cairns, "Along the road back to France 1940", *American Historical Review*, 64: 3 (1959), p. 583.

3 *The Last European War, September 1939/December 1941* (Garden City, New York: Anchor Press, 1976).

4 *L'Express*, 17 May 1980.

5 Survey in *L'Express*, 26 Aug. 1983 (international edition). See the commentaries by H. Rousso, in *La Mémoire des Français. Quarante ans de commémorations de la seconde guerre mondiale* (Paris: Editions du CNRS, 1986), p. 50; and by R. Frank, in A. Wahl (ed.), *Mémoire de la seconde guerre mondiale* (Metz: Centre de Recherche Histoire et Civilisation de l'Université de Metz, 1984), p. 290.

6 *Le Point*, 2 July 1990. See also R. Desquesnes, "1994: échos des commémorations en France", *Contemporary French Civilization*, 19: 2 (1995), 196n.

7 The standard works on this obsession are H. Rousso, *The Vichy Syndrome* (Cambridge, Massachusetts: Harvard University Press, 1991); and E. Conan and H. Rousso, *Vichy, un passé qui ne passe pas* (Paris: Fayard, 1994). The latter is now available in English: *Vichy: an Ever-Present Past* (Hanover, New Hampshire: University Press of New England, 1998).

8 The precipitating event in this controversy was the publication of a study of Mitterrand's early years: P. Péan, *Une Jeunesse française. François Mitterrand, 1934–1947* (Paris: Fayard, 1994). As many commentators noted, most of the revelations in this book had long been whispered about or even widely known. But the fact that Mitterrand chose (for reasons that are still the subject of debate) to cooperate with Péan gave the book an instant credibility and significance.

9 Péan, *Une Jeunesse française*, pp. 147–55.

10 Péan, *Une Jeunesse française*, pp. 113, 488.

11 *Vichy Syndrome*, p. 279.

12 A. de Saint-Exupéry, *Pilote de guerre* (Paris: Gallimard, 1942), p. 93.

13 Hoffmann, "The trauma of 1940", in J. Blatt (ed.), *The French Defeat of 1940. Reassessments* (Providence, Rhode Island: Berghahn, 1998), p. 360.

14 Hoffmann, "Trauma", p. 356.

15 "Martyrs' vengeance: memory, trauma, and fear of war in France, 1918–1940", in Blatt, *French Defeat of 1940*, p. 60.

16 *Les Français de l'an 40*, 2 vols (Paris: Gallimard, 1990).

17 *France and the Origins of the Second World War* (New York: St Martin's Press, 1996), pp. 37–59.

18 M. Margairaz, *L'Etat, les finances et l'économie. Histoire d'une conversion, 1932–1952*, 2 vols (Paris: Comité pour l'Histoire Economique et Financière de la France, 1991).

19 *1940. The Fall of France* (London: Cassell, 1967), p. 212. First French edition was 1965. A similarly expansive conclusion was reached by J. Gunsburg, author of one of the most searching reassessments of the 1940 campaign: *"Vaincre ou Mourir": the French High Command and the Defeat of France, 1919–May 1940* (Ph.D. thesis, Duke University, 1974), p. 626.

20 P. Kennedy, *The Rise and Fall of the Great Powers* (New York: Random House, 1987), p. 341.

21 "1940: fulcrum of the twentieth century?", *International Affairs*, 66: 2 (1990), 325–50. For the sake of the present argument, I will combine Reynolds' second and third points into a single one. The force of his argument has been acknowledged and amplified by A. Adamthwaite, *Grandeur and Misery: France's Bid for Power in Europe 1914–1940* (London: Arnold, 1995).

22 Reynolds, "1940: fulcrum", p. 348.

23 Beaufre, *1940*, p. 33.

24 See, for example, J. Charmley, *Churchill: the End of Glory* (San Diego, California: Harcourt Brace, 1993).

25 Y. Durand, *Vichy (1940–1944)* (Paris: Bordas, 1972), p. 145.

26 C. Ailleret, *L'Aventure atomique française* (Paris: B. Grasset, 1968), p. 114.

27 G. Hecht, *The Radiance of France. Nuclear power and national identity after World War II* (Cambridge, Massachusetts: MIT Press, 1998), p. 209.

28 M. Debré, *Trois Républiques pour une France. Mémoires*, 5 vols (Paris: A. Michel, 1984–94), vol. 2, p. 376.

29 "L'opinion française des années 1930 aux années 1940. Poids de l'événement, permanence des mentalités", in J.-P. Azéma and F. Bédarida (eds), *Le Régime de Vichy et les Français* (Paris: Fayard, 1992), p. 482.

30 "La réforme intellectuelle et morale de la France", in *Oeuvres complètes de Ernest Renan*, 10 vols (Paris: Calmann-Lévy, 1947–61), vol. 1, p. 401.

In tracking the consequences, rather than the causes, of defeat, this study ventures in a different direction from most books about 1940 – downstream, as it were, as opposed to upstream. Scholarly writing about the fall has been largely concerned with understanding why it happened. Whose were the crucial errors? Could the nation's military and political leadership reasonably have made different and better choices? What is the correct interpretative balance to be struck between the long-term or structural vulnerabilities of France's position and the short-term contingencies of the campaign? Questions such as these have stimulated, and continue to stimulate, intense debate and passionate disagreement. There has been far less debate, scholarly or otherwise, about the impact of defeat. Or perhaps it would be more accurate to say that this other issue has been subsumed within larger and more compelling controversies ignited by the four years of Occupation that followed defeat. As a result of this patchy historiography, the foregoing work has relied not on one scholarly literature but on several (as well as on other kinds of sources). My bibliographical comments will place particular emphasis on English-language works (on the assumption that those interested in French sources will be able to make use of the notes attached to the text).

The phony war and the defeat

Although the suspicion grows that historians have venerated Marc Bloch's book uncritically, the best starting point for understanding 1940 remains *Strange Defeat* (New York: Norton, 1968). Bloch's gently caustic memoir undoubtedly raised most of the questions that have guided historians' thinking ever since. His intuitions about the nation's internal fissures and its psychological and material unpreparedness for war have been explored (and, to a degree, modified) by the fine scholarship of Jean-Louis Crémieux-Brilhac: *Les Français de l'an 40*, 2 vols (Paris: Gallimard, 1990). Notwithstanding this study, the crucial phony war period remains relatively understudied, though there are useful older books such as G. Rossi-Landi, *La Drôle de guerre* (Paris: A. Colin, 1971), and important insights in recent biographies such as Elisabeth du Réau, *Edouard Daladier, 1884–1970* (Paris: Fayard, 1993). The most accessible and authoritative introduction to contemporary scholarship on the phony war and May–June 1940 is the collection of essays edited by Joel Blatt: *The French Defeat of 1940: Reassessments* (Providence, Rhode Island: Berghahn, 1998). A different kind of introduction is afforded by Jean-Pierre Azéma's collection of vignettes of the critical moments between July 1939 and December 1940: *1940. L'année terrible* (Paris: Seuil, 1990). There are too many narratives of the military and political events before and after May 10 to be listed here. Alistair Horne, *To Lose a Battle* (London: Macmillan, 1969) is characteristically readable, while Jean-Baptiste Duroselle, *L'Abîme, 1939–1945* (Paris: Imprimerie Nationale, 1982) is exceptionally lucid and carries great conviction. A brilliant, brief introduction to the politics of the *exode* is H. R. Kedward, "Patriots and patriotism in Vichy France", *Royal Historical Society Transactions* (5th series), 32 (1982), 175–92. In general, the *exode* has received less attention, especially from social historians, than its importance merits. A good point of entry into that experience, as into the experience of the phony war, is provided by diaries and memoirs, which abound. Of those available in English, the following are among the more interesting: D. Barlone, *A French Officer's Diary* (Cambridge: Cambridge University Press, 1943); Arthur Koestler, *Scum of the Earth* (New York: Macmillan, 1941); Jean-Paul Sartre, *The War Diaries* (New York: Pantheon, 1984); and Simone de Beauvoir, *The Prime of Life* (Harmondsworth: Penguin, 1965).

The causes of defeat

Here one turns from famine (in terms of historical scholarship) to feast. A very useful introduction to the large and complex literature on the roots of defeat is Robert J. Young, *France and the Origins of the Second World War* (New York: St Martin's Press, 1996). Perhaps the fundamental point of contention among diplomatic and military historians is the issue of inevitability. Put baldly, could better leaders have done better, or could different decisions in the field have produced a different outcome? A long tradition (stretching back to the moment of defeat and, in a sense, predating it) has viewed the defeat as an outgrowth of long-standing national decline and France's weak leadership and poor strategy in 1939–40 as all that one could expect of a polarised, fragmented, stagnating society, haunted by memories of the First World War. In recent years, this view has been reiterated by such leading French historians as Jean-Baptiste Duroselle and Serge Berstein. The critics of this "decadence" model have tended to come from outside France. Robert J. Young, *In Command of France. French foreign policy and military planning, 1933–1940* (Cambridge, Massachusetts: Harvard University Press, 1978) was one of the first to challenge what he termed "the curse of 1940, that irrepressible need to draw straight lines between the terrible military defeat and everything that had gone before it". An even earlier proponent of the sceptical view was John Cairns, whose influential articles – beginning with "Along the road back to France 1940", *American Historical Review*, 64: 3 (1959), 583–605 – encouraged historians to set sweeping condemnations of decline against the archival record. A fine example of what this approach can yield is Martin S. Alexander's sympathetic and well-informed study of General Maurice Gamelin, *The Republic in Danger* (Cambridge: Cambridge University Press, 1992). Anthony Adamthwaite has written a wide-ranging and scholarly synthesis of the entire interwar period that argues against decline and stresses the shortcomings of French grand strategy and political leadership: *Grandeur and Misery. France's bid for power in Europe 1914–1940* (London: Arnold, 1995). Lest one form the impression that this dispute pits declinist French scholars against revisionist foreign historians, it should be noted that important French studies (such as du Réau, *Daladier* (op. cit.), Robert Frankenstein, *Le Prix du réarmement français* (Paris: Publications de la Sorbonne, 1982), and Crémieux-Brilhac, *Les Français* (op. cit.)) have refocused attention on the initiative and resolve demonstrated by France's leaders in a period of difficult choices and severe constraints. On the other hand, some of the most trenchant criticisms of the French Command's strategy and of revisionist scholarship about it have come from non-French historians, like Nicole Jordan (see her essay in Blatt (ed.), *French Defeat* (op cit.), as well as her book *The Popular Front and Central Europe: the Dilemmas of French Impotence, 1918–1940* (Cambridge: Cambridge University Press, 1992)). A bracing, far from neutral, commentary on these debates is P. Jackson, "Recent journeys along the road back to France, 1940", *Historical Journal*, 39:2 (1996), 497–510.

Crisis of the 1930s

The trend of modern scholarship has been to rehabilitate aspects of the record of the Popular Front governments and their centre-right successors, without rehabilitating the record of the decade as a whole (which still seems, at a distance of more than half a century, a dismal one). On the Popular Front, the best work in English is Julian Jackson, *The Popular Front in France:*

Defending Democracy, 1934–38 (Cambridge: Cambridge University Press, 1988), which should be read in conjunction with Robert Frankenstein's indispensable study of rearmament, *Le Prix du réarmement* (op. cit). Also important is Richard Vinen's contentious but stimulating study: *The Politics of French Business, 1936–1945* (Cambridge: Cambridge University Press, 1991). On the Daladier government of 1938–40, there is no satisfactory study in English, but three important multi-author volumes in French: *Edouard Daladier, Chef de Gouvernement* (Paris: Presses de la FNSP, 1977); *La France et les Français en 1938–1939* (Paris: Presses de la FNSP, 1978); and R. Girault and R. Frank (eds), *La Puissance en Europe, 1938–1940* (Paris: Publications de la Sorbonne, 1984), to which should now be added E. du Réau's biography, *Edouard Daladier* (op. cit.). An influential book that reasserted a fundamentally negative view of France's record at a time when it seemed to be yielding to a more balanced view was Jean-Baptiste Duroselle's *La Décadence: la politique étrangère de la France, 1932–1939* (Paris: Imprimerie Nationale, 1979). A recent book that borrows Duroselle's decadence theme and deploys it with characteristic verve is Eugen Weber, *The Hollow Years: France in the 1930s* (New York: Norton, 1994). Among books that trace continuities from the 1930s forward into the 1940s, the following may be noted: Richard Kuisel's groundbreaking study of economic planning, *Capitalism and the State in Modern France* (Cambridge: Cambridge University Press, 1981); Vicki Caron's authoritative study of French refugee policy, *Uneasy Asylum. France and the Jewish refugee crisis, 1933–1942* (Stanford, California: Stanford University Press, 1999); Michel Margairaz's huge and definitive analysis of the revolution in the State's management of the economy, *L'Etat, les finances et l'économie. Histoire d'une conversion 1932–1952*, 2 vols (Paris: Comité pour l'Histoire Economique et Financière de la France, 1991); and the present author's *Rethinking France: Plans for Renewal, 1940–1946* (Oxford: Oxford University Press, 1989). This last work, like Kuisel's, was influenced by Stanley Hoffmann's brilliantly suggestive essay on the transformation of French politics and society between the 1930s and the 1950s: "Paradoxes of the French political community", in Hoffmann *et al.*, *In Search of France* (New York: Harper, 1965), pp. 1–117. A much-used synthesis which unites post-defeat and pre-defeat periods is J.-P. Azéma, *From Munich to the Liberation, 1938–1944* (Cambridge: Cambridge University Press, 1984).

Vichy and the Resistance

As virtually every bibliography of this kind acknowledges, the best book on the Occupation remains Robert Paxton, *Vichy France: Old Guard and New*

Order (New York: Columbia University Press, 1972). This classic work has retained remarkable freshness in spite of the fact that many of its generalisations have been refined and some even contradicted by more recent research. Paxton's work is now complemented by the able, up-to-date synthesis of Philippe Burrin, *La France à l'heure allemande 1940–1944*, translated as *Living with Defeat: France under the German Occupation, 1940–1944* (London: Arnold, 1996). For readers interested in understanding the current state of research in this academic growth field, the most comprehensive and reliable compendium is J.-P. Azéma and F. Bédarida (eds), *Le Régime de Vichy et les Français* (Paris: Fayard, 1992). A less forbidding work intended for a non-specialist audience is J.-P. Azéma and F. Bédarida (eds), *La France des années noires*, 2 vols (Paris: Seuil, 1993). John Sweets, *Choices in Vichy France* (New York: Oxford University Press, 1986) is a fine study of Vichy at the grass roots, one of the first in a now lengthy list of local studies. Other specialised works that were pioneering in their various fields and proved important for the present study are: Robert Paxton and Michael Marrus, *Vichy France and the Jews* (New York: Schocken, 1983); Pierre Laborie, *L'Opinion française sous Vichy* (Paris: Seuil, 1990); Bertram Gordon, *Collaborationism in France during the Second World War* (Ithaca, New York: Cornell University Press, 1980); and W. D. Halls, *The Youth of Vichy France* (Oxford: Oxford University Press, 1981). Halls' more recent work, *Politics, Society and Christianity in Vichy France* (Oxford: Berg, 1995), is an excellent synthesis. Miranda Pollard has written an important study of Vichy's gender politics (*Reign of Virtue* (Chicago: University of Chicago Press, 1998)), which should stimulate much further research. Along similar lines, Francine Muel-Dreyfus, *Vichy et l'éternel féminin* (Paris: Seuil, 1996), offers astute commentary on Vichy gender discourse and its prewar precursors. The struggles of daily life – for most of the population the most tangible consequence of military defeat – are best analysed by Dominique Veillon in *Vivre et survivre en France, 1939–1947* (Paris: Payot, 1995) and are also well discussed in Ian Ousby's very readable *Occupation: the Ordeal of France, 1940–1944* (London: John Murray, 1997). For prisoners of war, see Yves Durand, *La Captivité*, 3rd edn (Paris: Fédération Nationale des Combattants Prisonniers de Guerre et Combattants d'Algérie, Tunisie, Maroc, 1982) and for their wives and families, Sarah Fishman, *We Will Wait. Wives of French prisoners of war, 1940–1945* (New Haven, Connecticut: Yale University Press, 1991). Good biographical writing about the leading figures in Vichy, as about Daladier and Reynaud, is relatively sparse. Richard Griffiths, *Pétain* (Garden City, New York: Doubleday, 1972) and Geoffrey Warner, *Pierre Laval and the Eclipse of France* (London: Eyre and Spottiswoode, 1968) were written before most of the official archives were opened to researchers, but retain many virtues. The memoir and diary literature relating to Vichy is vast and naturally quite uneven in importance and reliability. Most is not translated. Nor is the best work on the Riom trial: F. Pottecher, *Le Procès de la défaite. Riom, février–avril 1942* (Paris: Fayard, 1989) and H. Michel, *Le Procès de Riom* (Paris: A. Michel, 1979).

Resisters thought and wrote a good deal about 1940, but it is not easy to reconstruct this thinking. In addition to the invaluable archival sources and clandestine publications cited in the notes, there are relatively few scholarly studies of the Resistance that engage the theme of this book directly. In English, the best work on the Resistance has been done by H. R. Kedward. His article "Patriots and patriotism" (op. cit.) and his fine book *Resistance in Vichy France* (Oxford: Oxford University Press, 1978) are indispensable. Also useful is his later, somewhat less accessible but equally magisterial, *In Search of the Maquis* (Oxford: Oxford University Press, 1993). Most of the major resistance movements have now received monograph treatment in France. A fine recent example is Laurent Douzou's study of Libération-Sud, entitled *La Désobéissance* (Paris: O. Jacob, 1995). One of the most substantial contributions to Resistance history during the past decade is Daniel Cordier's massive study of the Resistance leader Jean Moulin (which is far more than a mere biography): *Jean Moulin, l'inconnu du Panthéon*, 3 vols (Paris: J.-C. Lattès, 1989–93). Another brilliant biographical work is Jean Lacouture's *De Gaulle*, 3 vols (Paris: Seuil, 1984–86), translated as 2 vols (London: Collins, 1990). On Free France, two other fundamental sources are de Gaulle's famous *War Memoirs*, 3 vols (London: Weidenfeld & Nicolson, 1955–60) and a recent scholarly study by Jean-Louis Crémieux-Brilhac, *La France Libre* (Paris: Gallimard, 1996), which is the best of a surprisingly sparse crop of French studies of Free France. The defeat's impact on Resistance thinking about postwar reconstruction is discussed in Shennan, *Rethinking France* (op. cit.), Claire Andrieu, *Le Programme Commun de la Résistance: des idées dans la guerre* (Paris: Editions de l'Erudit, 1984), and Henri Michel, *Les Courants de pensée de la Résistance* (Paris: PUF, 1962). The intensity of such debates may be gauged by reading Léon Blum's wartime essay *À l'échelle humaine*, translated as *For All Mankind* (Gloucester, Massachusetts: Peter Smith, 1969) as well as Bloch, *Strange Defeat* (op. cit.).

Liberation and beyond

The most reliable overall guide to the period after Liberation is Jean-Pierre Rioux's *The Fourth Republic, 1944–1958* (Cambridge: Cambridge University Press, 1987). Peter Novick's study of the postwar purge, *The Resistance versus Vichy* (New York: Columbia University Press, 1968) is still essential reading, as is Henry Rousso's analysis of postwar memories of the Occupation (the most interesting parts of which deal with the fifteen years after Liberation): *The Vichy Syndrome* (Cambridge, Massachusetts: Harvard University Press, 1991). The field of "memory studies" has acquired a faddish aura in the last decade, but there is no denying that Rousso's book opened up new avenues of enquiry (although most of this enquiry has focused on the crimes committed by Vichy or on Resistance heroics, not on the defeat itself). Two studies with a narrower focus that proved particularly useful in the preparation of this book were: Richard Vinen, *Bourgeois Politics in France, 1945–1951* (Cambridge: Cambridge University Press, 1995); and C. Lewin, *Le Retour des prisonniers de guerre français* (Paris: Publications de la Sorbonne, 1986). A wealth of stimulating and well-informed observations about the "new" France of the postwar era and its relationship to the "old" France of 1940 is to be found in the synthesis that Robert Frank has produced of his research over the past two decades: *La Hantise du déclin. Le rang de la France en Europe, 1920–1960: finances, défense et identité nationale* (Paris: Belin, 1994).

INDEX

Abetz, Otto, 74
Adamthwaite, Anthony, 32
Addison, Paul, 137
Adler, Jacques, 129
Adrey, Georges, 6–7, 20n21
Air Force, French, 31, 33
Algerian war, 106
Alphand, Hervé, 139
Alsace-Lorraine, 21, 49, 132n6
Anglo-French Union (1940), 3, 47
anti-communism, 30, 51, 74–5, 77, 82,
    95–6, 106, 118, 141, 144–8
anti-semitism, 10, 16, 37, 51, 56–7, 60,
    68–9, 74–5, 128–30, 144–5, 159
armistice (1940), 3–4, 48–52, 99, 158
Armistice Commission, 49
Army, French
    in Second World War, 2–3, 5, 9, 13, 27,
        33–4, 37, 49, 72, 100
    under Fourth Republic, 103, 150
Aron, Raymond, 35, 39, 91
Aron, Robert, 39
Astier de la Vigerie, Emmanuel d', 46n78
atomic weapons, 131, 135, 165
Au Pilori, 120
Auriol, Vincent, 81

Bank of France, 31, 33, 139
Bardoux, Jacques, 35
Bartov, Omer, 160
Baudouin, Paul, 53, 93, 96, 99
BBC *see* British Broadcasting Corporation
Beaufre, General André, 161–3
Beauvoir, Simone de, 30
Belgium, 2, 10, 21n44
Belin, René, 29, 56
Benoist-Méchin, Jacques, 50
Bergery, Gaston, 29
Bichelonne, Jean, 55
Bidault, Georges, 149
Blanchard, Maurice, 115
Bloch, Marc, 14, 29, 47–8, 102, 160

Bloch-Lainé, François, 55, 139
Blum, Léon, 69–71, 73–4, 77, 80–1, 93
Bonnet, Georges, 29, 77, 142–3
Bourdan, Pierre, 88
Bouthillier, Yves, 53, 65, 96, 98–9
British Broadcasting Corporation (BBC), 5,
    59, 115, 121–2
British Expeditionary Force (BEF), 2–3, 11,
    17, 34
Brossat, Alain, 87
Brossolette, Pierre, 121, 125
Bullitt, William, 28
Burrin, Philippe, 74
business, French, 31–2, 35–6, 38, 70, 79,
    130, 140

Cagoule, 89
Caillot, Monseigneur, 13
Canada, 52, 149
Catroux, General Georges, 51–2
Ceux de la Résistance, 82
Chamberlain, Neville, 30, 33
chantiers de la jeunesse, 120
Charte du Travail, 70
Chobaut, Hyacinthe, 13, 18
Christian Democrats, 95, 98, 102–4, 138, 145
churches, 117
    Catholic, 13, 40, 70, 143–4
    Protestant, 22n63, 122
Churchill, Winston, 33, 58, 137, 142, 149,
    162, 164
cinema, 32, 161
civil servants, 55, 68, 79
Clément, René, 161
CNR *see Conseil National de la Résistance*
Cochet, General, 16
collaborationism, 50–1, 56, 73–5, 120–1,
    124–5, 127
Combat, 78, 91
comités d'entreprise, 138
Commissariat Général aux Questions Juives
    (CGQ J), 57, 130